The Holy Spirit and the Church

SERIES EDITORS
A. T. B. McGowan and John McClean

The Rutherford Centre for Reformed Theology (RCRT), based in Scotland, has established "The Ecclesiology Project" to enable some serious reconsideration of the Reformed doctrine of the church. The project is carried out in partnership with the Theological Commission of the World Reformed Fellowship (WRF).

On many of the doctrines of the Christian faith, there is broad agreement within the community of Reformed Christians. If we were considering the Trinity, the Person and Work of Christ, the doctrines which make up our understanding of salvation (effectual calling, regeneration, justification, adoption, repentance etc.) then the disagreements among us would be minor. When it comes to the doctrine of the church, however, there is no such agreement. We believe that there is a great need today for clarity in our understanding of the church, not least its nature and purpose.

In the seventeenth century, the ministers and theologians who wrote the *Westminster Confession of Faith* had a very "high" view of the church. They affirmed that the church is "the kingdom of the Lord Jesus Christ, the house and family of God, out of which there is no ordinary possibility of salvation." In the twenty-first century, many people have a very "low" view of the church, seeming to regard the church almost as an optional extra. Within the community of churches that trace their origins back to the sixteenth-century Reformation, both of these views are represented and also everything in between. How then should we formulate a doctrine of the church that is true to our roots and that is also fit for purpose in the twenty-first century?

In this series there will be several monographs on the subject, two of them being on aspects of the unity of the church, which we believe to be a vital topic in our divided church situation. Given our Reformed beliefs that the church should be confessional and that its worship should conform to the "Regulative Principle" (the idea that we may only do in worship what God commands), we are including in the series the WRF Statement of Faith (a new Reformed confessional statement) and a new edition of the *Reformed Book of Common Order*. Also included will be the papers from the Edinburgh Dogmatics Conferences of 2021, 2023 and 2025.

We hope that you will both enjoy and benefit from this series.

A.T.B. McGowan, editor
Director of the Rutherford Centre for Reformed Theology (www.rcrt.scot)

John McClean, deputy editor
Vice Principal of Christ College, Sydney (https://christcollege.edu.au)

The Holy Spirit and the Church

Papers from the Edinburgh Dogmatics Conference 2023

Edited by
JOHN McCLEAN

Series Editors:
A.T.B. McGowan and John McClean

PICKWICK *Publications* · Eugene, Oregon

THE HOLY SPIRIT AND THE CHURCH
Papers from the Edinburgh Dogmatics Conference 2023

Rutherford Centre for Reformed Theology Ecclesiology Series

Copyright © 2025 Wipf and Stock Publishers. All rights reserved. Except for brief quotations in critical publications or reviews, no part of this book may be reproduced in any manner without prior written permission from the publisher. Write: Permissions, Wipf and Stock Publishers, 199 W. 8th Ave., Suite 3, Eugene, OR 97401.

Pickwick Publications
An Imprint of Wipf and Stock Publishers
199 W. 8th Ave., Suite 3
Eugene, OR 97401

www.wipfandstock.com

PAPERBACK ISBN: 979-8-3852-5415-6
HARDCOVER ISBN: 979-8-3852-5416-3
EBOOK ISBN: 979-8-3852-5417-0

Cataloguing-in-Publication data:

Names: McClean, John, editor. |

Title: The Holy Spirit and the Church : papers from the Edinburgh Dogmatics Conference 2023 / John McClean.

Description: Eugene, OR: Pickwick Publications, 2025. | Rutherford Centre for Reformed Theology Ecclesiology Series. | Includes bibliographical references and index.

Identifiers: ISBN 979-8-3852-5415-6 (paperback). | ISBN 979-8-3852-5416-3 (hardcover). | ISBN 979-8-3852-5417-0 (ebook).

Subjects: LCSH: Holy Spirit. | Church. | Reformed Church—Doctrines. | Spirituality—Reformed Church. | Ecclesiology.

Classification: BT121.3 H56 2025 (print). | BT121.3 (ebook).

10/08/25

Contents

Introduction		vii
Abbreviations		xv
Contributors		xvii
1	The Communion of the Saints in the Fellowship of the Spirit JOHN MCCLEAN	1
2	"It has seemed good to the Holy Spirit and to us": Church, Scripture, and Discerning the Spirit MICHAEL ALLEN	20
3	The Holy Spirit and the Digital Church: A Discussion of Calvin, Pentecost, and Hybrid Ecclesial Practices MARK J. CARTLEDGE	33
4	Prioritising the Spirit in Our Churches: Toward a Comprehensive Third Article Ecclesiology GREGORY J. LISTON	52
5	The Holy Spirit and the Apostolicity of the Unholy Church PAUL T. NIMMO	73
6	The Eschatological Spirit and the Church: The Promise of an Ongoing Struggle CORNELIUS VAN DER KOOI	89
7	Taking the History of the Church Seriously: Pneumatic Dissonance and Its Partial Resolution EPHRAIM RADNER	99
8	Ecclesiological Pneumatology over the Last 50 Years MARK W. ELLIOTT	115

Bibliography 131
Index 143

Introduction

The 2023 Edinburgh Dogmatics Conference focused on the theme of "The Holy Spirit and the Church." It is tempting to observe that these are both unusual topics for a conference in the Reformed theological tradition. In recent generations Reformed theology has a reputation of ignoring both. That is not true of the deeper tradition of Reformed theology, which has had a robust account of the work of the Spirit and high ecclesiology. The papers at the conference returned to those themes recovering some of the riches of older theology and also exploring the challenges and implications for the faith in twenty-first century.

The following chapters was each a paper at the conference. They retain something of the directness of papers which were read to an audience. We are thankful to each of the contributors for the work of preparing the papers, revising them for publication and reviewing the various stages of editing.

John McClean explores the communion of the saints as an aspect of the work of the Spirit. He sets out a pneumatological account of the communion of the saints tracing the work of the Spirit to realise in human lives and communities the purpose of the Father and the work of Christ. This communion is enacted in personal relationships between believers in local communities, but is also global, historical and heavenly, and progressive in all these aspects. It has an eschatological orientation fulfilled in the communion of God and his people in the New Creation.

McClean argues that this account shows that the communion of the saints is a fundamental description of the nature of the church. The visible church is always an expression of the greater reality of the communion of the saints which exists in the "here and now." The church is the church when it is not gathered, and congregations have fellowship with and duties toward one another. The reality of communion in the Spirit calls Christians to consider how we express in concrete ways our fellowship with believers broadly, because together we share in the glorious grace of God.

Michael Allen reflects on the words of the apostles—"It has seemed good to the Holy Spirit and to us" (Acts 15:28)—asking how the Spirit directs the church in moral decisions. Luke Timothy Johnson's influential proposal is that Acts 10–15 is a model for church discernment. Allen argues that Johnson is right to highlight the passage, yet his proposal fails on three counts.

First, the apostolic decision does not abrogate or annul the Old Testament, rather James considers that the conversion of Gentiles conformed with the prophecy of Amos which led the council to recognise that circumcision law was foretold to conclude. Further, the ethical instruction for Gentile believers (Acts 15:20, 29) is drawn from Scripture (Gen 11, Lev 17–18). Second, the inclusion of Gentiles in the covenant is part of a new creation, but it is not a rejection of "nature." God's grace rebuilds and restores nature and human life and calling. We should see how grace advances upon nature, but never consider grace antagonistic to nature. Third, Acts 15 does not set New Testament Spirit against Old Testament Word. The Triune God works in perfect unity, Word and Spirit together, and his ways are discerned in that unity. This is grounded in key claims of Trinitarian theology.

Allen concludes that the work of the Spirit is in unity with the whole of Scripture, with God's purposes in redemption of creation and, most of all, in the Triunity of the work of God himself. The Spirit will guide the church in fresh reading of Scripture, directing it to a restoration of creation and fulfilment of human destiny as it shares in true Light and Word of God. So, with care, the church can discern the mind of the Spirit.

Mark Cartledge reflects on digital church as it has developed over some time and was highlighted during the pandemic. He aims to set out a pneumatology that relates Reformed ecclesiology with digital ecclesial expressions.

First, he samples Calvin's thought, which affirms that the church is both the outward aid for faith through the preaching of the Word and the due administration of the sacraments, and is the society and body of Christ reflecting the whole number of believers. In this Church the Holy Spirit sustains and matures believers. Calvin makes little connection between the church and the Day of Pentecost. Cartledge argues that a stronger connection would lead us to focus on the corporate experience of the Holy Spirit and widen the focus from the Word and Sacraments. The church is not, first and foremost, an external aid to faith but a community participating in the life of the Trinity through the Holy Spirit. Calvin's ecclesiology is thin and insufficiently Pentecostal.

Introduction

Digital church comes in many forms, Cartledge focusses on the "hybrid service" and considers how it may reflect the Calvinian view of the church augmented by Pentecostal perspectives. He notes that a digital platform allows people to gather and provides an extension of fellowship, it also enables them to share in the sacramental sung worship—though probably not as fully as in person. People can listen effectively to a sermon online but may miss the corporate attentiveness and awareness of the Spirit's movement. He recognises that sharing the Lord's Supper online is contentious but notes that Calvin's view of "spiritual feeding" seems to allow for it. Finally, he asks if a hybrid service contributes to the public life of the community as a witness. He notes ways in which community can be extended and enhanced, but also draws attention to what is lost compared to the whole community meeting in person. He suggests that life is now lived in "physical-digital hybridity" and that the Spirit is leading the church into this space to witness to the kingdom. The chapter concludes with a series of questions which churches and theologians need to ponder in the ongoing reflection on digital church.

Gregory Liston worked as a management consultant before he was a pastor and he notes that the experience of church ministry seemed far too similar to his first career. As antidote to this mundane experience of church he offers a third-article ecclesiology which will bring the work of the Spirit in the church to the forefront of understanding and practice.

The first step in this discussion is to move from a Spirit Christology to ecclesiology. Spirit Christology supplements Chalcedonian Christology with a fuller emphasis on the work of the Spirit in the incarnation, which allows a better appreciation of Christ's true humanity. This in turn suggests that, with Barth, we should see how the work of the Spirit in the church correlates with his work in Christ. Both are conceived and sustained in communion, conformed to God, directed and empowered by the Spirit. In turn the Spirit is displayed and mediated by Christ and the Church. The relations of the Spirit to Christ and the Church are not identical but are similar. This highlights that the Church exists as the Spirit enabled union of the incarnate Christ with human community and is marked by a "Christotelic impetus." By the Spirit, Christ is revealed in and through the Church.

Liston then looks at the Church in the light of the Trinity. In the Triune life of God, the Son is "empersoned" by the Spirit, in time the Son is incarnate by the Spirit and so, in turn, the Son is embodied in the Church by the Spirit and then Christ is formed in the members of the Church by the Spirit. This helps us to realise that our prayer and worship are not produced by our efforts and enthusiasm but are the Triune life of God expressed through those in communion with him.

The fourth step is to consider the church eschatologically—as the Spirit mediated anticipation of the kingdom. Following Torrance, Liston argues that by the Spirit "new time"—Christ's past, present and future—impacts on the Church. He appropriates these in turn to Christ's roles as prophet, priest and king. In particular, he highlights that the Spirit displays in the Church the future kingdom of Christ in qualities of truth, life, justice, and love. Liston focusses on the Eucharist as the way in which the Church experiences and practices the kingly presence of Christ by the Spirit.

The final step in the reflection deals with the relation of church and mission from the same perspectives. Christologically, the church not only embodies Christ but draws the world to Christ as she suffers for and with him. From a trinitarian perspective, the pattern of prayer and worship in which the love of Christ is offered and returned is also the pattern of mission as the people of God go out to love the world and gather for Christ to be formed in them. Eschatologically, as the church is transformed by the presence of the kingdom it is also a transforming presence in the world.

Liston concludes by reflecting on how these theological insights changed his experience of pastoral work from the stress of thinking church depended on him to the joy of sharing in what God is doing in his church and how they enable the church to rediscover its true spiritual identity in a time of weakness.

Paul Nimmo's chapter confronts the problem of how the Church can be "on mission" when its reputation is so tarnished by scandal. He directs attention to the notes of the Church in the Niceno-Constantinopolitan Creed, particularly holiness and apostolicity.

The Church is holy because the Triune God is holy which consists in his disposition toward purity and against sin. God not only is holy but elects his Church to be holy and makes it so which brings with it an ethical imperative. Yet there is a terrible contradiction that the holy Church can be so unholy. If holiness is a mark which identifies the true Church, we might wonder if a Church ever exists. So the Church is *simul sanctus et peccator*—entirely holy by way of its union with the holiness of Jesus Christ and entirely sinful on the basis of its failure to live in obedience to his commands. Its holiness is alien, in Christ not in itself.

The Church is apostolic because it is commissioned by God and shares in the same covenant as the apostles appointed to testify to and enact Christ's love as it hears and obeys the Word of God. Yet the Church with this commission is the one which is unholy.

It is the work of the Holy Spirit which holds together the holiness of the unholy Church and its apostolicity. The Spirit is present in the Church to sanctify it. Nimmo highlights three aspects of this work. 1) The Spirit relates to fallen human creatures as they are—the unholiness of the Church is no obstacle. 2) This is the proper work of the Spirit redeeming fallen creation and empowering the church for mission. 3) Yet this is not a work which can be summoned or appropriated to creaturely action, the Spirit works in the Spirit's way and time. The Spirit is at work in the witness of the Church, but not controlled by that. Thus, the holiness and apostolicity of the Church rests entirely on the work of the Spirit.

Nimmo concludes that the Church must always begin with repentance not only before God but also to the world it has failed. It must constantly renew its commitment to receive the Word of God brought by the Spirit and to serve the world in humility. In dependence on the Spirit the Church must continue prayerfully, for only by the Spirit does God take the flawed acts of the Church and transform them into apostolic witness.

Cornelius van der Kooi takes up the theme of the eschatological Spirit. He reminds us that the biblical understanding is that the Spirit is promised in the New Age and his presence in Christ and the Church marks the coming of that promise. Against that background, he points out that the Heidelberg Catechism declares that Christ is anointed by the Spirit to be our Prophet, Priest and King, and that each Christian shares in that anointing and in its three-fold office. Van der Kooi comments that in the New Testament the Church receives the Spirit, not just the individual believer.

By the Spirit, the Church shares in the rule of Christ. It exists as the people who have been drawn into the kingdom of life—signified by baptism. The eschatological Christian identity is ec-centric grounded in the promise of the new authority of Christ, it also brings transformation for those to whom kingdom is given. The signs of the kingdom are the fruits and gifts of the Spirit. Van der Kooi comments particularly on the gifts which come in many forms, though he warns of the danger of Western Christians failing to recognise gifts of healing.

The Church also shares in Christ's priestly ministry offering a "living sacrifice of thankfulness" displaying Christ's mercy to one another in the Eucharist and to the world in service. It shares in Christ's prophetic office, not only in the preaching in the ministry of the Word but also in congregational singing, family worship and in speaking in tongues. The Spirit may well enable the Church to speak God's word in many other forms. The Spirit of Christ is at work so that the Church may taste his grace, now.

Ephraim Radner considers the disappointing experience of the church divided and fractured and how that might relate to the work of the Spirit. He contemplates the asserted unity of the Church against its apparent disunity and asks if we do know what constitutes unity and if we can measure it. The cognitive dissonance created by the contrast of supposed unity and historical division generates many responses—shifting churches, disconnecting from church, and theological adjustment.

Radner sets out to rethink "the pneumatic guarantee" of the unity of the Church. He points out that this connection is not so clear in Scripture, since the Spirit gives the "first fruits," a "deposit." This leads to the key theological claim that in this life the Spirit is associated with the beginning, the first instalment, the partial, rather than fullness. The work of the Spirit has to be understood mereologically (Gk. *meros*, part)—by considering the relation of the part to the whole. By the Spirit we know in part (1 Cor 13:9–12) and possess in part. The part suggests a whole but does not yet reveal it. Radner proposes that the work of the Spirit is to stabilize and order the dissonance rather than resolve it, enabling the church to move toward its fulfilment. This is consistent with the Biblical testimony that the Spirit enables patience and endurance (Rom 5:1–5; 8:22–25; 1 Cor 13). Recognising the mereological work of the Spirit will draw attention to what is required for ecclesial survival—catechesis, prayer and worship. Radner doubts that unity (at least a total unity) is one of these. Rather the Spirit enables the church to live in sin and fracture, looking to Christ in whom alone are the part and the whole fully resolved historically. The church now, by the Spirit, bears the suffering of division as a witness to fullness of grace.

In the final chapter Mark Elliot offers review of discussion of the Holy Spirit and the Church in recent theology (post-1965). This is not a question of practical theology, but to understand how we follow the Nicene-Constantinopolitan creed and affirm that the church is one, holy, catholic and apostolic. Protestant theology has typically downgraded the importance of the church over against the Word and treated the Nicene marks as impossible ideals, at best. Zahl has emphasised that Pneumatology should emphasise the dynamic work of the Spirit in Christian experience rather than the more static "participative" view.

Elliot first reviews the remarkable variety of Catholic contributions, particularly prompted by landmark statements of Vatican II. On one side are the maximalists. For instance, in his 1986 *Dominum et vivificantem* John Paul II affirmed that the church is the creation of the Spirit, yet after this it is the instrument of grace and the work of the Spirit is directed to the individual heart. The church is pure, and through it God purifies sinners. There is little appreciation of the Church as community, nor of the work of the Spirit to purify the church. Schnackenburg takes a similar view of the church as mediating the work of Christ, though Elliot notes that this does not fit with the Ephesisans texts to which he appeals. Schillebeeckx, in contrast, is a minimalist and holds that the Church is, or should be, in constant repentance, which includes the questioning of its authority and the inclusion of dissent. As such it is nucleus and beginning of the kingdom, but not identical with it.

Moltmann is the first Protestant theologian to be considered. He stresses that the Spirit makes the Church, and turns it outward in mission. The Church is the means of God's self-mediation, as it points away from itself to the Kingdom. Elliot wonders if this does not serve to protect the church from repentance and change.

Initially, Pannenberg's ecclesiology was focused on the Word which the church receives and passively repeats, speaking as it hears. This Word shows the church to be a sinner and makes it clean. In *Systematic Theology* his ecclesiology was more pneumatological and hence more dynamic. The Spirit is a gift to the church in anticipation of the eschatological outpouring, and the church is the protype of the cosmic renewal. In this movement, in creation and in the church, the Spirit lifts humans ecstatically over their own particularity to grasp what is beyond them. Elliot considers that in this Pannenberg begins with New Testament texts but ends with a natural theology which absorbs the particular in the general.

Tom Greggs' recent *Dogmatic Ecclesiology*, seeks to ensure that the Church is only identified with Christ by the constant work of the Spirit. As such, the Church exists for God and the world, not for itself and is an act of God. The visible church subsists in this invisible action and the church is an object of faith in the inseparable invisible and visible aspects. The Spirit makes the church the body of Christ to share in his priesthood to the world, as such it enjoys intimacy with Christ but remains distinct from him. Greggs understands that as the church exists due to the act of God by the Spirit, the Spirit and the whole Trinity is revealed in and through this act. Elliot's reservation is that the church needs to understand what it means for the Spirit to be at work in the church and be able to test itself before God, rather than presume that it has a prophetic task to the world.

Elliot's concluding reflections are that with the gift of the Spirit the church is a co-worker with God. We do need to recognise the Nicene properties as the basis for critical assessment of the church. The reformation marks of the church will make ecclesiology too clerical, the four attributes provide a better basis for engagement with practical theology.

As you enjoy the chapters in this volume, you will notice several themes emerging. First, it is clear that the church must be understood as the work of the Spirit—it is not a human creation, but God's. This means that the church is properly an object of faith and confession and an appropriate theme of serious theological reflection. While there is a place for understanding the church "from below," asking the questions for practical theology; each contribution considers the church as enacted by God through the Spirit and understood in light of revelation. Second, each of these chapters, in one way or another, affirms that the Spirit applies the work of Christ and creates a communion of people with Christ and one another. Recovering a pneumatological approach is not to question a Christological understanding. Third, each of the chapters highlights that the Spirit is not only the Creator of the church, but the one who sustains and enlivens. There is a strong sense through the volume that a pneumatological ecclesiology is dynamic and will question a static and institutional view of the church. Fourth, this is far from being a volume of triumphalistic ecclesiology. Several of the contributors wrestle with the failure and sinfulness of the church and each chapter recognises the need for the church to be humble, dependent and penitent. Fifth, the work of the Spirit is to enable to the church to serve God in the world—mission matters to the Spirit. This is expressed in different ways through the chapters, but is a common recognition. Finally, several chapters highlight that Spirit is eschatological, he is the reality and downpayment of the age to come. So the dynamism of the Spirit anticipates the new creation and for all the realism about the state of the church, there is also hope in the Spirit.

We hope that your understanding and appreciation of the church of the Spirit is enriched as you read and reflect.

Abbreviations

ATR	*Anglican Theological Review*
DPL	*Dictionary of Paul and His Letters*
IJST	*International Journal of Systematic Theology*
JAPA	*Journal of the American Philosophical Association*
JTS	*Journal of Theological Studies*
NDT:H&S	*New Dictionary of Theology: Historical and Systematic*
PRRI	Public Religion Research Institute
RISU	Religious Information Service of Ukraine
RTR	*Reformed Theological Review*
SJT	*Scottish Journal of Theology*

Contributors

JOHN MCCLEAN is Vice-Principal and Lecturer in Systematic Theology at Christ College, the theological college of the Presbyterian Church of Australia in Sydney. He is co-chair of the Theology Commission of World Reformed Fellowship. His doctoral work was on the thought of Wolfhart Pannenberg and he has since published *From the Future*, an introduction to Pannenberg's thought. He has research interests in a range of topics in theology and theological ethics.

MICHAEL ALLEN is the John Dyer Trimble Professor of Systematic Theology and Academic Dean at Reformed Theological Seminary in Orlando. He has written and edited many books, most recently writing *The Fear of the Lord: Essays in Theological Method* and *The Knowledge of God: Essays on God, Christ, and Church* (both published by T. & T. Clark) and editing *The New Cambridge Companion to Christian Doctrine*. He serves as a general editor for the New Studies in Dogmatics series by Zondervan Academic and for the T & T Clark International Theological Commentary series. He ministers as a teaching elder in the Presbyterian Church in America and serves as theologian-in-residence at NewCity Orlando.

The Revd Professor MARK J. CARTLEDGE, PhD, FRSA, is Principal of London School of Theology and Professor of Practical Theology. He is a minister in the Church of England, a practical theologian and a scholar of Pentecostal and Charismatic Christianity. His recent books include: (co-editor), *Sisters, Mothers, Daughters: Pentecostal Perspectives on Violence Against Women* (Leiden: Brill, 2022); *The Holy Spirit and Public Life: Empowering Ecclesial Praxis* (Lexington Books / Fortress Academic Press, 2022); and (co-editor), *The Holy Spirit and the Reformation Legacy* (Pickwick Publications, 2020). He is currently co-editing *Pentecostal Public Theology: Engaged Christianity and Transformed Society in Europe* (Palgrave Macmillan, 2024).

Greg Liston is a Senior Lecturer in Systematic Theology at Laidlaw College in Auckland, New Zealand. His research interests focus on the role of the Spirit in the life of the church, and exploring how the interaction between science and theology raises fundamental questions about reality and the nature of time. In addition to numerous journal articles, he is the author of *The Anointed Church* (with Fortress Press) and *Kingdom Come* (with T. & T. Clark). Before taking up his current role, Greg's journey has included PhDs in both systematic theology and quantum physics, being the senior pastor of a local Auckland suburban Baptist church, and strategic management consulting. Greg is married to Diane and has two children, Emily and James.

Paul Nimmo holds the King's (1620) Chair of Systematic Theology at the University of Aberdeen, having previously held positions at Cambridge and Edinburgh. His monograph, *Being in Action: The Theological Shape of Barth's Ethical Vision*, was awarded a John Templeton Award for Theological Promise, and he has since published *Barth: A Guide for the Perplexed*, and co-edited *The Cambridge Companion to Reformed Theology* and the *Oxford Handbook of Karl Barth*. He is the Senior Editor of *International Journal of Systematic Theology*, and English-language Editor of the Karl Barth Translation Project. An ordained elder in the Church of Scotland, he is currently Convenor of its Theological Forum and a member of the CPCE delegation for ecumenical dialogue with the Roman Catholic Church.

Prof. Dr. **Cornelis van der Kooi** (1952) is emeritus Professor of Systematic Theology at the Vrije Universiteit Amsterdam. He published (together with G. van den Brink) a new handbook *Christian Dogmatics* (Eerdmans 2017), originally in Dutch (2012) and widely acclaimed. In 2014 he delivered the Warfield Lectures in Princeton, now published as *This Incredibly Benevolent Force: The Holy Spirit in Reformed Theology and Spirituality* (Eerdmans 2018). Other major publications are *As in a Mirror: John Calvin and Karl Barth on Knowing God. A Diptych* (2002, ET 2005). He was the editor of the critical edition of Barth's second commentary on the letter to the Romans (2010). He functions as a theological linking pin between the reformed tradition and evangelical/charismatic renewal movements and is one of the founders of the Herman Bavinck Center for Reformed and Evangelical Theology at the VU (HBCRET). Together with his wife Margriet van der Kooi he published *Good Tools are Half the Job: The Importance of Theology in Chaplaincy and Pastoral Care* (Eugene OR: Wipf & Stock, 2021). In 2018 he was appointed at the Erasmus University Rotterdam on the relation between theology and economics.

Contributors

EPHRAIM RADNER (PhD, Yale University) is Professor of Historical Theology at Wycliffe College, a seminary of the Anglican tradition at the University of Toronto. He is the author and editor of several books on the theology of the church, biblical interpretation, and the Holy Spirit, most recently, *A Profound Ignorance: Modern Pneumatology*; and earlier, *The End of the Church, Leviticus, A Brutal Unity, Time and Word,* and *A Time to Keep,* a work on human mortality. A volume on Christian politics, *Mortal Goods*, appeared in 2024. He is currently co-editing the *Oxford Handbook on Jewish Christianity and Messianic Judaism*. A former church worker in Burundi and an Anglican priest, he has served parishes in various parts of the United States and has been active in the affairs of the global Anglican Communion. He is married to the Rev. Annette Brownlee, Wycliffe College's Chaplain, and they have two children.

MARK W. ELLIOTT was schooled in Glasgow. For university he went to read Law at Oxford, then he studied Divinity at Aberdeen and gained his PhD in Patristics at Cambridge University. He then taught at the universities of Nottingham, Liverpool Hope, St Andrews, and Glasgow and is now Professor of Biblical and Historical Theology at the University of the Highlands and Islands (Highland Theological College) as well as Professorial Fellow at Wycliffe College, Toronto. His recent projects include *History of Scottish Theology* (co-edited with David Fergusson, Oxford University Press, 2019) and *Providence: Biblical and Theological* (Baker, 2020). He is editor of the Mohr Siebeck series, History of Biblical Exegesis.

1

The Communion of the Saints in the Fellowship of the Spirit

JOHN MCCLEAN

ROBINSON-KNOX ECCLESIOLOGY

THE ECCLESIOLOGY OF DONALD Robinson (1922—2018) and Broughton Knox (1916–1994) has had a significant influence in Sydney Anglicanism and wider reformed circles in Australia and beyond.[1] I want to highlight some features of this approach which I think arise in part from a lack of a substantial reflection on the work of the Spirit in the existence of the church. That will serve as a starting point for an exposition of the communion of the saints in the fellowship of the Spirit.

Donald Robinson and Broughton Knox taught together at Moore College in Sydney from the mid-1950s to the mid-1970s.[2] The synthesis of their

---

1. I reflect on the Robinson-Knox approach because it is a prominent feature in my local theological context.

2. Knox was first appointed as a lecturer at Moore College in February 1947, he completed his DPhil at Oxford (1950–1954) and returned to Moore in 1954 as vice-principal and became principal in 1959. He retired as principal in 1985 and finished teaching in 1988. Donald Robinson was first appointed to lecture part-time in 1952,

views of the church is the source of this distinctive ecclesiology, and it has often been termed *Robinson-Knox ecclesiology*. Their approach was shaped by two major concerns. The Church of England dioceses in Australia were negotiating a constitution to form the Anglican Church of Australia. At the same time, the ecumenical movement was at its zenith. Both these factors raised questions about the theological status of denominational structures and church unity.[3]

Their ecclesiology developed from a study of the word *ecclesia* and its relation to Christ. They argued that the church is the assembly of people gathered to and by Christ.[4] The Christological gathering theme climaxes in a passage such as Hebrew 12:22–24 in which believers are assured that they "have come" to a heavenly assembly "the ecclesia of the firstborn." God's church is the gathering of his people around Christ in the heavenly places which is then manifest in local gatherings. Matthew 18:20 in which Jesus says that where two or three gather he is present is a key text.

> *The church is where Christ is. On earth, that is where two or three are gathered together in His name . . . . In heaven, it is where He is, seated at the right hand of the throne of God.*[5]

This approach undercuts much of the Australian Anglican and ecumenical discussions. It implies that, at best, the "Anglican Church of Australia" can be named a church in a derived and conventional sense. It is not theologically speaking, a church; and cannot claim the powers of a church. Knox is explicit that denominations are "structures . . . to assist the fellowship between congregations," and "must not exercise the duties of the congregation on behalf of the congregation" and "must be careful not to exercise jurisdiction within the congregation." He argued that "what is needed as a first step is . . . handing back to the congregations those functions and responsibilities which they had in the New Testament and the early centuries." Knox suggests this would result in simplified denominational structures, which could be far more easily united. Though since the denominations are not churches, this unity is a subordinate concern.[6]

---

and took a full-time role in 1954. In 1959 he became vice-principal and continued in his full-time teaching till he became the Bishop of Parramatta in 1973. He continued part-time teaching until he became the Archbishop of Sydney in 1982.

3. See Kuhn, *Ecclesiology*, 30–46 for a detailed discussion of this context.

4. Knox, "The Church, the Churches," 15, identifies this as "The most important passage in Scripture about the church" and argues that *epi* in Matt 16:18 should be translated as "at" or "in front of."

5. Robinson, "The Church in the New Testament," 4–5.

6. Knox, "The Church, the Churches," 23. Robinson explains that his view is that "a

The Robinson-Knox claims about denominations are not unusual among Congregationalists, though they are surprising for Anglicans, especially from one who later became a bishop. More idiosyncratic was what we might term "ecclesial occasionalism" which holds that the visible church exists only when it is meeting. Robinson contrasts the church in heavenly and earthly forms: the heavenly is "uniform" (it exists "only in one place) and "continuous" ("offering perpetual praise as it hears without intermission the name and glory of God declared in its midst by Christ"). The earthly church is "multiform" (it is "wherever two of three are gathered together in Christ's name") and is "intermittent."[7]

Knox's comments on church membership show the implications of this occasionalism. He explains that "the unity of the visible church consists of accepting into full membership of the congregation all true believers who happen to be in the congregation at the meeting of the congregation."[8] In his view the church has no other function but to meet as the fellowship of Christ's people, so there is no need nor warrant for any other qualification for membership than "being one of Christ's people and being present." Knox allows that the company of those who usually meet may "wish to club together to transact business beyond being a church." That further business, I take it, would include appointing elders or calling a minister as well as managing finances. For such purposes it may be necessary to have "explicit membership or a membership roll," yet Knox is clear that "it is not a church roll but a roll of persons with certain qualifications who are also church members." Elsewhere he concedes that "it is possible to speak of elders of a gathering . . . when there is no gathering going on at the moment."[9] Yet this is a concession, and the emphasis is clear—the visible earthly church is constituted when it meets.

---

body like the Church of England in Australia was simply not a church in any sense in which ekklesia is used in the New Testament, and that it was a confusion of categories to seek to relate it to the holy catholic church . . . I had no objection to the use of the title Church of England as such; it had grown up through long usage and everyone knew what it referred to. But it seemed important not to transfer to this national or denominational structure prerogatives and dignities which belonged to the ekklesia of God." Robinson, "The Church Revisited," 11.

7. Robinson, "The Church of God," 236. Knox argues that "Church . . . in the Greek New Testament always refers to an actual assembling" and "fellowship . . . only exists when it is experienced" for it "consists of a word spoken and responded to in the context of receiving one another and appreciating one another," (236). Knox, "De-mythologising the Church,"54.

8. Knox, "The Church, the Churches," 22.

9. Knox, "De-mythologising," 54.

The Robinson-Knox view, in its original form, thus holds that neither polity nor community are strictly part of the existence of the church. The congregationalism has been challenged, most directly by pointing to New Testament passages which on a plain reading refer to the visible church at something beyond the local level (Acts 9:31; 1 Cor 10:32; 12:28).[10]

In contrast to the Robinson-Knox view it is almost a truism in ecclesiology that the church is a community. While older discussions often did not make this point while largely assuming it, it has come to the fore more recently, and any number of contemporary ecclesiologies emphasize the community aspect.[11] The metaphor of the "body" uses a common Graeco-Roman description of a society or community.[12] Not surprisingly then, the occasionalism of Robinson-Knox view has been tempered by later exponents of the position.[13] Similarly, while views vary as to the appropriate polity of the church, it is almost universally acknowledged that polity is a feature of the church.[14]

This paper is not, primarily, an assessment of the Robinson-Knox view. Rather, their ecclesiology serves as a starting point for a larger dogmatic discussion, prompted by an observation about a striking aporia in their approach. Robinson-Knox ecclesiology is developed Christologically—church is the company of people gathered around Christ and in Christ. In contrast they have little to say of the work of the Spirit in the church. Knox refers to

10. Fields, "Ecclesia as Gathering Only?," 49–69. The rest of my discussion will assume that this criticism is valid and that there is no reason why the term *ecclesia* should only be applied to local congregations and the heavenly gathering.

11. Van der Kooi and van den Brink, *Christian Dogmatics*, 573–83 develop their initial discussion of church as the "eschatological community." Greggs, *Dogmatic Ecclesiology*, Vol. 1, 30 worries that his initial presentation of church as "an event of the act of the Spirit of God" may not indicate sufficient interest in a particular community as the locus of the work of the Spirit. So, he examines "the abductive socio-poiesitic nature of the church as a community," (32). The Spirit brings attraction to God and with that and on that basis attraction to other believers, so community is "grounded in the divine presence of the activity of the Holy Spirit." Webster, while cautious of thinking of church as a mode of human sociality affirms that "Election generates a polity, a common life," Webster, "On Evangelical Ecclesiology," 19–20. Allison wants to avoid voluntarism which suggests that churches exist because people choose to join them but insists that "the covenant community comes about first and foremost according to the new covenant that God establishes with his people," Allison, *Sojourners and Strangers* 128.

12. Fung, "Body of Christ," 77–78.

13. E.g., Cole, "The Doctrine of the Church," 3, affirms that believers are related to one another by common membership in the people of God. Although they are only "church" when gathered, there are real continuing relationships both locally and globally. See also Foord, "We Meet Again! In Heaven or on Earth?" 225–34.

14. See for example Bavinck's discussion of church's government and the relation of the church as an organism and institution; H. Bavinck, *Reformed Dogmatic*, 4:329–32.

the work of the Spirit, but primarily as the one who makes Christ present when two or three believers are gathered.[15]

This paper here is an attempt to fill that gap, and to suggest how ecclesiology might look different if it takes seriously the communion given and formed by the Holy Spirit. I will argue that some of the features in the Robinson-Knox view which have been challenged on exegetical grounds would not have been developed if our view of church was pneumatological as well as Christological. The thesis of this paper is that as we are given fellowship with the Holy Spirit in Christ, so we are given communion with others; and this communion with the saints is fundamental to the life of the church.

THE COMMUNION OF THE SAINTS

Roman Catholic feminist theologian Elizabeth Johnson contends that the communion of saints "is one of the least developed" doctrines.[16] There are no treatises from the early or medieval church on the doctrine. Catholic theology focused on the place of individual saints and piety directed toward them. *Lumen Gentium* gave the first conciliar treatment of the doctrine, but this remains "more of a sketch."[17] There are only a handful of significant monographs on the doctrine in the last hundred years.[18]

In the Greek speaking church *koinonia ton agion* meant participation in the holy elements of the Eucharist.[19] In the West the Latin *communio sanctorum* came to designate "fellowship with holy persons."[20] Particularly in

---

15. Knox "The Church and the Denominations" 47, "These local gatherings... were manifestations of the Church of Christ. Christ had gathered them, and He Himself was present according to His promise where two or three were met together in his Name. Thus they were gathered round Christ through his Spirit and consequently nothing was lacking for a complete church of Christ." Kuhn, *Ecclesiology*, 161–62 argues that Knox, in particular, had an important pneumatological aspect to his thought and that "Knox intended to stress the special promise of Christ's presence by the Spirit when believers gather, over and against the continual presence of the Spirit in the lives of believers" (194). This is a limited account of the work of the Spirit, and is only occasionally explicit in Knox's discussion.

16. Johnson, *Friends of God*, 9.

17. Johnson, *Friends of God*, 9.

18. Bonhoeffer, *Communion of Saints*; Emry, *L'unite des croyants*; Gaurdini, *The Saints in Christian Life*; Johnson, *Friends of God*; Fiddes, Haymes, Kidd, *Baptists and the Communion of Saints*; Delorenzo, *Work of Love*; Trozzo, Kit, and Ating, eds. *Communion of Saints in Context*.

19. See Delorenzo, *Work of Love*, 8, who refers to Kelly, *Early Christian Creeds*, 389–90; Wood, "Sanctam Ecclesiam Catholicam", 228; and Berard Marthaler, *The Creed*, 330.

20. There is some dispute as to how quickly and fully this transition took place. Delorenzo, *Work of Love*, 9 follows Kelly, *Early Christian Creeds*, 394–400. Badcock,

Gallic Christianity, this referred to communion with the redeemed already in heaven, in the first instance with the faithful martyrs, in time with other illustrious believers.[21] According to Delorenzo, "*Communio sanctorum* was first believed implicitly and practiced devotionally—almost instinctively—before it was confessed explicitly and handed down in the creed."[22] Fellowship with the faithful dead was recognized as a gift of the Spirit in which God sanctifies the life of faith.[23]

The Catholic Catechism now includes all of these elements in the "communion of the saints"—communion in holy things (the faith, the sacraments, graces, goods and love) and holy people (in all three states—pilgrimage, purgatory and glory). It also includes the intercession of the saints for the church, the communion of the church with the saints and also the church's prayer for the dead.[24]

The Reformation challenged much of this doctrine. It excluded the doctrine of purgatory which in turn removed any place for prayer for the dead. It rejected any teaching about the intercession of the saints "for the way it disrupts the gospel, overshadowing Christ in whom God's gracious mercy has been poured out."[25] The Reformation critique of idolatry and superstition rejected veneration of the saints and especially of relics. The result was that the theme of communion with the saints was focused on the visible church.[26] Thus, the Westminster Confession states that "All saints that are united to Jesus Christ their head by his Spirit, and by faith, have fellowship with him in his graces, sufferings, death, resurrection, and glory." They are "united to one another in love" and share "in each other's gifts and graces" and are to serve each other and to keep fellowship in worship together and care in outward needs (WCF 26.1-2).

The Reformation affirmation of the unity of the church militant and triumphant was developed under the discussion of the invisible church.[27]

History of the Creeds, 243-72, argues that the original eucharistic meaning was preserved. See Lamirande, "The History of a Formula," 15-38.

21. Delorenzo, *Work of Love*, 10 following Kelly. See Delorenzo's helpful short portrait of the spiritual and theological significance of fellowship with the faithful in heaven and how this developed into a devotion to the saints.

22. Delorenzo, *Work of Love*, 15.

23. Delorenzo, *Work of Love*, 14.

24. *Catholic Catechism*, 949-59.

25. Johnson, *Friends of God*, 2.

26. "The fellowship of the saints . . . came to mean the common life of any given congregation of believers, as well as the acceptance of the traditional teachings of the leading theologians and martyrs of the past," Bray, "Communion of Saints," 196.

27. Turretin, for instance, in the discussion of the invisible church responds to the

Heppe summarises "living believers and those asleep are aware of being purified in the community of their hope in the Lord, in the community of intercession for all members of the Church and in the community of the same gifts of the Holy Spirit."[28] So, the theme is not absent from Reformed theology, but has had little development. It is worth considering, then, how Reformed theology gives a pneumatological account of the communion of the Saints. In what follows I offer eleven dogmatic statements which seek to set out how the Spirit grants us fellowship with one another in the economy of the gospel.

1) Participation in the Spirit Brings the Realization in Human Lives of the Purpose of the Father and the Work of Christ.

The work of the Spirit in our fellowship is an aspect of the personal mission of the Spirit. In the indivisible work of the Triune God, there are two movements proper to the persons—the incarnation of the Son, and the outpouring of the Spirit to indwell the people of God. Our communion with the Spirit is the result of the Spirit coming from the Father and the Son.

Fellowship with the Spirit is fellowship with the Son and the Father. The inhabitation of the church by the Spirit forms it as the temple of the Triune God. The New Testament speaks most often of the indwelling of the Spirit (John 7:38–39; Rom 8:11, 14–16; 1 Cor 1:21–22; 3:16; 6:19; Gal 4:6; Eph 1:13–14; 2:22; 2 Tim 1:14; 1 John 2:27; 3:24; 4:13). It speaks also of the indwelling of the Son (John 14:3,18, 20, 23, 28; 17:23; 26; Rom 8:10; 2 Cor 13:5; Gal 2:20; Eph 3:17; Col 1:27; Rev 3:20) and more pervasively of union with Christ. Sometimes life in Christ and union with him are explicitly related to the presence of the Spirit (John 14:15–17, 26; Rom 8:10; Eph 3:16–17). There are also references to the Father indwelling believers (John 14:20, 23) and some references to God indwelling which are likely to refer to the Father (Eph 2:22; 2 Cor 6:16; 1 John 4:12–13, 15–16). Most of these relate the presence of the Father to that of the Son and the Spirit.

That the presence of the Spirit is the presence of the Father and the Son is a key part of the New Testament witness to the Trinity. As such, it is a demonstration of the principle of inseparable operations which affirms

critique of the doctrine which argues that there can be no society unless people know each other, and to do so they must see each other. He argues that "there is a society and union between the church triumphant and militant, the spirits made perfect and those who have gained the goal in heaven and travellers on earth," though they do not see each other. He adds that "I know Paul and other saints, not by external and visible signs, but by the communion of the Spirit." Turretin, *Institutes of Elenctic Theology*, 40,

28. Heppe, *Reformed Dogmatics*, 659.

that the work of God outside himself is undivided as Father, Son and Spirit act together with one will and one power. What the Father does, so the Son does; what the Son does, so does the Spirit.[29] This prohibits us from divorcing or dividing the work of the persons; positively we must seek to wonder at and bear witness to the unity of the work of God.

Some discussions raise the question of whether there is tension or even a contradiction if we affirm a personal mission of the Spirit to believers and distinct fellowship with the Spirit, Son and Father. If the Son and the Father are present to us by the Spirit, can we also know them in their distinct persons. If we cannot know the persons distinctly, then it would be difficult to present the communion of the saints as distinctly a work of the Spirit. It is, however, a pseudo-problem. God's gift of his presence follows the Trinitarian pattern. In the coming of the Spirit, we are united to the Son and because he lives, we also live. With the presence of the Spirit and the Son, we know and call on the Father. In this communion we know the three-in-one.[30]

In this work of communion the Spirit brings to perfection what is intended by the Father and achieved by the Son. The Triune purpose was to have a people who belong to God, who live for him in unity with one another. That comes about as we are drawn to Christ and his work by the Holy Spirit.

2) Participation in the Spirit Is a Mystery That Cannot Be Fully Analyzed.

The fellowship of the Spirit has consistently been termed "mystical communion," with the implication that it cannot be fully described. In the following discussion I consider what we *can* say about the nature of this communion, but it is important to preface that by noting that no description will be comprehensive. We should exercise a proper reserve as we recognise a limitation to how fully we may describe the communion of the Spirit. Bavinck, commenting on the Spirit's work of regeneration, says that "in all that God reveals, we finally encounter an impenetrable mystery at the point where

---

29. Teer, "Inseparable Operation," 339.

30. Calvin famously recognised this when he reflected on his delight in the passage from Gregory of Nazianzus "I cannot think on the one without quickly being encircled by the splendor of the three; nor can I discern the three without being straightway carried back to the one." Calvin, *Institutes* 1.13,17, p. 141.

the eternal touches the temporal, the infinite the finite, the Creator the creature."[31]

3) Participation in the Spirit Is a Personal Communion Involving Hearing, Speaking and Personal Knowing.

How do we describe, as far as we can, the nature of our fellowship with the Holy Spirit?

Scripture describes our communion with the Spirit in terms analogical to communion between human persons. First and foremost, it is a communion of love. The Augustinian tradition describes the Spirit as the gift of love because that is an extension of the personal properties of the Spirit as the gift and bond of love between the Father and the Son.[32] Our communion with the Spirit is characterized by God's love for us and our love for him in response.

Second, participation in the Spirit is verbal—we are spoken to and we speak. The Spirit *speaks* to God's church. Here I am particularly thinking of what the Reformed tradition has called the illuminating work of the Spirit. This work of the Spirit involves the 'internalisation' of revelation. Believers receive God's word and are internally transformed so that they know God and live according to his will. Paul prays that his Colossian readers will be "filled with the knowledge of [God's] will through all the wisdom and understanding that the Spirit gives" (Col 1:9, NIV).[33] In this way the Spirit brings a through-going transformation of people in their orientation, attitudes and actions through an ever-deepening communion with God through Christ by the Spirit in love.[34] He brings the personal, transformative knowledge of God in the word into the inner experience of the church as the Spirit speaks in and through God's word.

---

31. Bavinck, *Reformed Dogmatics*, 4:93. Cf "Here we have union which we are unable to define specifically. But it is union of an intensely spiritual character consonant with the nature and work of the Holy Spirit so that in a real way surpassing our power of analysis Christ dwells in his people and his people dwell in him." Murray, *Redemption: Accomplished and Applied*, 116.

32. For defences of this view see Levering, *Engaging the Doctrine of the Holy Spirit*, 62–74; Köstenberger, Allison, *The Holy Spirit*, 193–205.

33. See Dunn, *Colossians and Philemon*, 71, who comments that here *pneumatikos* "spiritual" means "given by and manifesting the Spirit."

34. Rabens, *The Holy Spirit and Ethics in Paul* offers a careful study of the transforming work of the Spirit. He shows that Paul understands that "believers are transformed by means of deeper knowledge of and an intimate encounter with the (glory of) the Lord . . . by the Spirit" (190).

As the Spirit speaks to the church, so also the church speaks by and in the Spirit. Galatians 4:6 and Romans 8:15 offer a wonderful pairing. The Galatians text refers to the Spirit sent into our hearts by the Father, speaking in and to believers, crying "Abba, Father." The Spirit of adoption assures us that we are children of God and repeats Jesus' language of prayer in us. Romans 8:15 shows the corresponding response: by the Spirit we cry "Abba, Father." So as the Spirit speaks in and to us, so we speak praising and calling on God.

Speaking does not exhaust the work of the Spirit in the church, but it is central, and helps to characterize the personal presence of the Spirit. We do not best think of the Spirit as a 'force' which drives or arouses us but as a person with whom we have communion as he speaks to us and enables us to speak. In that, the Spirit does his work of transforming us by love.

The inhabitation of the Spirit is a unique personal communion. On the one hand it is communion with the one who infinitely transcends us. It is inconceivable and wonderful that the Sovereign Lord God should take up residence in human persons and communities, even if to refer to *inhabitation* is still to speak analogically.

Simultaneously, this is personal communion with one who is within us, not over against us. This is a unique feature of communion with the Spirit. All other communion is with another who is identifiably distinct from us and in some sense apart from us. We see each other's bodies and hear words that address us from the outside. The incarnation offers an encounter with someone who is apart from us. Jesus was present in one place, and not another; he met people and spoke to them. As we read the Gospels we share in such an encounter. The Spirit, however, is within us. At the same time, it is important to stress that the Spirit is not identical with the human spirit, his voice is not our inner voice.[35]

---

35. "The Holy Spirit is so actively involved in our lives, subjectively, that we can take his presence for granted or identify him with our own inner self. Domesticating the Spirit to an individualistic mysticism, the Holy Spirit becomes one's inmost voice. But again, this is a distortion of a truth. The Holy Spirit is the person who works within us, even to the point of indwelling us and interceding in our hearts. But the Holy Spirit is not our spirit, and his voice is not to be confused with our own. The Spirit is a divine person within us, not a divine part of us," Horton, *Rediscovering the Holy Spirit*, 26.

4) Participation in the Spirit Is Immediately Corporate as It Is Individual.

Relatively few discussions of the indwelling Spirit or union with Christ highlight the corporate dimension. A typical Reformed treatment deals with the inhabitation of the Spirit in the *ordo salutis,* particularly in the discussion of regeneration, and these are characteristically, and perhaps notoriously individualistic.[36] Berkouwer observes that "Reformed theology has frequently dealt with this "mystical union" but he finds "no special concern about the implications of this doctrine for the unity of the Church."[37] Scripture does not describe the gift of the Spirit as granted to individuals who are then, as a second movement, drawn to one another in communion. Rather, the Spirit comes to individuals as he comes to the Church, and he comes to the Church as he comes to individuals. This was demonstrated at Pentecost when the Holy Spirit came like a mighty rushing wind filling the whole house and as divided tongues of fire to rest on each believer. The Spirit was given to all together and to each individually. That Baptism signifies and seals the reception of the Spirit, incorporation into Christ and membership of the body of Christ highlights that the gift of the Spirit is both corporate and individual.

All of salvation is achieved and determined for us by the person and work of Christ and the gifts of salvation are given to us as we are united to Christ by the Spirit. In relation to the communion of the saints, such a pattern is very clear in Ephesians 2. Christ has created unity in himself, removing the "dividing wall of hostility," "setting aside the law," reconciling Jews and Gentiles "through the cross" so that "he is our peace" (vv. 14–16). The one new humanity exists in Christ. On that basis Christ has proclaimed peace and given access together "to the Father by one Spirit." That is the

---

36. John Murray's discussion of the work of the Spirit, including the chapter on union with Christ, does not highlight the corporate dimension, though it might seem to be implied in almost all his comments about union with Christ.

37. Berkouwer, *The Westminster Larger Catechism* offers some correction to this individualizing tendency. It begins the application of the redemptive work of Christ (Q58–90) with a treatment of the visible and invisible church (Q61–62) affirming that only those who are members of the invisible church are saved because they enjoy union and communion with Christ "in grace and glory" (Q65). The *ordo salutis* is then developed as an account of the union and communion of the invisible church with Christ (Q67–90). It is not clear that this arrangement substantially effects the doctrine of the Catechism, but it at least provides the right context for an exposition of the *ordo salutis*. It is fair to note that some recent discussions do better at noting the corporate dimension of inhabitation, e.g. See Billings, *Union with Christ*, 123–65; Campbell, *Paul and Union with Christ*, 288–89; Johnson, *One with Christ* 189–211; Gorman, *Participating in*, 37; Cole, *He Who Gives Life*, 219–21; Allison, *Sojourners and Strangers*, 117–20.

unity of believers comes from the person and work of Christ, realised by the Spirit. Believers are bound to one another in the Spirit because there is one body of Christ. That gift of unity is not subsequent to the gift of salvation, it is an aspect of salvation.

The claim that the gift of the Spirit is at the same time individual and corporate is a crucial one for my account of the communion of the saints. My case is that participation in the communion of the saints is a necessary entailment of union with Christ.

5) Participation in the Spirit Is Enacted in Loving, Hearing, Speaking, and Personal Knowledge Between Believers.

At this point we consider directly the communion of the saints. What is the life we share together?

Since our communion with one another is fellowship with the Spirit, then the characteristics of that fellowship are reflected in our communion. That is, the communion of the saints is shared love in and through the exchange of words.

Paul calls on the church to keep the unity of the Spirit (Eph 4:3) and then expands on this unity. The church has received gifts from the ascended Christ. While Paul does not name the Spirit as the one who brings the gifts no doubt this is his work. In this case, the gifts are people who serve with God's word (Eph 4:11). Their task, by the word, is to equip the whole church to serve, so that together the church will move to its appointed end. The description is theologically potent and draws in many of the themes I have already noted. The goal is that "the body of Christ may be built up," which consists of "unity in the faith and in the knowledge of the Son of God" and "attaining to the whole measure of the fullness of Christ" (Eph 4:12–13). Maturity is contrasted with doctrinal instability and described as "speaking the truth in love" as a means of together growing into Christ (Eph 4:14–16). Other passages parallel this description—the work of the Spirit enables the church to speak and hear God's word so that it grows in love into the likeness of Christ (Col 3:9–17; Rom 12:3–21; 1 Pet 1:22–2:10).

Berkouwer insists that the body of Christ must live in "concrete fellowship." The fellowship of the Spirit cannot be an abstract truth. There can be no theoretical "contemplation" of being "in itself," an isolated "essence" of the Church as a "mystical" reality. Rather, there is an indissoluble connection with the concrete life of the Church on earth, directed to a unique "representation" of Christ's work of salvation and of His fullness.[38]

---

38. Berkouwer, *The Church*. 88.

His exposition refers to Ridderbos' discussion of the indicative-imperative connection, and a look at that passage helps to expand what Berkouwer has in mind.[39] Ridderbos argues that in Pauline theology the imperative rests on the indicative and, conversely, that the imperative does not exist apart from the indicative. He states that "in the new obedience the new life must become evident, and without the former [obedience] the latter [life] cannot exist."[40] Berkouwer comments that "these radical statements are decisive also for the church's being." That is union with Christ creates the possibility of the concrete communion of the saints and cannot exist apart from such communion.[41]

Berkouwer captures the sense of the New Testament. To be in Christ by the Spirit is immediately to live in fellowship with his body. When the Spirit came from the risen Christ, believers devoted themselves to the teaching of the apostles and the fellowship of shared worship, generous welfare and joyful hospitality (Acts 2:42–47). Christian gatherings in Acts are marked by the presence of the Holy Spirit with signs and wonders along with teaching and exposition of Scripture, breaking bread and baptism, prayer, community and mission.[42] We could supplement this with an examination of the way in which descriptions in the NT epistles imply concrete fellowship in the Spirit.

Bonhoeffer, too, stresses the place of the fellowship in constituting the Christian life, and the concrete and demanding nature of such fellowship.

> *The Christian comes into being and exists only in Christ's church. He is dependent upon it, that is, upon the other . . . Each . . . sustains the other in active love, intercession and forgiveness of sins through complete vicarious action, which is possible only in the church of Christ, resting as it does in its entirety upon the principle of vicarious action, that is, upon the love of God.*[43]

The commonplace experiences of church life—Christians welcome one another, encourage and admonish, confess the faith, sing, pray, teach, forgive, share gifts, visit, support the poor and suffering, submit to one another—that is the community of the saints in and by the Spirit. This is the mode in which the unity created in Christ is realized among us.

---

39. See Ridderbos *Paul*, 253–58.
40. Ridderbos, *Paul*, 256.
41. Berkouwer, *The Church*, 90.
42. White, "Gathered Together," 60–79.
43. Bonhoeffer, *Communion of Saints*, 136; and see Green, "Human Sociality and Christian Community," 113–33.

6) Participation in the Spirit Creates Local Communities.

The Robinson-Knox occasionalism leaves us wondering about the status of the relationship of believers when they are not gathered. Yet the work of the Spirit is not only to physically gather the saints, but in and with those gatherings he forms communities. Brothers and sisters who meet for worship are bound together by the Spirit, sharing in his life together. Such is the import of the claim that the body of Christ in the Spirit has "concrete fellowship."

A distinctive note of the work of the Spirit is that he creates and recreates the particular.[44] The work of the Son in creation and redemption is to provide the form and foundation—he is the logos (the rationale), he is the firstborn and the head (Col 1:15,18). He is the representative and substitute. The work of the Spirit is to bring into existence the particular realities created and recreated in and for Christ. A new humanity is formed in Christ, individuals and communities are formed in that new humanity by the Spirit. Greggs emphasizes that the Spirit works in time and space to bring people into fellowship with each other in immediate communities.[45]

The New Testament witnesses to the Spirit's work in forming local communities in the careful attention in the epistles to the shared life of churches in cities around the Mediterranean. The instructions in Romans 12 serve as an example: believers have different gifts to be used for the good of one another, they are to love sincerely in devotion to one another, honouring one another, sharing with "the Lord's people who are in need" and showing hospitality (Rom 12: 6–16). This presumes that life in the Spirit is shared not only in specific gatherings but also in an ongoing community life. The work of the Spirit establishes and sustains ongoing commitment between believers who are part of specific congregations.

7) Participation in the Spirit Creates Global Fellowship.

The Spirit also brings believers in their congregations into wider unity with the whole church. Greggs puts it thus, "Congregations are not simply in and of themselves the body of Christ but—being fully churches—are nevertheless both the body of Christ and a part of the body of Christ whose fullness is expressed across space and time."[46]

---

44. Greggs, *Dogmatic Ecclesiology*, 1 :21.
45. Greggs, *Dogmatic Ecclesiology*, 1:334.
46. Greggs, *Dogmatic Ecclesiology*, 1:351.

This is the obvious implication of the Ephesians 4 text concerning the unity of the church: "There is one body and one Spirit, . . . you were called to one hope . . . ; one Lord, one faith, one baptism; one God and Father of all" (Eph 4:4). Those great theological realities are one not only within the local congregation, but globally. There is and can be only one Triune God, there is only one hope of salvation and so only one faith and one baptism. While Paul's immediate application of these truths is to the local congregation, they must also imply that all churches share in the same fellowship.

In the New Testament fellowship between congregations was expressed in common apostolic oversight (Acts 14:23; 15:22; 2 Cor 11:28; Col 1:24–2:3; 1 Pet 1:1); greetings (Rom 16:5ff; Col 4:15); the exchange of writings (Col 4:16); the exchange of personnel (Col 4:12; Rom 16:1, 3; Acts 18:2); financial support (Rom 15:25ff; 2 Cor 8:19) and maintaining common practices (1 Cor 4:17; 7:17; 11:16; 13:33, 34; 16:1).

The nature of this fellowship, granted and sustained by the Spirit builds upon the concrete fellowship in congregations. It often consists of words exchanged as well as concrete gifts. We can conceptualize the fellowship of the "universal visible church," yet this always exists in concrete and conscious fellowship between specific congregations and believers. It is often primarily expressed between representatives of congregations, yet it reflects a connection between the congregations.

This aspect of the communion of the saints means no single congregation may consider itself to be "the church" alone. While this does not immediately require a particular polity, it does show the necessity of concrete connection between congregations.

8) Participation in the Spirit Gives Historical Continuity.

Greggs emphasizes that the communion of saints is "the basis and theological grounds for the engagement with the tradition and teaching of the church."[47] When we attend to the teaching, witness and confession of past generations, we participate concretely in the communion of the saints by the Spirit. We do not simply consider historical artefacts but read or hear the voices of brothers and sisters with whom we are bound by the Holy Spirit.

---

47. Greggs, *Dogmatic Ecclesiology*, 261, deals with this theme so well that I will not expand on it here.

9) Participation in the Spirit Unites Us in Worship with the Saints in Glory.

The predominant theme in Catholic and Orthodox discussions of the communion of the saints is the relationship of the church militant with the church triumphant. Vatican II reaffirms that the church is united with the dead and prays for them as well as seeking their prayers. It emphasizes the unity of love and the power of the example of those who have died in Christ and the shared worship of the earthly and heavenly church.[48] How do we think about this in a Reformed account of the communion of the saints? Is there a concrete and experiential communion with the church triumphant by the Spirit.

Those in the intermediate state of glory continue to live in and by the Spirit. He is the deposit and guarantee of life in glory (2 Cor 1:22; 5:5; Eph. 1:13-14), believers now are the first fruits of the Spirit anticipating the eschatological harvest (Rom 8:23). He is the Spirit of life (Rom 8:1-13), the Spirit of adoption (Rom 8:14-17) and the Spirit of glory (1 Pet 4:14; cf 2 Cor 3:18).[49] The Spirit as the perfecting cause continues his work in glory. Since those now in glory share in the same Spirit as believers in this life; we have a warrant for affirming that together we share in the communion of the Spirit.

The Catholic view is that this fellowship consists in an exchange of spiritual goods between believers and the dead in Christ. In this life, the Church prays for those in purgatory, and the saints pray for the Church. There are good reasons to reject the doctrine of purgatory.[50] Yet, there is a basis for affirming a continued shared life of worship. The book of Hebrews stresses that in Christ believers now have access to God in the heavenly temple (Heb 4:16; 7:19; 10:19-22; 13:10). Hebrews 12 expands this to assure believers that they now worship with those in glory. They *have come* to "Mount Zion, to the city of the living God, the heavenly Jerusalem" which is characterized by the great joyful assembly of angels, God, the Judge, Jesus the mediator of a new covenant and, particularly, to "the church of the firstborn" and "the spirits of the righteous made perfect" (Heb 12:24). So, through participation in Christ, Christians now share in heavenly worship with the faithful who have completed their pilgrimage.

John's visions in Revelation imply something similar. He sees the twenty-four elders, representative of the people of God, joining with the

---

48. Flannery, ed. *Vatican Council II: The Basic Sixteen Documents* §§50-51, pp. 75-78.
49. Cole, *He Who Gives Life*, 238-39.
50. Venema, *The Promise of the Future*, 63-74.

heavenly host in praise (Rev 4:4–10).[51] Later he sees the 144,000 which is the incalculable multitude in God's presence, praising him (Rev 7:9–17). Beale concludes that "the picture does not primarily connote the idea of a select group of martyrs, but encompasses the entire company of the redeemed."[52] The same company appears in Revelation 14 singing a new song of praise (Rev 14:3). Each of these visions show the whole church, triumphant and militant, sharing in heavenly worship. When the church is seen from the heavenly perspective it encompasses all who have faith in Christ and shows us in common worship.

Reformed theology, then, can and should affirm a communion of the church militant with the church triumphant. As we praise God by the power of the Spirit, we join our voices with the heavenly assembly who are also filled by the Spirit. Such a biblical insight should frame our understanding of gathered worship.

10) Participation in the Spirit Is Progressive.

Ephesians 4 reminds us that participation in the Spirit is progressive. The church is indwelt with the Spirit and exists in the Spirit. This will and must result in growth. The NT discussion of progress is Christological—we grow in the full stature of Christ, and the new self is "being renewed in knowledge in the image of its Creator" (Col 3:10). We should not think of sharing more and more fully in the Spirit, but that in the Spirit we come to know and imitate Christ more fully, and this must happen together. So, in local, global, historical and heavenly dimensions we pray for and expect that there will be a growing communion of the saints in the fellowship of the Spirit. Of course, this is not always observable. The concrete communion of the saints in love and faith seems often to diminish rather than progress. The expectation of progress should not be a reason for presumption nor for idealism. It should be an encouragement to continue to keep the unity of the Spirit in the bond of peace and to strive that in Christ the whole body with all its parts working together may "build itself up in love."

11) Participation in the Spirit Has an Eschatological Orientation.

Greggs stresses that the church is a provisional community. It witnesses to Christ's death, resurrection and ascension in the past; and anticipates his

---

51. Beale, *The Book of Revelation*, 322.
52. Beale, *The Book of Revelation*, 438.

return and kingdom. As an institution, the church will come to an end with the fullness of the kingdom. Even between the resurrection and return it is "always passing at any given moment in time and space." He views the communion of the saints as the counterpoint to such provisionality. Even though the church is passing away and will end it exists "within the everlasting communion of saints."[53]

I am not convinced that the church and the communion of the saints stand in such contrast. If the church in our experience of time and space is united with the heavenly church, then the change in form at the eschaton is perhaps not so great. Nevertheless, the main point is correct. The visible church exists within the everlasting communion of saints, and it anticipates the consummation of that communion in the New Creation.

CONCLUSION

What do we learn from a consideration of the communion of the saints in the fellowship of the Spirit?

This exposition highlights that the church exists in the triune economy and is particularly the result of the mission of the Holy Spirit. Since this is the context for the existence of the church, then the communion of the saints is a fundamental description of the nature of the church, and all else we say about the church should relate to it. The visible church is always an expression of the greater reality of the communion of the saints. Because we are always in fellowship with Spirit, then we are also in fellowship with the saints. In the visible church this is expressed in concrete fellowship, which is both local and universal.

Thus, a consideration of the communion of the saints as the fellowship of the Spirit challenges both the ecclesial occasionalism and congregationalism of the Robinson-Knox view. The church is the church when it is not gathered—though it must gather in concrete fellowship. Believers are bound to one another and have particular and specific duties to one another, gathered and scattered. Further, congregations which are the primary concrete realisation of the communion of saints, have in turn specific fellowship with and duties toward one another.

The study offers wider and more important implications. It calls us to consider how we can express in concrete ways our fellowship with believers in our own congregations, in our denominations and other communions and in the wider church. Because fellowship is expressed in words grounded on the Word of God, we cannot ignore doctrinal differences. We must be

---

53. Greggs, *Dogmatic Ecclesiology*, 247.

discerning about how we can express fellowship within our convictions about biblically ordered faith and practice. Yet the truth of the communion of the saints calls us to seek such fellowship broadly, rather than narrowly.

This exposition underlines the serious duty named in Ephesians 4:3—"Make every effort to keep the unity of the Spirit through the bond of peace." Preserving unity in truth and love is an imperative for the local church, wider visible church, even in our unity with past generations of saints and in continued sharing in their glorified worship. Most of all this theme brings us again to wonder that as the church of God, in our various relations with each other, we share in the glorious grace of God.

2

"It has seemed good to the Holy Spirit and to us"

Church, Scripture, and Discerning the Spirit

MICHAEL ALLEN

BIBLICAL MODELS FOR ECCLESIAL DISCERNMENT: THE RELATIONSHIP OF THE JERUSALEM COUNCIL TO CONTEMPORARY QUANDARIES

THE CHURCH FACES A host of issues. They appear all over the globe and take various local forms, to be sure, but they cluster around a host of issues. We navigate issues of morality regarding the use of our bodies or of various technologies. We debate approaches to politics and power and public agency. We seek consensus pertaining to the task of education, of building and sustaining families, and so forth. In many of the countries of Europe and North America, these conversations happen at a time of growing distrust and heightening polarization. Often those cultural conditions can impact the church as much as the ballot box or the town square.

Christians have been here before. Not exactly here, of course, but situations and circumstances very much like what we face here and now. Christians have regularly lived in contexts where our sexual ethic does not match native custom or where biblical concerns pertaining to wealth and power seem to run aground the virtues of that host culture. Examples of discernment—especially of discernment in the face of supposed turning points—are sought by a range of thinkers. When we know we have challenging theological demands ahead, we are wise to honor the fifth commandment and ask what we might learn from our spiritual fathers and mothers. We are wiser still to remember always what the first commandment suggests, namely, how the lord in Scripture might model an approach to discernment for us, by which we might tackle our contemporary challenges.

"It has seemed good to the Holy Spirit and to us" (Acts 15:28). These words offer the promise of a Spirit-inspired unity and, further, its roots in a Spirit-enlightened discernment. For many recent interpreters, these words and that account of the Jerusalem Council provide the pertinent scriptural model for how a divided church might discern its way through moral and cultural quandaries, more specifically, how the Spirit might help bring clear judgment to situations where there's debate as to how to apply the Word to new contexts.

In his 1983 book *Scripture and Discernment: Decision Making in the Church*, Luke Timothy Johnson argued that Acts 10–15 serves as a key analogue and the judgment of the Jerusalem Council in Acts 15 models an approach to pneumatological discernment that can and should be emulated by churches today. The approach of Johnson has been influential, with Stephen Fowl, Sylvia Keesmaat, and Eugene Rogers amongst those who claim to follow his lead.[1]

Johnson views the New Testament as midrashic in origin and best read as analogous to the Talmud.[2] As Paul rarely models how he makes decisions (though 1 Cor 5:1–5 is an exception), Acts 15 is "unique in the New Testament for the fullness of the attention it gives to the decision-making process."[3] Reading the text well involves facing three difficulties. Historically, does this refer to one or more meetings? And how does this history relate to what is reported in Galatians 2?[4] Literarily, how do we catch the intention of the text? What does its narrative context in Luke and Acts reveal?[5] Theologically, what

---

1. Fowl, *Engaging Scripture*, 97–127; Keesmat, "Welcoming in the Gentiles," 30–48; and Rogers, *Sexuality and the Christian Body*, 49–66.
2. Johnson, *Scripture and Discernment*, 38–39.
3. Johnson, *Scripture and Discernment*, 68–69.
4. Johnson, *Scripture and Discernment*, 73–75.
5. Johnson, *Scripture and Discernment*, 76–77.

is normative in this text: a process, a judgment, or a narrative?[6] How might we hear and obey this text: as a ruling, a protocol, or an inspiration?

Johnson observes the Council hearing of signs and wonders occurring among the Gentiles (15:12; see also parallels in 2:19, 22, 43; 5:12; 6:8; 7:36; 14:3).[7] Peter realizes that Jews will be saved like the Gentiles, as opposed to perceiving that Gentiles come in as do the Jews.[8] Why? "Narrative is their only argument."[9] To what effect? "Experience of God's activity stimulates the church to reread the Scripture and to discover ever new ways in which God maintains continuity with Godself."[10]

"Taking the texts seriously means that in our ecclesial—as well as personal—decisions we are willing to take our stand over against as well as under the text."[11] Johnson finds subjectivity less a threat than what he deems the "inertia" of tradition and the status quo.[12] Prophetic discernment is crucial then. Later Johnson adds: "The teaching office of the church requires the voice of prophecy to be alive if it is not to grow distended: through prophets the living Jesus can speak in new ways. And the preservers of tradition need also to hear the voices of theologians whose task is not so much to preserve as it is to extend the boundaries of our understanding of the mystery of Christ."[13] How can one discern appropriately? He accents the distinctiveness of the church as a rubric for analysis, given that holiness involves being set apart.[14] Whatever case studies might be considered, ranging from debates about sexuality to ordination to wealth and possessions, the church should seek to discern the distinctive path that breaks with the wider culture.[15]

---

6. Johnson, *Scripture and Discernment*, 78.

7. Johnson, *Scripture and Discernment*, 102–3.

8. Johnson, *Scripture and Discernment*, 103.

9. Johnson, *Scripture and Discernment*, 103. Keesmat follows suit with a singular focus upon story as the theologically authoritative facet of Scripture, "Welcoming in the Gentiles," 32.

10. Johnson, *Scripture and Discernment*, 107.

11. Johnson, *Scripture and Discernment*, 43.

12. Johnson, *Scripture and Discernment*, 111.

13. Luke Timothy Johnson, *Living Jesus*, 38.

14. Johnson, *Scripture and Discernment*, 125.

15. I do not have space here to explore this element sufficiently, but one needs to distinguish between distinctiveness relative to cultures that are or are not yet influenced significantly by Christianity (acknowledging, of course, that no culture has been completely or consistently Christianized, on which see Augustine, *The City of God*, bks. 18–19). To aim for a distinctive posture relative to the Greco-Roman world is one thing, to do likewise relative to Christendom or to a significantly Christianized society is notably (though not completely) different. Johnson does not note any element of that sort of distinction.

While the Council can and must serve as an orienting model for how discernment should occur, I hope to show that Johnson's proposal runs afoul of three concerns. First, I will show how his proposal fails to trace the conciliar judgment that the Old Testament was not being rejected but that certain portions of the Old Testament foretold a later fulfillment of other elements of the Old Testament. In so doing, we can observe an exercise in intertextual exegesis that nowhere contrasts Spirit with the Old Testament. Second, I will analyze the way in which Johnson's argument implies an uncoupling of grace from nature and of new creation (or recreation) from creation itself. In as much as it does so, it fails to match the way that both Old and New Testaments relate the end to the beginning. Third, I will show the way in which Johnson's approach bespeaks trinitarian disunity, wherein the Spirit trumps the Word, and thereby misses the differentiated oneness that marks the inner life of the one living and true God revealed as Father, Son, and Holy Spirit. While there is counsel to be taken from this council, a more textured account, attendant both to the immediate details and to the wider doctrinal frame in which it appears, must be sought.

INTERTEXTUAL EXEGESIS: THE RELATIONSHIP OF OLD AND NEW

First, the Jerusalem Council seeks to relate Old Testament moral teaching to a seemingly new ecclesial situation, and the Spirit's guidance does not lead them to discern the abrogation or annulment of the Old Testament but its nuanced fulfillment according to its own stated prompts.

It should not be surprising that intertextual exegesis was constitutive of apostolic preaching and of conciliar judgment. It was elemental to the very message of Jesus Christ. He not only foretold the necessity of his suffering and glory, but chastised the despairing disciples on the Emmaus Road for being foolish and slow to believe not what he spoke but "all that the prophets have spoken!" (Luke 24:25). Later on that Easter day, he twice relayed what he had spoken to his disciples to "everything written about me in the Law of Moses and the Prophets and the Psalms," which "must be fulfilled" (Luke 24:44). He had earlier offered now famous instruction that one "not think that I have come to abolish the Law or the Prophets; I have not come to abolish them but to fulfill them" (Matt 5:17). Unsurprisingly, when Paul spoke of that death and resurrection occurring "according to the Scriptures" in 1 Cor 15:3–5, he was largely rehearsing the final lesson conveyed by Jesus in Luke 24:46–49. The apostles caught the intra-textual bug and never were satisfied simply to follow the Spirit away from the words of the prophets. And early Christians caught this essential element of early Christian thought, as evidenced by Irenaeus of Lyons's inclusion of the significance that the gospel occur "according to the Scriptures" in his *Demonstration of the Apostolic Preaching*. That text not only comments on this line in particular, but structures the entire work into two parts that itemize the elements of the gospel and show their roots in the writings of the prophets. I do not mention Irenaeus randomly either, for his litany of the gospel ends with the inclusion of the Gentiles.[16] He too has learned this from the apostles and ultimately from Jesus (see Luke 24:47). When Luke's second work, the Acts of the Apostles, begins to describe the gospel witness from Jerusalem to Judaea, to Samaria, and to the ends of the earth, it is not portrayed as inventing something. It is expanding on the final line from his characterization of Jesus in his gospel account.

Acts 15 manifestly models this intratextual concern, which can be explored in conversation with Fowl and Keesmat's extension of the argument originally offered by Johnson. Stephen Fowl argues that James's argument "articulates for the community the sense of the Spirit's work."[17] He rightly notes that it is not merely the gravity of his person that carries the day but the shape of his argument. So far, so good. But it is not merely the Spirit's witness in recent experience which confirms James's judgment. He labors to manifest that experience's conformity with scriptural precedent. James said: "Simeon has related how God first visited the Gentiles, to take from them a people for his name. And with this the words of the prophets agree" (Acts 15:14–15). He quotes Amos 9:11, 12 as a prophetic foretelling of what Peter, Paul, and Barnabas have attested to have recently occurred (Acts 15:16–17). It is remarkable that James mentions that experience as the starting point for conversation: he says "the words of the prophets agree" with this narrative of Gentile conversion, rather than that the story of Gentile conversion conform to the Scriptures. Even so, the word order does not undo the link.[18] Experience is not superseding scripture, as has been suggested by other accounts.[19]

---

16. Irenaeus, *Demonstration of the Apostolic Preaching*, 66–67 (ending part 1), and 92–100 (ending part 2).

17. Fowl, *Engaging Scripture*, 112.

18. Peterson, *Acts of the Apostles*, 430–32; *contra* Keesmat, "Welcoming in the Gentiles," 38.

19. Keesmat, "Welcoming in the Gentiles," 36, where she states that "there is *absolutely no biblical precedent* for welcoming in Gentiles without being circumcised and following Torah. The Pharisees who opposed Paul had both scripture and tradition on their side." Later Keesmat argues that James raises scriptural references only by bringing in indirect texts that suit his purposes (39).

Scripture is seen to have attested to its own eventual culmination: the requirement of circumcision for membership in God's people was only for a time but was foretold or figured to conclude eventually. "Only because the new experience of Gentile converts proved hermeneutically illuminating of Scripture was the church, over time, able to accept the decision to embrace Gentiles within the fellowship of God's people."[20] Scripture interprets Scripture, in the deliberation of the council, as Amos contextualizes the laws of the Pentateuch within a certain (past) phase of redemptive history. While Fowl may be right that the "plain sense" of certain texts may seem to push one way, the Jerusalem Council saw other texts (like Amos) offering a "plain sense" that offered eschatological qualification of those earlier texts.[21] In no case did the council or experience reject the "plain sense" of Scripture. Because of the experience witnessed and its conformity to biblical teaching, the council renders a judgment agreeable to James's suggestion: "my judgment is that we should not trouble those of the Gentiles who turn to God" with things like circumcision and observance of the Israelite law (Acts 15:19, 28).

The ethical teaching that is offered is also rooted in the biblical writings of the people of God. There are debates as to the precise roots of the commands "to abstain from the things polluted by idols, and from sexual immorality, and from what has been strangled, and from blood" as James puts it, and to "abstain from what has been sacrificed to idols, and from blood, and from what has been strangled, and from sexual immorality" (Acts 15:20, 29). Some argue that these commands point back to the Noahic laws given in Genesis 11.[22] Others believe they are all given to resident aliens in Leviticus 17–18.[23] Undoubtedly, they are biblical teaching regarding the behavior of non-Israelites (either outside the covenant or coming into the covenant). We can say, then, that not only in its moral restraint but also in the particularity of its ongoing ethical requirements, the Council looks to Scripture to shape its judgment: Gentile converts are to obey as the Old Testament says they should (provided the Old Testament is read in such a way that its own eschatological prophecies about the redemptive-historical inclusion of Gentiles, as Gentile believers rather than as Israelites, is given due attention).[24] Luke Timothy Johnson himself acknowledged that other decision-making passages in Acts 1:15–26; 4:23–31; 6:1–6; and 9:26–30 involve scriptural interpretation and narrative perception "interpenetrating"

20. Hays, *Moral Vision*, 399.
21. Fowl, *Engaging Scripture*, 126.
22. Bruce, *The Book of the Acts*, 295–96.
23. Fowl, *Engaging Scripture*, 113.
24. Bauckham, "James and the Jerusalem Council," 462–63.

and "intermingling."[25] The literary context of Acts 10–15 sets the stage, then, for what we find in Acts 15. Narrative perception follows from re-immersion in the authoritative claims of the Scripture. The story has not moved along past prior Scripture, but Scripture itself is seen to clarify and constrain their sense of this new time and its attendant responsibilities for faithfulness and polity.

NATURE AND GRACE: THE RELATIONSHIP OF CREATION AND RE-CREATION

Second, the Jerusalem Council seeks to relate Old Testament moral teaching to a seemingly new ecclesial situation, and the Spirit's guidance does not lead them to discern the contradiction or separation of grace from nature but the restoration of fallen creation to its newly recreated destiny.

Johnson's model leads to a cataclysmic juxtaposition: in rather than out, child rather than stranger, heir rather than dog, friend rather than enemy. It can be construed by a range of pairings—and others might be added, each appearing in one scriptural register or another—but they each involve the removal or clearing of prior ground at the Spirit's behest. Johnson acknowledges the position of the Gentiles previously: "Gentiles were 'by nature' unclean, and were 'by practice' polluted by idolatry."[26]

The gospel does work an apocalyptically invasive salvation. It makes enemies into friends and even family. It resurrects the dead. But that is not yet a sufficient account of the way the gospel is depicted in the New Testament (or even in Acts 7:2–53). The gospel works that apocalyptically invasive salvation in a way that is wholly owing to God's intervention and yet completely fitting with prior divine order. The language of necessity repeatedly gestures in this direction. In his account of the Emmaus Road, Luke conveys the first response of Jesus to his despairing disciples: "Was it not necessary that the Christ should suffer these things and enter into his glory?" (24:26). It is not enough to forgive and forget. It will not suffice to determine to move on. God's justice and holiness demand that forgiveness and new resolve take the form of addressing the just demands of God's own law. It is not for nothing that Paul will speak in Rom. 3:24–26 of God demonstrating his own justice in being both just and the justifier.

Such is the way of atonement, and so also is the way of covenant inclusion. Not only the Jerusalem Council but two other texts are often identified

---

25. Johnson, *Scripture and Discernment*, 84–85.

26. Johnson, *Scripture and Discernment*, 147; see also Rogers, *Sexuality and the Christian Body*, 53.

"It has seemed good to the Holy Spirit and to us"

as showing God's concern in grace to act contrary to nature. First, Gal 3:28 locates the distinction of Jew and Gentile alongside others such as male and female, slave and free. "In Christ Jesus you are all sons of God, through faith. For as many of you as were baptized into Christ have put on Christ. There is neither Jew nor Greek, there is neither slave nor free, there is no male and female, for you are all one in Christ Jesus" (Gal 3:26–28). While contemporary eyes might fix upon the series from back to front, the first pair is the one discussed repeatedly and at length across the New Testament. In fact, Eugene Rogers contends that "it may come as a surprise to modern Christians that that pair is far and away the most important of the series."[27] Rogers is right about its significance, though his account wrongly conveys a singular focus upon God acting *para physin* ("contrary to nature"). In Galatians 3, the passage goes on to reassert the nature of old covenant identity: "If you are Christ's, then you are Abraham's offspring, heirs according to promise" (Gal 3:29). Children will be adopted anew, then, but the one family persists. Second, Rogers employs the language of Rom 11:24, where Gentiles,[28] who are *kata physin* or "contrary to nature," are grafted into the olive tree of God's people. Again, the particular metaphor of the olive tree does convey a crucial facet of God's covenantal action throughout Romans 11. Relative to that image in that specific context, Gentiles are grafted in *kata physin*. And yet Paul has already offered another parallel account in Romans 9–10, where they are not grafted in so much as truly identified as those welcomed by God when they call upon him and even as those called mysteriously by God to be Abraham's children? Romans 9:24 is so blunt as to identify that electing call as relevant to those "not from the Jews only but also from the Gentiles." In this first approach to the Jew/Gentile issue, Paul inscribes Gentiles within the old nature of the covenant even if that demands our acknowledgement that assumptions about who was in or out were too simplistic and perhaps even wrong. In a second approach, Paul turns to the language of acting *kata physin* to show that Gentiles are truly redeemed in a new manner.

The danger here is that we would construe the New Testament teaching on nature and grace monolithically as a contrariety and nothing more. Whether in the form of Johnson and Rogers' arguments or the guise of some recent apocalyptic theologians, such claims might lead to a sense that grace or new creation is altogether unrelated to or contrary with nature.[29] In such

---

27. Rogers, *Sexuality and the Christian Body*, 47.
28. Rogers, *Sexuality and the Christian Body*, 65.
29. For assessment of so-called apocalyptic theology, see Hill, "Apocalyptic Theology"; and Allen, *The Fear of the Lord*, 103–16.

a vantage point, the judgment of the Council and others like it in the New Testament point to Jesus as novel. And yet the very passages that Johnson or Rogers turn to consider are themselves located in contexts that exude more and insist also on relating grace not only discontinuously but also continuously with nature. They call us to a far more challenging discernment of continuity amid discontinuity and vice versa.

The saving work of Christ does involve new creation, and yet that does not dispel concern for the restoration of creation. After hearing the testimony of Peter and Paul, James himself quotes from Amos 9, a passage that reiterates the importance of return, rebuilding, and restoration. "After this I will return, and I will rebuild the tent of David that has fallen; I will rebuild its ruins, and I will restore it" (Acts 15:16). Return and restoration serve as first and final markers of divine commitment to the old nature of covenant promises, with a doubled reference to building (the tent and the ruins) in the center. James does delimit the ongoing application of certain Mosaic judicial demands for these Gentile Christians, and yet he frames his approach as anything but sheer apocalyptic change or singular focus upon novelty. With this nonidentical repetition of the old nature of covenant loyalty, the heritage of the covenant itself is rebuilt and restored. When God returns, nature will be restored anew, and human life and vocation will be rebuilt.

Just as theologians must tend to ways in which grace really does advance upon nature, so we must also avoid the error of reducing their relationship to one of antagonism.

TRIUNITY: THE RELATIONSHIP OF WORD AND SPIRIT

Third, the Jerusalem Council seeks to relate Old Testament moral teaching to a seemingly new ecclesial situation, and the Spirit's guidance does not lead them to discern the Spirit leading away from the prior revelation of the Word but to the Spirit's unified witness to the wholeness of that Word's own speech.

Johnson's account would have an Old Testament Word countered or abrogated by a New Testament Spirit. It is a revelational parallel to a more common trinitarian understanding (or misunderstanding) of the saving work of God. Too often, the incarnate Son is perceived by Christians as trumping what is most kindly construed as the justice of God and often taken in a more suspicious mode to be the miserly or vindictive posture of his heavenly Father toward sinners. Such an approach finds its seeming motivation in that the Bible speaks of sinners as God's enemies and objects of wrath. Further, Christ is conveyed as compassionate, often especially for those marginalized and maligned by charges according to divine and scriptural law. It is not surprising then that the incarnate Son is viewed as including those whom the Father had previously been seen to exclude.

But Christ's saving work was according to the will of the one who sent him. You may or may not find the language of a covenant of redemption or *pactum salutis* useful here—that is another topic for another day, and one that involves a host of complexities—but all of us surely need some way to alert ourselves to the myriad scriptural signs of the Son's errand to earth being neither a solo effort nor an individual mission and never ever construed as an intercessory counterpoint to the posture of the Father toward sinners. Rather, his particular mission was performed by the power of the Spirit and according to the plan and pleasure of the Father. Here is love, not that Jesus came apart from the Father and Spirit but that he manifests the whole Godhead's merciful resolve to do good to enemies such as us.

And it is not only the atoning work of the Son that must be viewed in such a harmonious and unified portrait of the Trinity. The inclusion of the Gentiles—more specifically, the salvation of elect Gentiles in Christ, as perceived by the Jerusalem Council—also occurs as much according to the Word as it is discerned by the Spirit. The Spirit neither draws attention away from the Word nor suggests a contrary position to that of the Word. Here we do not return to the intertextual question of the relationship of the Old to the New Testament but to the deeper trinitarian question of how this Spirit relates to that Word and whether we can find contrapuntal actions within the missions of the Godhead.

The Holy Spirit will be known as the Spirit of Jesus and the very own Spirit of Christ, names which convey the integral and essential union of the two persons within the mystery of the Godhead. This essentially integral union can be appreciated by means of the language of three trinitarian concepts. They might be likened to a three-stranded cord, playing a cumulative role in informing and locating our approach to the pneumatology at play in Acts 15. First, the procession of the Holy Spirit terminates in the visible mission of the Holy Spirit, which thereby betokens something of the character whereby the Spirit manifests the one divine life in particular hypostatic form. Second, the Word and Spirit share in the one divine will. Third, the three persons of the triune Godhead, in as much as they are defined relatively by their processions and not something else, share together in external works. Here I only have time to comment briefly upon each element of this three-stranded cord.

First, the Spirit proceeds not merely from the Father but from the Father and the Son. Here, irrespective of historical happenstance regarding its creedal insertion, I take the Western concept of the *filioque* as essential to a full and orderly account of biblical trinitarianism. The Spirit is none other than the lordly, divine one spirated by Father and Son. That procession means that even the distinctiveness of the Spirit—his personal *propria*—itself stems from his personal relation to Father and Son and cannot be thought otherwise. While he flows forth from Father and Son in a way that is distinctly his own, it nonetheless remains to be said that even this personally distinctive element itself can be construed only by means of interconnection with and overflow from Father and Son. Not for nothing, then, does Jesus in his farewell discourse say of the Spirit's coming that "he will not speak on his own authority, but whatever he hears he will speak" (John 16:13). This unity of mission and pedagogy has metaphysical and intra-trinitarian roots.

Second, this Spirit shares the one divine will with both the Father and the Son. The Spirit does not will apart from the Son or the Father. The Spirit is sent by Father and Son, to be sure, but this economic manifestation (what we call his visible mission) truly does make manifest his oneness with Father and Son and offer visibly a sign of the Godhead's inviolable volitional unity. That inviolable volitional unity manifests outwardly and, by analogous extension, in the sending of the Spirit in the divine economy. Interestingly, in the farewell discourse, Jesus says he "sends" the Spirit (15:26; 16:7) and that the Spirit is "sent . . . from the Father" (15:26). Father and Son each stand behind the sending of the Son, though the manner in which they each issue forth the Spirit eternally and send him forth economically will be attested diversely: the Father doing so as Father or in a Fatherly way, the Son doing so as Son or in a Sonly manner.

Third, the external works of the triune God are undivided, in as much as all three persons share the divine life and are hypostatically distinguished only by their own relations of origin or procession. In a real sense, this rule follows from the prior two claims, namely, that personal properties follow from the relations of origin and, thus, cannot be observed apart from the shared divine life, and also that the three persons share one will. In volitional unity and personal coinherence expressed via the divine processions, the inner life of God is marked by an inviolable unity. But we speak not only of the inner divine life, for these realities are made evident also in the external works or missions of the Godhead. This divinity—not merely its contrast to creation, but also its personal relations—is made visible in those works. This Godhead—not merely its high holiness, but also its simplicity and unity—is manifest in that divine economy.

These three intra-divine realities being true, the discernment of the Spirit in the divine economy cannot take one away from the Word, for the Spirit is sent of the Word with the Father, shares the same will with the Word and Father, and works not apart from or divided from the Word and Father.

Each constituent element attests to this unified life and being on its own, and all three serve to offer overlapping and triangulated testimony to an inner divine life that itself also surely exceeds our capacity for comprehension. However hard it may be to attest fully the nature of this unity, we can signal ways which obviously fall short. In particular, one would pertain to the current concern and deserves mention. A supplementary or juxtaposed relationship of Spirit's revelation to the Word's illumination would run amiss of this cluster of trinitarian teaching.

CONCLUSION: THE SERVICE OF SYSTEMATIC THEOLOGY TO ECCLESIAL DISCERNMENT

"It has seemed good to the Holy Spirit and to us": these words rightly stand as a banner over successful theological discernment by the church. Yet they assume much, which we are wise not simply to presume. They assume clarity about that Spirit, his relationship to the whole of Scripture, to the saving work of Christ and its implications for a fallen creation and fallen human nature in particular, and to the Father and Son in the inner life of the Trinity. If we presume too much here, we can fail to discern the spirits and wrongly assume the identification of the Holy Spirit with our own judgment or our tribe's own spirit. Here as ever, the church which aims to discern as she must and to practice scriptural discernment about the weighty moral challenges of our day will be well served by tending to the discipline of systematic theology. Systematics or dogmatic reasoning will alert her to the range of concerns about which she must always be concerned, lest she rush forward presumptively and allow her assumptions to go unscathed and idolatrously. Such concerns include:

- We need the Spirit to guide our reading of Scripture, but we need also to see that guidance as a genuinely fresh reading of Scripture itself.
- We need the Spirit to illumine our grasp of how grace recasts nature, but we need also to perceive that illumination as a restoration of creation and the fulfilment of a long-awaited destiny for human nature and the whole of creation.
- We need the Spirit to enlighten our grasp of the good news of the one true God, but we need also to receive that enlightenment as not only coordinated with but a sharing in the true Light, who himself came into the world.

We need to discern what seems good to the Holy Spirit and to the church, yet we dare not venture forth as if there won't be treacherous paths to misperceive and real temptation to presume too much.

Systematic theology can help prompt our ecclesial discernment, then, to keep our eyes ever on the whole counsel of God, to attend to scripture's own priorities and categories, to watch for ways in which scripture employs ordinary language in sometimes extraordinary fashion, and to catch the coherent connections between the diverse teachings of the Word. Systematic theology is not a means of grace and guarantees nothing. But systematic theology helps us discern better what seems good to the Spirit and to the church of Christ. Hopefully this systematic argument has helped to refine the way in which we gather what is going on behind and among the determinations evident in the Jerusalem Council as attested by Acts 15.

3

The Holy Spirit and the Digital Church
A Discussion of Calvin, Pentecost, and Hybrid Ecclesial Practices

MARK J. CARTLEDGE

INTRODUCTION

I AM ONE OF those rare people who belongs to one tradition but spends most of his time researching another tradition. By background and conviction, I am an Evangelical Anglican, and my understanding of Reformed theology is, in large part, mediated by that tradition, especially but not exclusively through the work of Thomas Cranmer, the great English reformer, and his liturgy. As an undergraduate at London Bible College, I was led through large portions of Calvin's *Institutes* and I still use the same copy that I purchased back in 1984, complete with my own (rather odd) 39-year-old annotations! Despite my early studies in historical theology, my academic work over the years has been shaped by two main areas. The first is practical theology, so I write not as a systematician but as a practical theologian, who has nevertheless engaged with a variety of systematic theological loci in my own work. I am interested in systematics, even if I position myself at the edge of the discipline. The second area is my research focus, namely the study of contemporary Pentecostalism and the Charismatic Renewal movement, often using empirical research methods drawn from the social sciences but framed within empirical theology associated with Nijmegen in the Netherlands. Recently, I have developed an interest in digital expressions of Christianity, especially the notion of digital ecclesiology and the idea of digital Pentecostalism.[1] In this chapter, I attempt to bring together a number of these different features (Calvin, Pentecostal theology and digital ecclesiology) as will be obvious as I proceed.

The COVID-19 pandemic brought many changes to church life in 2020–21. It brought physical lockdowns, working from home, the use of masks, hand gel and social distancing measures, to name the obvious things that people experienced. It also brought huge pressures on health care, educational institutions, government, law and order and civic life. The church as an important worldwide institution responded in different ways but was subject to the restrictions place upon her by governments around the world. In the UK the government did not regard clergy as essential workers. Thus, church buildings closed and clergy, like everyone else, worked from home. In this world of home working, church services and meetings went online. Either services were live-streamed from inside a church building with a lone minister or they were broadcast from the living room, with break-out Zoom rooms for "virtual coffee" afterwards.

In this season of lockdown, the wider church was exploring what it meant to "do" or "be" digital church. For many independent churches with the technology already in place this was a fairly easy transition, but for those more traditional churches it was either a mad scramble to get the hardware and then become competent to use it or simply to close up and wait for the pandemic to pass.[2] Of course, there had been ongoing development of internet, cyber, virtual or digital church for some time.[3] Indeed, in parts of the world, some creative experiments had taken place and were already in various stages of development. But the pandemic thrust all of us into this world of the digital interface around worship with differing levels of competence and enthusiasm. Now, in a post-pandemic reality, it is worth pondering how

---

1. My recent publications in this area include: "Digital Pentecostal Sacramentality"; "Pentecostalism and the Eucharist in a Digital Age"; "Empirical Theology as Theological Netnography"; "Studying Digital Pentecostalism"; and "Virtual Mediation of the Holy Spirit."

2. For a discussion of the "digital divide" among American churches during the COVID-19 pandemic, see Campbell, "When Churches Discovered the Digital Divide."

3. Some examples include: Wilson, *The Internet Church*; Campbell, *Exploring Religious Communities Online*; Estes, *SimChurch*; Drescher, *Tweet if You [Heart] Jesus*; Wise, *The Social Church*; Spadaro, *Cybertheology*; Thompson, *The Virtual Body of Christ*; Hutchings, *Creating Church Online*; Schmidt, *Virtual Communion*; and Campbell and Dyer, *Ecclesiology for a Digital Church*.

Reformed ecclesiology is still wrestling with digital expressions of church. And in particular, it could be asked: *What are the constructive opportunities for articulating a pneumatology that is sensitive to both Reformed ecclesiological interests and digital ecclesial expressions?*

In order to begin to answer this question, the chapter will (1) review some key points from Calvin's ecclesiology, noting the role that pneumatology plays in his construction; (2) revisit the day of Pentecost narrative and observe the role of the Holy Spirit and the nature of the church as described by Luke; and (3) consider how a Pentecost-informed Reformed ecclesiology might be adaptive to contemporary digital expressions.

THE HOLY SPIRIT AND CALVIN'S ECCLESIOLOGY

In this section, I shall consider the language that Calvin uses to describe the nature of the church and her relationship with the person of the Holy Spirit in Book IV of his *Institutes*.

For Calvin, the church is the external means by which God invites us into the society of Christ and holds believers in that society. She is given that the preaching of the gospel might flourish and as an outward aid for the increase of faith of individual believers.[4] In order to do this, God instituted pastors and teachers, that there might be an agreement between faith and right order. In this context, sacraments were instituted as "useful aids" to foster and strengthen faith and as a divine accommodation to our fleshly weakness, so that we might draw near to God.[5] In this way the church functions as a mother, guiding, caring and supporting her children as they mature in the faith.[6] The church as the society of Christ is a universal body, includes the elect (the visible church is always mixed in composition), who are united to Christ and called to participate in the one God and Christ.[7] In this outward expression of the church, there is a diversity of graces, yet one community, united as one body to the common head, who is Christ.[8] Believers are united to the steadfastness of Christ and trust in the promises of salvation offered through him.

The church is the means by which the faithful are educated, built up in the body of Christ, becoming mature.[9] It is through the holy assemblies that

---

4. Calvin, *Institutes* 4.1.1, 1011.
5. Calvin, *Institutes* 4.1.1, 1012.
6. Calvin, *Institutes* 4.1.1, 1012; 4.1.4, 1016.
7. Calvin, *Institutes* 4.1.2, 1014.
8. Calvin, *Institutes* 4.1.3, 1015.
9. Calvin, *Institutes* 4.1.5, 1016.

church doctrine is taught, the authority of the Word experienced, and the doctrine of salvation embraced. The Holy Spirit is given to enlighten believers' minds to understand such doctrine. The church includes those in God's eternal presence, adopted by Christ, as well as those being sanctified by the Holy Spirit and includes the saints on earth as well as the elect throughout history. The church comprises "the whole multitude over the earth professing to worship the one God and Christ."[10] Only God knows who is "in" the church, but we should assume a "charitable judgement, whereby we recognise as members of the church those who, by confession of faith, by example of life, and partaking in the sacraments, profess the same God and Christ as us."[11] For Calvin, there are two marks of the church: (1) "where we see the Word of God purely preached and heard"; and (2) "the sacraments administered according to Christ's institution."[12] And, "[w]herever two or three are gathered in my name, there I am in the midst of them" (Matt 18.20).[13] The church universal, therefore, is "a multitude gathered from all nations, it is divided and dispersed in separate places, but agrees on the same truth of divine doctrine, and is bound by the bond of the same religion."[14] This means that different individual churches around the world are part of the same universal church, provided that they have both the ministry of the Word and the sacrament. Wherever the Word is received and has a "fixed abode," it is shown to be effective, providing food for the souls of believers.[15] There should be public edification of the faithful in a manner that is decent and in order.

According to Calvin, these signs are how we may judge between a false and true church.[16] They are regarded as a "perpetual token" by which the true church may be distinguished from the false church.[17] The church is founded on the teaching of the apostles and prophets, since Christ "reigns by his Word alone."[18] This is why Christ uses ministers of the church, to

---

10. Calvin, *Institutes* 4.1.7, 1021.

11. Calvin, *Institutes* 4.1.8, 1022–23.

12. Calvin, *Institutes* 4.1.9, 1023.

13. Calvin, *Institutes* 4.1.9, 1023. Nimmo, "Reformed Ecclesiology," 164 states that in the Reformed tradition the "church is conceived as a concrete and identifiable gathering of members."

14. Calvin, *Institutes* 4.1.9, 1023.

15. Calvin, *Institutes* 4.1.10, 1024.

16. Calvin, *Institutes* 4.2.1, 1041.

17. Calvin, *Institutes* 4.2.1, 1041.

18. Calvin, *Institutes* 4.2.4, 1046. Thus "the Word of God" takes functional priority over the sacraments, see Ralston, "Preaching Makes the Church," 130. For Calvin, according to Ralston, the meaning of the phrase "the Word of God" is multivalent: referring to Scripture, the gospel and Jesus Christ. Also see Parker, *Calvin*, 131.

declare his will and act as ambassadors to the world.[19] Acknowledging the different terminology used in Scripture, Calvin regards Presbyters as the designated ministers of Word and sacrament.[20]

The sacraments are an aid to our faith and are related to the preaching of the gospel. As Calvin states:

> *It seems to me that a simple and proper definition would be to say that it is an outward sign by which the Lord seals on our consciences the promises of his good will toward us in order to sustain the weakness of our faith; and we in turn attest our piety toward him in the presence of the Lord and of his angels and before men. Here is another briefer definition: one may call it a testimony of divine grace toward us, confirmed by an outward sign, with mutual attestation of our piety toward him.*[21]

Following Augustine, the sacrament is a visible sign of a sacred thing, of an invisible grace.[22] The Word and the sign are always linked because the Word is a promise and the sign an appendix to it, which seals and ratifies it.[23] This means that the Word must explain the sign, and the preaching of the Word helps us to understand the meaning of the sign.[24] Sacraments by themselves thus require preaching to elicit faith and are never bare but always linked to doctrine. Faith rests on the same Word as a foundation, while the sacraments are like columns which are built on that foundation.[25] As Calvin says, "[w]e have determined, therefore, that the sacraments are truly named the testimonies of God's grace and are like seals of the good will that he feels toward us, which by attesting good will to us, sustain, nourish, confirm, and increase our faith."[26] Faith is the work of the Holy Spirit, who illuminates our minds and allows us to see spiritual things and opens our hearts to receive both the Word and the sacrament.[27]

Therefore, the sacraments are intended to confirm and increase our faith, as instituted by the Lord.[28] Again, Calvin states:

19. Calvin, *Institutes* 4.3.1, 1053.
20. Calvin, *Institutes* 4.3.8, 1060.
21. Calvin, *Institutes* 4.14.1, 1277.
22. Parker, *Calvin*, 149.
23. Calvin, *Institutes* 4.14.3, 1278.
24. Calvin, *Institutes* 4.14.4, 1279.
25. Calvin, *Institutes* 4.14.6, 1281.
26. Calvin, *Institutes* 4.14.7, 1282. Calvin's view is sometimes classified as "symbolic instrumentalism"; see Nimmo, "Reformed Ecclesiology," 171–72.
27. Calvin, *Institutes* 4.14.8, 1284.
28. Calvin, *Institutes* 4.14.9, 1284.

> But the sacraments properly fulfil their office only when the Spirit, that inward teacher, comes to them, by whose power alone hearts are penetrated and affections moved and souls opened for the sacraments to enter in. If the Spirit be lacking, the sacraments can accomplish nothing more in our minds than the splendour of the sun shining upon blind eyes, or a voice sounding in deaf ears. Therefore, I make such a division between Spirit and sacraments that the power to act rests with the former, and the ministry alone is left to the latter—a ministry empty and trifling, apart from the actions of the Spirit but charged with great effect when the Spirit works within and manifests his power.[29]
>
> Therefore, Word and sacraments confirm our faith when they set before our eyes the good will of our Heavenly Father toward us, by the knowledge of whom the whole firmness of our faith stands fast and increases in strength. The Spirit confirms it when, by engraving this confirmation in our minds, he makes it effective. Meanwhile, the Father of Lights [cf. Jas 1.17] cannot be hindered from illumining our minds with a sort of intermediate brilliance through the sacraments, just as he illumines our bodily eyes by the rays of the sun.[30]

The Word and the sacrament work equally in confirming faith since there is an "indissoluble bond" between the preaching of the Word and the inward illumination and moving of the mind by the Spirit.[31]

Christ is the matter or the substance of the sacraments, for in him they have all their firmness and they do not promise anything apart from him.[32] The sacraments "foster, confirm and increase the true knowledge of Christ" in us so that we are able to "possess him more fully."[33] They have the same office as the Word of God, namely to set forth Christ to us.[34] Indeed, for Calvin, "[t]he Holy Spirit (whom the sacraments do not bring indiscriminately to all men [sic] but whom the Lord exclusively bestows on his own people) is he who brings the graces of God with him, gives a place for the sacraments among us, and makes them bear fruit."[35] Thus, Calvin contrasts the inner grace of the Holy Spirit with the outer ministry of the church as an

---

29. Calvin, *Institutes* 4.14.9, 1284.
30. Calvin, *Institutes* 4.14.10, 1286.
31. Calvin, *Institutes* 4.14.11, 1286.
32. Calvin, *Institutes* 4.14.16, 1291.
33. See Parker, *Calvin*, 149, for a discussion of *caro vivifica Christi*, "the life-giving flesh of Christ"; but also see n.63 below.
34. Calvin, *Institutes* 4.14.17, 1292.
35. Calvin, *Institutes* 4.14.17, 1293.

institution.[36] He thereby focuses on the work of the Holy Spirit in the hearts of individual believers.[37]

In summary, it could be said that the *church is referred to as the following*: (1) an outward aid for faith; (2) the society of Christ, the body of Christ; (3) includes the elect (the visible church is always mixed); (4) marked by the preaching of the Word of God (becoming a "fixed abode") and the sacraments being duly administered; (5) where two or three are gathered; (6) reflects the whole multitude from over the earth dispersed in many places; and (7) where there is public edification of the faithful. In this church, the *Holy Spirit functions to*: (1) illuminate believers' minds to understand doctrine; (2) sanctify them; (3) open the hearts of believers to allow the sacraments to enter into them; (4) confirms and strengthens faith; and (5) makes the sacraments bear fruit.

THE DAY OF PENTECOST

When considering the relationship of pneumatology to ecclesiology, it is important to examine the day of Pentecost as the key event in the establishment of the community that is called the church. Overall, the Reformed tradition has failed to consider this event as clearly as it might have done. It is interesting that in the edition of the *Institutes* that I am using the word "Pentecost" does not appear in the index! Reference to the Holy Spirit does appear but when it is cross-referenced with Acts chapters 1–2, there are three main areas to note.[38] (1) For Acts 1:8 Calvin refers to apostles being equipped with "arms and tools which they had to have," thus the Holy Spirit is considered a kind of instrument.[39] (2) For Acts 2.3 he simply refers to the apostles experiencing the power of a miracle "under tongues of fire."[40] (3) For Acts 2:4 he discusses confirmation as a devaluation of baptism and relates it to a discussion of Acts 8:16, saying Luke "has in mind the receiving of the Spirit, by which manifest powers and visible graces were received. Thus, the apostles are said to have received the Spirit on the day of Pentecost."[41] Therefore, it is fair to say that the connection between Pentecost and the church in Calvin's ecclesiology is somewhat thin! However, I would suggest

---

36. Calvin, *Institutes* 4.14.17, 1293.

37. For a discussion of Calvin's understanding of the Lord's Supper and pneumatology, see McDonnell, *John Calvin*, 249–93.

38. See Calvin, *Institutes*. 1670.

39. Calvin, *Institutes* 4.13.12, 1063.

40. Calvin, *Institutes* 4.15.8, 1309–10.

41. Calvin, *Institutes* 4.19.8, 1456.

that the Pentecostal narrative has much to tell us about the Holy Spirit and the church and can be used as a source for constructive theology. So, let us read this particular biblical text with an ecclesiological gaze.

The first thing to notice is that there was a gathering of people. Luke tells us that there were 120 people in an upper room (Acts 1:15). They were gathered all together in one place (Acts 2:1); and it was a sufficiently large enough space to hold such a gathering. The disciples were comprised of all sorts of people, including the apostles, but not limited to them. The Holy Spirit came upon all of them corporately as a single body in a single place, suggesting that the coming of the Holy Spirit is given corporately to the body before being given to individuals. Of course, we are told by Luke that the Holy Spirit came like a rushing wind and filled the entire house, suggesting the physical mediation of the Holy Spirit in the space where the disciples were sitting together.[42] It was not just human individuals that experienced the coming of the Holy Spirit, but there was a filling of physical space with the intensity of the Spirit's presence. Tongues of fire appeared on individuals as if to mark out each person as receiving the Spirit's presence in a new way. Pentecostals associate this action with their doctrine of the Baptism of the Holy Spirit, an overwhelming sense of the Spirit's presence, eliciting a sign, namely speech in tongues, or glossolalia, which in this instance Luke indicates is also xenolalia (real unlearned human languages).[43] All of them began to speak in tongues as the Spirit enabled them (Acts 2:4).[44] There was a spilling out from the upper room into the public space because a crowd gathered, became bewildered because they heard many different languages being spoken and wondered how it could be the case that uneducated Galileans spoke such a diversity of languages. A single, unified experience of the Holy Spirit had produced a cacophony of sound that represented different languages, cultures and people (Luke refers to Parthians, Medes, Elamites; residents of Mesopotamia, Judea, Cappadocia, Pontus, Asia, Phrygia, Pamphylia, Egypt, Libya, Cyrene, Rome; Cretans and Arabs). These very different groups were united in hearing the disciples "declaring the wonders of God" (Acts 2:11). In other words, *they were praising God in unity and diversity.* It could be suggested that, according to Luke, this is the first mark

---

42. Cartledge, *The Mediation of the Spirit*, 90–98.

43. Macchia, "Spirit Baptism."

44. Cartledge, *Charismatic Glossolalia*, 61–63; and for an interpretation of glossolalia as a sacrament based on Calvin's theology, see 195–97. Calvin appears to restrict the speakers to the apostles, see Calvin, *The Acts of the Apostles*, 52–53, and does not focus on the nature of the speech as doxology, 54.

of the church.[45] As the Holy Spirit constituted the church, the people of God in union with her Lord praised God for his mighty acts.[46]

This event also needed interpretation and explanation. This is what Peter does when he speaks to the crowd that had gathered (Acts 2:14–36). The allegation that glossolalic speech is the result of "new wine" is refuted because of the time of day. It was too early in the morning to be associated with drunkenness. Instead, Peter uses Scripture to interpret experience by explaining that "this" experience is related to the "that" of biblical prophecy, namely Joel 2.28.[47] This experience is in fulfilment of an eschatological promise that God would pour out his Holy Spirit upon his people as a mark of the last days. All people may receive the gift of the Holy Spirit (irrespective of gender, age, or social status).[48] With this gift comes the ability to speak prophetically and receive the gift of salvation.[49] Peter continues by saying that this gift is the fulfilment of the life, ministry, death and resurrection of Jesus of Nazareth. The people who are speaking in tongues and declaring the wonders of God are witnesses to his resurrection (Acts 2:32). This Jesus has been exalted through the ascension and is seated at the right hand of God. As the anointed one, he has received the Holy Spirit again, but this time so that he might "pour out" the person of the Holy Spirit upon the church. He is both Lord of the Spirit and Lord of the church. This is a gift received from the Father and given to the church; thus, the Holy Spirit unites the triune God in covenant with his people. The crucified one is both Lord and Messiah (Acts 2:36). *The Word spoken by Peter interprets the sign of the Holy Spirit* in the doxological community, such that it becomes an invitation to join this new community. Indeed, that is exactly what happens. The hearers are "cut to the heart" (*katanyssomai* with *tēn kardian*, Acts

---

45. Higton, *Christian Doctrine*, 310–14, in a discussion of catholic marks of the church (one, holy, catholic and apostolic), treats unity by means of worship and, in effect, regards worship as the first mark of the unified church.

46. Zizioulas, *Being as Communion*, 21–22, argues that the Holy Spirit constitutes the church as the eucharistic community. In Reformed theology, the church is often regarded as constituted by divine action as a creature of the divine Word, *creatura verbi divini*, see Schwöbel, "The Creature of the Word," 122–26. More recently, on the constitution of the church by the Holy Spirit, see Greggs, *Dogmatic Ecclesiology*, 12–18. For a discussion of the role of the Holy Spirit in liturgy, see Mangina, "Ecclesiology and Pneumatology," 352–54.

47. Cartledge, *Encountering the Spirit*, 125–30.

48. See Cartledge, *The Holy Spirit and Public Life*, 124–28.

49. Turner, *Power from on High*, 401–27. Specifically, Turner states, 427, "We may thus safely claim that he [Luke] thought the Spirit was *the principal* divine power maintaining, developing and extending Israel's salvation/transformation, and that without the gift of the charismatic Spirit of prophecy the sort of 'salvation' he had in mind would simply evaporate from Israel like the departure of the cloud of God's glory and presence."

2:37),⁵⁰ and Peter is asked what they must do.⁵¹ He replies that they need to repent, be baptised so that their sins might be forgiven and they too might receive the gift of the Holy Spirit. This is a promise that is for them and for their children and all who are far off (Acts 2.39). When interpreted and explained, the sign of the Holy Spirit becomes the basis for evangelism and incorporation into the community. It is what might be called an expression of "doxological mission": praise flows out into explanation, which then flows back through incorporation into community.

The people of God as a community are reconstituted in covenantal union with the triune God. According to Acts 2:42, there were four main characteristics of community life: (1) attention to the apostles' teaching; (2) fellowship; (3) the breaking of bread; and (4) prayer. This is augmented by (5) signs and wonders; (6) sharing of common resources according to need; and (7) worship: in the temple, by means of the breaking of bread at home and praise of God, thus returning to doxology again (Acts 2:43–47). As a result of this community life, many others were "saved" and joined the community. These characteristics suggest a vibrant community that was able to move between the Jewish worship practices associated with the temple but instructed now by the new teaching of the apostles, just as Peter had illustrated, with home meetings around meals and including the Lord's Supper. Prayer was followed by dramatic answers, which provoked a sense of awe and wonder. The needs of the community were met, even if that meant selling possessions and pooling resources for the sake of others. There was a genuine participation in the lives of others, which was attractive, and the Lord used it to draw new people into the community. *The community of the church was alive unto God, each other, and their neighbours, providing a locus of participation between God and his people.*

When we bring this description into dialogue with the account of Calvin's ecclesiology, as noted above, a number of points are worth observing.

In some respects, this description given by Luke is different to that given by Calvin. The church is not primarily an outward aid for personal

---

50. Johnson, *The Acts of the Apostles*, 56; Calvin, *The Acts of the Apostles*, 77, does acknowledge the power of the Holy Spirit to touch "with a feeling of grief," which was followed by obedience to Peter's counsel. The language appears to be principally "affective" in nature. Those responding are not persuaded primarily by an intellectual argument but convicted powerfully through Peter's words inspired by the Holy Spirit.

51. Interestingly, Ralston, "Preaching Makes the Church," 135, acknowledges the role that preaching plays in the creation of the church; he suggests that the church is a creature of both "the Spirit and human preaching." He acknowledges that the Spirit falling on the disciples calls the church into being and that the community is expanded via the preaching of Peter. However, he completely misses doxology, which, I am arguing, is the first mark of the church according to the day of Pentecost narrative.

faith. Rather, she is a community that participates in the life of the triune God through the Holy Spirit. The primary mark of the church is not the preaching and hearing of the Word *per se*, but Spirit-inspired doxology, which is nevertheless focused on the ascended Christ. The church is primarily a community of praise. She exists for the praise of her creator and redeemer. All other functions flow from this central one and not *vice versa*. There is attention to the Word interpreting the sign, the teaching of the apostles and the breaking of bread, which would have included the Lord's Supper. However, for Luke, these are meant to explain what the Lord has done in the outpouring of the Holy Spirit to constitute the church. Luke does not use the language found in Calvin explicitly, such as the "illumination of minds" or the "opening of hearts" (although the metaphor of cutting/piercing is used) or the "bearing fruit." However, all these ideas could be regarded as implicit in the narrative of Luke and so, at least, should not be regarded as antithetical to it.

In other respects, Luke's description appears to accord with Calvin's ideas. The church is a new society united to Christ and while Luke does not use the concept of a body explicitly (as Paul does), it coheres well with the idea because of the unity and diversity of its members. While each member may indeed be counted among the elect (on the basis of a charitable assumption), this is not language that is emphasised by Luke on the day of Pentecost.[52] There is indeed a gathering of more than two or three people, in this case it was initially 120, which then became over 3000, and then even more, although it is probable that they would have gathered in smaller groups in homes. But the point is clear enough, the church is also marked by a gathering of some sort. The different languages suggest that the presence of the Holy Spirit "poured out on all flesh" is for *all* people (not just the apostles), dispersed in many places. Indeed, the book of Acts charts just how this happens in the early church, as the gospel message is proclaimed throughout the Mediterranean world. Clearly, there is a public edification of the faithful because there is gladness and generosity within the community, which translates into the goodwill of wider society towards the church (Acts 2:46–47).

DIGITAL ECCLESIAL EXPRESSION

Heidi Campbell describes digital ecclesiology as "the study of the structure and practices of the Church in online or digitally-enhanced contexts, and

---

52. See the discussion from a Pentecostal perspective by Macchia, *The Spirit-Baptized Church*, 59–104, although it comes with a fairly heavy dose of Barth!

the theological implications of the online-offline or hybrid church experiences this creates."[53] Additionally, John Dyer brings some specific terminological distinctions which are useful.[54] He suggests that (1) "online church" refers to any use of digital media by Christians, including digital worship services as well as the use of social media platforms; (2) "broadcast church" refers to a service delivered primarily through a one-way medium such as live streaming; (3) "interactive church" refers to services and group activity that uses two-way interactive media; (4) "virtual church" refers to a service or activity that meets in a fully virtual environment, such as Second Life, Roblox or metaverse; and (5) "hybrid church" refers to a local church that includes both digital and in-person experiences. For our purposes, I regard option (4) as raising very specific (although interesting) questions that fall beyond the purview of this study because fully virtual environments are not normally what most congregations are considering when thinking about digital practices. To be even more specific, let me confine my reflections to worship services for the sake of greater focus; and let me address hybrid services that are a combination of online and broadcast experiences.

On a typical Sunday morning, post-COVID-19, many congregations have resumed their in-person services while at the same time using Zoom, Teams or Facebook live software to broadcast the service and include interaction of some kind. Let us suppose that for a typical church service at a fictional congregation called "St Andrew's Church" this includes: (1) the broadcast of the service; (2) interaction sections during the service with online participants able to (a) offer online exclamations during the sung worship or preaching; (b) make online contributions via testimony, Scripture verses or prophetic words; (c) identify online prayer requests via the chat room function, which are then picked up and used within the in-person context; (d) contribute online notices for inclusion at the end of the service; and (3) a self-contained post-service coffee meeting for those who are online and who wish to socialise via digital means. In this example there is a combination of broadcast and interactive experiences in a hybrid manner.

There are several areas that can be considered for reflection. I shall limit my comments to five main points.

First, there is clearly a *gathering of people from dispersed places in one event of fellowship*.[55] The addition of digital platforms enhances and diversifies the nature of the gathering. It could be argued that Calvin's emphasis on the church as a gathering of people from multiple places can be easily

---

53. Campbell and Dyer, "Introduction," xiv.
54. Dyer, "Exploring Mediated *Ekklesia*," 5–8.
55. See Chow and Kurlberg, "Two or Three Gathered Online."

extended to the idea of multiple spaces that (from our historical vantage point now) includes digital spaces. Online broadcasting of public worship means that individuals and groups from around the world can now participate digitally from their own contexts, whether that is in their own homes or in another church building. In this example of hybridity, the basic gathering is in-person, and this is not supplanted by the digital environment. Rather, it is enhanced and developed by it. There is an extension of fellowship through the online environment, which would have been impossible previously. Clearly, the experiences of both groups of people are affected by the other. The online group could not experience this kind of corporate worship except for the gathered in-person group. And what happens in the in-person worship event in a sense determines the range and nature of what is experienced online. There is both continuity and discontinuity. While the gathered in-person group benefits from the digital presence of people online through their contributions (a-d above), which are mediated via the leader/s (and which need to be planned carefully), it is not the same as online people being in the same physical space. Inevitably, there is a different experience of worship. There is also a division between both groups at the end, when post-service coffee is experienced somewhat differently. But this will always be the case, as some people stay to socialise in a physical setting, while others leave. The service has ended and so people go their own way.

Second, the *praise elements of sung worship are obviously heard and experienced online*. How this works, of course, will depend on the nature of St Andrew's Church. Let us suppose it is a contemporary charismatic evangelical congregation, with lots of songs or hymns sung together. At the beginning of a service there may be four or five different songs/hymns used without a break, creating different moods among the worshippers as the sequence progresses. The flow of these songs/hymns can begin with initial lively ones, which provoke exuberance, with arms waving and people dancing, some people waving flags and moving around the physical space. This mood of celebration is important in Pentecostal and charismatic worship and is magnified within large gatherings of thousands of people in a single physical location.[56] Sung worship tends to close with reflective songs as people sit or kneel as they transition into a more meditative mood. This phase in the sequence tends to be associated with more intimate language and corporate stillness. In this latter stage, worshippers may be moved affectively by an intense experience of the Holy Spirit, which includes bodily postures such as kneeling, lying down, perhaps weeping with hands held out in front symbolising the reception of grace. Obviously, it would be harder

---

56. See Althouse and Wilkinson, "Musical Bodies in the Charismatic Renewal," 37.

for people at home in their living rooms to experience the full corporate mood of sung worship. The celebratory action of being carried along among a sea of people, perhaps dancing with others, waving flags and arms cannot be replicated easily in a living room with a single individual. Therefore, it could be said that the atmosphere may not translate very well via a digital modality. But, in principle at least, each person online could sing along with the music and participate kinaesthetically as they wished and, as the home furnishings allow, through clapping, raising arms, dancing, sitting, standing or kneeling. Certainly, if they see and hear others engaged in these practices the continuity of activity can be experienced even if there is also a discontinuity because of the online mediation.[57]

While Calvin does reference affectivity in relation to the sacraments (as noted above), the Reformed tradition has not tended to emphasise it in relation to "sung worship times." But the sacramentality of this phase of worship has been noted by Pentecostals and links back to the essence of their ecclesiology as rooted in the day of Pentecost narrative (as also noted above).[58] Therefore, it could be argued, using Calvin's reasoning, that there is also the possibility of the Holy Spirit so moving hearts and minds during this phase of worship that hearts might also be lifted to heaven, to participate with the heavenly host in their sung worship of the Lord Jesus Christ. Revelation chapter 4 gives us a glimpse of what this looks like in the heavenly realm. For many Pentecostals, they see sung worship as providing a mystical union between the church and her Lord, which is just as powerful and as nourishing in the faith as other elements of worship.

Third, *the preaching of the Word can be heard in the same way as those in-person participants would hear it*, if there are no technical glitches.[59] Of course, the whole worship experience is subject to technological issues, but if the highlight of the worship event is the reception of the preached Word, then it becomes a significant component to get right. Listening to a sermon digitally as an experience is very similar to being there in the in-person space. People at home can follow along with their Bibles opened and taking notes if they so wish. Indeed, it could be argued that a home experience might be enhanced since the discomfort of a church pew might be missing. It is possible that St Andrew's Church, being charismatic and evangelical in nature, may well have taken out the pews and installed individual comfortable chairs! The comfort advantages are clear enough. But, again,

---

57. It could be suggested that all the main elements of a theology of sung worship could be present but experienced differently, see Lord, "A Theology of Sung Worship."

58. For a sacramental reading of Pentecost, see Vondey, "Pentecostal Sacramentality," 95–98; also see Cartledge, "Digital Pentecostal Sacramentality."

59. See Bekkering, "From 'Televangelist' to 'Intervangelist,'" 101–7.

what may be missing is the spiritual impact of the sermon on the gathered congregation. There can be a specific interaction between the preacher and the congregation that creates a corporate sense of attentiveness to the Scriptures and an awareness of the moving of the Holy Spirit that may be missed when translated into an individualised home environment. This is an important aspect to note. Just as sung worship can create an affective connection between members of a congregation, so the reception of a Word preached from the Scriptures can also create a powerful shared experience among congregational members of the Holy Spirit speaking to hearts not just minds.[60] There may be a similar educational experience as the sermon builds knowledge of the Scriptures. The affective dimension of the preached Word may not be always noted by Calvin, but it has been observed by more pietistic strands of Evangelicalism and it is clearly present in Pentecostalism. It is often associated with "conversion" practices in Evangelicalism and Pentecostalism. As noted above, it is also highlighted in the day of Pentecost narrative and for this reason deserves to be taken seriously. The hearing of the Word preached online may be accompanied by a diminished affective dimension because of the lack of a strongly inter-personal context, but it may yet be present depending on the digitally mediated power of the Holy Spirit in the lives of those hearing the preached Word.

Fourth, *the mediation of the sacraments digitally is a contentious matter*. Obviously, it is impossible for matter to be mediated digitally (at least for now). Water, bread and wine cannot be transported digitally from one in-person setting to another. Nevertheless, the action of the Holy Spirit is not so restricted, and this is an essential feature to note. Most, if not all, Pentecostals have no problem whatsoever in conceiving the work of the Holy Spirit through digital means and this includes the sacraments (or ordinances as many prefer to call them).[61] In terms of our discussion of Calvin's ecclesiology, and indeed for most churches, the question, it would seem, revolves around "due" administration of the sacraments and what that actually means? To focus on Holy Communion, online participants cannot receive the elements directly from the hands of the minister who is leading the in-person service. Instead, they consume the elements that they have placed as an extension of the liturgical act that the minister performs remotely to them.[62] This spatial discontinuity may be a problem for

---

60. A theology of Pentecostal preaching would tend to contrast itself with Evangelical preaching that is characterised as modernist and rationalist, see Martin, "Introduction," 15.

61. See Cartledge, "Virtual Mediation of the Holy Spirit" and "Pentecostals and the Eucharist in a Digital Age"; also Addo, "Join the Holy Spirit on Zoom."

62. This is the argument of Burridge, *Holy Communion in Contagious Times*, 240,

some people, who feel that physical proximity to the eucharistic president is necessary for due reception of the sacrament. But does Calvin's view of the Lord's Supper actually necessitate such a thing, when the feeding on Christ is a mystical and transcendent one? If, according to Calvin, there is a true "spiritual feeding" on the ascended Christ by means of the Holy Spirit then physical proximity to the in-person consecrated elements may not be needed.[63] Provided that the participants hear the words of institution and intend to "feed on Christ in their hearts by faith,"[64] then I would suggest that Calvin's view, at least in principle, does allow such a practice.[65] Indeed, I would suggest that this is *the* theological gem contained within Calvin's understanding of the Lord's Supper, whereby there is a true (= real) feeding on the body and blood of Christ, one that is mystical and transcends the physicality of the actual eating of the bread and the drinking of the wine. This mystical union with and participation in Christ transcends physicality *even as it is mediated by it*.[66] The transcending of physicality also allows for pneumatological mediation via the digital "space" online. Of course, in an ecclesial tradition with a range of views (as in my own Church of England tradition), it may be prohibited because of a theology of the "real presence," which is regarded as an essential part of the ecclesial tradition.[67]

---

who suggests that the consecration of the elements of bread and wine might be extended to elements in the home via the computer screen, since they could be regarded as falling within the "zone of intention" of the president of the Eucharist.

63. Inevitably, there is a debate regarding whether Calvin believed in the "real" presence of Christ in the elements. Personally, I am persuaded that Calvin did *not* believe that there was a corporeal presence. See Tylenda, "Calvin and Christ's Presence in the Supper" and Niesel, *The Theology of Calvin*, 223. However, for a different position on Christ's bodily presence in the elements, and as a prerequisite for the believer's ascent to Christ in heaven, see Kaiser, "Climbing Jacob's Ladder." For the view that Calvin might have been nearer to Zwingli than Luther after all, see Lane, "Was Calvin a Crypto-Zwinglian?"

64. For the liturgical text used by Calvin, see "The Manner of Celebrating the Lord's Supper."

65. Recent research tends to suggest that lay Evangelicals within the Church of England and Free Church traditions are more accepting of online home communion using one's own elements of bread and wine. See Francis and Village, "This Blessed Sacrament of Unity?"; and Village, "Attitude toward Virtual Communion."

66. Farwell and Moore-Keish, "Sacramental Theology," 486, raise the concern that the Reformed view of the Lord's Supper "spiritualizes" the meaning because it separates physical embodiment, "effaces corporate embodied ritual" and favours a "purely individual communing with the invisible Christ." In my view, embodiment is never lost, even in the digital mediation, and in the hybrid practice envisaged here it is always regarded as an auxiliary mode by those people who are usually part of the physical assembly.

67. See Burridge, *Holy Communion in Contagious Times*. For recent Pentecostal eucharistic theology, see Green, *Toward a Pentecostal Theology of the Lord's Supper*; and for broader Pentecostal sacramental theology Tomberlin, *Pentecostal Sacraments*.

Fifth and finally, it can be asked: *does such a hybrid service contribute to the rich public life of the community as a form of witness?* Certainly, it can contribute to praise and prayer and include a potentially more diverse group of people (e.g., the elderly, house bound and disabled). This is important and many churches have been surprised during the COVID-19 lockdown periods just how much worship was accessed beyond the usual range of people who attended in-person services. However, some aspects are challenging if not impossible. It is simply not possible to feed the homeless digitally, or play football at the youth group, although computer games are indeed possible. The in-person/digital discontinuities are obvious, but this may lead to creativity around what can be achieved. With technology, it is possible to preach virtually, teach in the Sunday school and participate in meetings and parish councils. Hybrid events are increasingly accepted in a post-pandemic world and so there is a greater continuity that would have been thought impossible before the pandemic. It is certainly the case that people can have fellowship with others gathered online. Again, this is an important dimension that should not be underestimated. New relationships can be forged that can, over time, create impact through community activities. Churches that began fully online pre-pandemic have often felt the need to take their fellowship to physical in-person locations, due to the development of relationships among themselves. With the use of smart phones as the norm for most people, physical-digital hybridity will lead to creative ways of navigating the public space and developing new ways of witnessing in and to the world. In this regard, it could be said that the guidance of the Holy Spirit is required. Just as the Gentiles were included in the early church because the preaching of the gospel had crossed certain geographical and cultural boundaries (Acts 10:1–48; 15:28—"it seemed good to the Holy Spirit and to us"). So, it could be that the Holy Spirit is enabling the contemporary church to cross physical-digital boundaries for the sake of her witness to the gospel of the Kingdom of God. It is here that we see the need to bring the concept of ecclesial witness into conversation with public theology and the public spaces in which the church operates. Digital spaces intersect with and influence physical and concrete realities. Increasingly, we need to be prepared to move our public theology online and develop digital public theology that makes sense of all "public" domains.[68]

---

68. For a discussion of public theology, see van Oorschot, "Public Theology Facing Digital Spaces."

CONCLUSION

I began this discussion by asking: *What are the constructive opportunities for articulating a pneumatology that is sensitive to both Reformed ecclesiological interests and digital ecclesial expressions?* In order to answer this question, I attempted to outline some of the basic features of John Calvin's ecclesiology and in particular the role that the Holy Spirit plays in relation to the marks of the church.[69] This ecclesiology was then augmented by reviewing the ecclesiology embedded in the day of Pentecost narrative, which is consistently ignored or downplayed by the Reformed tradition.[70] From this interaction, it could be proposed that the marks of church are: (1) doxology; (2) ministry of the Word (teaching and proclamation); and (3) community (fellowship, sacraments, prayer, manifestations of the Holy Spirit's power and care for the needy). All these marks can be expressed through a hybrid model of digital church as exemplified by the hypothetical St Andrew's Church, in the evangelical, charismatic tradition. It could be said that there are major challenges for the church as she adapts to digital expressions, and we have noted some of them. Given this pneumatological enhancement (or, dare I say, a "pentecostalizing") of Calvin's ecclesiology, it would seem that there are no real obstacles to the expression of hybrid church as outlined above. Indeed, it could be argued that such a Pentecost-informed ecclesiology, as a *pneumatological ecclesiology*, has great potential for the life, work and witness of the church in a digital age.

There are, of course, many aspects to this proposal that invite further consideration, debate and possible revision. Here are a few questions to begin the theological conversation:

- How can the sources of the Reformed tradition be used to inform our theological constructions today in ways that allow us to critique them not just honour them?

- How do contemporary readings of Scripture allow us to interrogate these sources of Reformed theology in new and creative ways?

- What insights can we glean from the broader Christian tradition, including new and emerging theologically rich traditions, such as Pentecostalism, that are able to inform our own traditions in their expressions today?

---

69. For discussion of Calvin's pneumatology in relation to contemporary theology, see Cartledge and Jumper, *The Holy Spirit and the Reformation Legacy*, chaps. 9 and 10.

70. For example, see Kristanto, *Ecclesiology in Reformed Perspective*, 66, who only refers to Acts 2:42 in a discussion of fellowship. It also seems to be missing from the discussion by Maruyama, *Calvin's Ecclesiology* (with no entry for "Pentecost" in the index).

- How do the new developments in our world, such as the digital revolution, enable us to address basic theological questions (e.g. the nature of worship, pneumatology and ecclesiology), in fresh ways, allowing us to resource the church's life and mission in the contemporary world?

I look forward to exploring how these ideas might be developed as the conversation continues.

4

Prioritising the Spirit in Our Churches
Toward a Comprehensive Third Article Ecclesiology

GREGORY J. LISTON

INTRODUCTION

IT IS THE CHALLENGING heart cry of many contemporary pastors and ministers that although they feel called to a distinctively Spiritual vocation, their actual day to day role is primarily mechanical—managing and maintaining an organisation. It is a cry I empathise with, for it is a situation I have lived through. Before I was a senior pastor, I worked as a management consultant.[1] But whether consulting or pastoring, my everyday activities were surprisingly similar. In both roles I was concerned with strategy, competitive advantage, vision casting, personnel management, logistics, and balance sheets. All these are necessary and important, but what became increasingly obvious during my first seven-year stretch as a pastor is that what I was doing each day was not significantly different from my previous and entirely

---

1. My first pastoral role was as the senior pastor of a 500-person Baptist church in suburban Auckland. Prior to this I worked for a large American-based management consulting firm.

secular occupation. To be honest, it felt like my main role as a pastor was simply to keep the machinery of the institutional church running.

Throughout the duration of this ministry, I began to question more and more explicitly and urgently whether church could be different. Isn't church supposed to be something miraculous, something supernatural, something intrinsically spiritual? But, growing simultaneously, another question was also demanding attention: what would a genuinely miraculous and intrinsically supernatural church look like? How would it work? Realising that I didn't have a good answer to this simple but important question, I resigned from being a pastor and started researching, first as a PhD student and then as a theology lecturer. What motivated me was the question of what it would mean to be a truly Spiritual church.[2] What would a contemporary western church look like if we lived and acted as if the Holy Spirit wasn't just an optional extra but was deliberately and intentionally placed at the forefront of everything we thought and did and said as a church. What if church was more than an institution, and our goal wasn't just to keep the machine running? What if our churches were intrinsically Spiritual and irreducibly supernatural?

This paper represents a summary of my reflections on this topic over the last decade. Most of my research effort during this period has been spent examining this crucial subject, and a couple of books and several articles have arisen.[3] Given the opportunity to speak at a conference explicitly focusing on *Spirit and Church* and to contribute to a volume specifically arising from this conference provided an excellent opportunity to reflect at a high level on what my research over the last decade has determined. Consequently, this chapter presents the overarching sweep of my current understanding of what it means to intentionally place the Spirit at the forefront of everything we are and do as the church. To this end, the paper will divide into five sections. First, it will explore the insights arising for ecclesiology from Spirit Christology. What can we learn about the Spirit's role in the church's life from exploring the Spirit's role in Christ's life? The second section will abstract out from that preliminary question to introduce the broad methodology known as Third Article Theology. How does it practically work to give the Spirit priority in our theological thinking, and how can we apply that kind of approach to an exploration of ecclesiology? The third section uses the Trinity as a vantage point. What can we say about the Spirit's role in the church through examining the Spirit's role in the Trinity?

---

2. In this essay the term Spiritual with a capital S is used to refer specifically to being guided, motivated, and empowered through the Holy Spirit.

3. The two books are Liston, *The Anointed Church*; and Liston, *Kingdom Come*.

The fourth section explores the intrinsically pneumatological relation between the church and the coming kingdom. How does the Spirit draw back into the church's present reality anticipations of the life to come? And the final section explores the implications such a pneumatological focus has for mission. How does the church's intrinsically pneumatological nature affect the way we go about interacting with the world around us?

The overall intent of this exploration is to outline an understanding of the church that is thoroughly orthodox and fits within a traditional reformed perspective, but also is an understanding that intentionally prioritizes the Spirit in both theology and practice. What that means is the following analysis will intentionally build on the work of people who have gone before. Developing an explicitly Third Article Ecclesiology[4] does not mean correcting the valuable ecclesiological work done by previous theological giants like Calvin, Barth, Torrance, and others. But it does mean complementing their work with an understanding that deliberately brings the Spirit to the forefront of our theological understanding and ecclesial practice.

FROM SPIRIT CHRISTOLOGY TO PNEUMATO-ECCLESIOLOGY

What can we learn about the role of the Spirit in the church's life, from exploring the role of the Spirit in Christ's life? As Kärkkäinen asserts, "The only way to construe a viable pneumato-ecclesiology is to reflect very carefully on the relationship between Christ and the Spirit on the one hand, and on the relation of the Spirit to the church on the other hand, and then try and see these three as mutual entities that inform each other."[5] To repeat the same sentiment more concisely . . . how can a Spirit Christology inform a pneumato-ecclesiology?

Many people simplistically equate Spirit Christology with adoptionism.[6] These scholars incorrectly assume that Spirit Christology means

---

4. As discussed in more detail later in this essay, the preliminary phrase *Third Article* as used here refers specifically to the third article of the Nicene Creed, which begins with a reference to the Holy Spirit. Third Article Theology has a pneumatological focus, therefore, but it distinguishes itself from traditional pneumatology by looking *through* rather than *at* the Spirit. So, in this particular case, Third Article Ecclesiology is a theological methodology that looks through the Spirit to illuminate the doctrine of ecclesiology.

5. Kärkkäinen, *Toward a Pneumatological Theology*, 93.

6. A recent example of this is the volume by Allison and Köstenberger who suggest that Spirit Christology requires the Holy Spirit to be the sole agent in the incarnation. See Allison and Köstenberger, *The Holy Spirit*, 353.

replacing the *Logos* with the Spirit as the way Christ's divinity is interpreted, with the result that Christ was nothing more than an anointed human being. While there have been theologians in the last 50 years or so who have used the language of Spirit Christology in this way,[7] such an interpretation of the phrase is not my understanding or intent. Indeed, most contemporary scholars employing the language of Spirit Christology deliberately distance themselves from this kind of flawed replacement understanding.[8]

Spirit Christology, in the way that I and an increasing number of theologians are using the phrase, is not a replacement of *Logos* Christology, but a complement to it.[9] Viewed in this way, Spirit Christology argues that to have a fully orthodox, fully Chalcedonian understanding of who Jesus Christ was and is as God incarnate requires that we pay attention not just to the *Logos* but also and equally to the Spirit. Indeed, it argues that paying insufficient attention to either the *Logos* or the Spirit leads to a deficient Christology. So, a *Logos* Christology without sufficient reference to the Spirit leads to a docetic understanding of Christ, which is the direction the tradition has often leant. While a Spirit Christology without sufficient reference to the *Logos* leads to an Ebionitic understanding, which is the way some recent theologians have leant in an overreaction to the tradition. The only way to gain a truly Chalcedonian understanding is to hold a *Logos* Christology and a Spirit Christology together as intentionally complementary.

In terms of the implications of this for ecclesiology, many theologians have explored the correlations between Christ and the church. Because the church is Christ's body, it makes perfect sense that the church's life should in some way parallel Christ's life. Perhaps the preeminent example of this analytical approach is Karl Barth's work developing an intentionally Christological Ecclesiology.[10] But because of the significant emphasis traditionally on *Logos* Christology over Spirit Christology, most scholars who have explored this relationship have compared a *Logos* Christology and the church. Barth fits into this category. The insights that arise from doing this comparison have been important and valuable, but they can and should be

---

7. See for example Hawthorne, *The Presence and the Power*.

8. See for example Habets, *The Anointed Son*; and Del Colle, "Spirit Christology: Dogmatic Issues," 3–19. Also, and particularly, see the overarching summary in Sánchez, *Introduction to Spirit Christology*, 115–50. This chapter refers to both ancient and modern scholars to make a resounding case for the complementarity of *Logos* and Spirit Christologies.

9. For a more detailed explanation of the argument made in this paragraph, see Liston, "A 'Chalcedonian' Spirit Christology," 74–93.

10. See particularly Bender, *Karl Barth's Christological Ecclesiology*.

complemented by the insights that arise when we explore the relationship between a Spirit Christology and ecclesiology.

But recognizing the value of this previous analysis means that explorations of this new and complementary relationship can intentionally leverage off the insights and approaches of those who have already examined the relationship between a *Logos* Christology and the church. Barth, for example, mines the correlation between Christ and the church by specifically noting unity, differentiation, and asymmetry between the two poles. Hunsinger argues that there is "virtually no discussion of divine and human agency in the *Church Dogmatics* that does not conform to this scheme."[11] So the complementary exploration of the parallels between Spirit Christology and pnemato-ecclesiology can utilise this Barthian approach, by examining the pneumatologically inspired parallels between Christ and the church—their unity, discontinuities, and asymmetries. At least five such parallels exist:

The Spirit conceives (Christ and the Church)

The Spirit sustains the communion (of Christ and the Church)

The Spirit conforms (Christ and the Church)

The Spirit directs and empowers (Christ and the Church)

The Spirit is displayed and mediated (by Christ and the Church)

For each of these, the areas of unity, discontinuity, and asymmetry between Christ and the church can be exegetically and systematically examined in detail. For example, there are clear parallels between the way the Spirit conceived Christ at the incarnation and the way the Spirit conceived the church at Pentecost, but there are also some clear differences and distinctions between those two events, with one of those clear differences being the asymmetric relation between them—the Spirit only conceived the church as a result of or because or through the Spirit conceiving Christ at Pentecost.

Consequently, analysis at this point would proceed by setting up this unity / discontinuity / asymmetry grid, applying it to each of these pneumatologically enabled parallels, and then from that basis completing some detailed exegetical and systematic work to determine what those parallels affirm and deny about the role of the Spirit in the church. This paper will not delve into this level of detail, however. In contrast, at this point, and several points later, having outlined the method by which a question can be answered, this paper leaps over the detail of applying the method, to

---

11. Hunsinger, *How to Read Karl Barth*, 185. For a more detailed examination of this use of correspondence, see Bender, *Karl Barth's Christological Ecclesiology*, 1–16.

focus on the derived answers and implications that arise from utilizing this approach.[12]

Passing over the detailed work of applying the method, then, and arriving at the conclusion that arises from doing such analysis, there are some fundamental insights that emerge from doing this comparison. Four key groups of insights can be affirmed. Exploring the parallels between a Spirit Christology and a pneumato-ecclesiology answers the question *What is the Church?* by asserting that the church's ontological nature is found in the Spirit enabled union that exists between the incarnate Christ and the human community. It answers the question *Who is in the Church?* by asserting that the church is comprised specifically and particularly of those humans who have been united by the Spirit to Christ. In other words, the church is the unique context in which the Spirit unites humanity to Christ. It answers the question *How is a Church recognised?* by asserting that a church is recognised as a community having a pneumatologically enabled Christotelic impetus, an overall momentum towards Christlikeness. And it answers the question *What does the Church do?* by asserting that the Church is cruciform in shape (molded by suffering), missional in purpose, narrative in character, and relational in identity. All these insights could get unpacked in much more detail, but the overarching point to recognize is that some fundamental affirmations about the church directly emerge from exploring the parallels between a Spirit Christology and a pneumato-ecclesiology.[13]

Perhaps the key affirmation that emerges from exploring the relationship is that through the Spirit, Christ can be seen in the church. T. F. Torrance explains this point (albeit without explicitly recognising the pneumatological means through which it happens) by noting that "wherever the Church shows forth His death until He comes and presents its body a living sacrifice, there the image of Christ is to be seen and His Body is to be discerned in the Church."[14] Peterson illustrates the same idea using the word *inscape*.[15] He writes winsomely about how some painters or photographers merely capture the reality in front of them (landscape artists). Others, however, convey the inner truth of what is really going on (inscape artists). When a portrait or photo does more than merely convey reality but beautifully captures the genuine inner essence of what they are portraying,

---

12. At each stage where significant detail is skipped, footnotes will point to where the exegetical and systematic work can be examined. For this particular point, a detailed examination of the unity, discontinuity, and asymmetry between Spirit Christology and a pneumato-ecclesiology can be found in Liston, *The Anointed Church*, 121–54.

13. For more detail see Liston, *The Anointed Church*, 155–79.

14. Torrance, "Atonement and the Oneness of the Church," 259.

15. See Peterson, *Practise Resurrection*. 141–42, 46.

this is inscape. Applying this idea to Christology, there are some who looked at Jesus, and seeing only a human, decided there was nothing there worth noticing. But there were a small number who saw through the human component (inscape!) and recognised something of immeasurable worth: God himself. In a similar way, some look at the church and see only the human side. This is the landscape view. But there are those who see through the human component (inscape!) and so recognise something in the church of immeasurable worth. The church through her obedient suffering reveals Christ to the world.

One of the premier insights of my research journey over the last decade is that this idea of inscape—that by the Spirit we can look through the church and see Christ—is foundationally important not just as a theological affirmation, but as a practical skill. This is perhaps the core reality that marks out a church as truly Spiritual and intrinsically supernatural. A church that intentionally prioritises the Spirit consists of people who have intentionally and practically become skilled at looking through the church and seeing Christ there. The more we can learn to use pneumatologically enabled eyes to deliberately and intentionally see that Christ is present and at work in our Christian communities, this is fundamentally what sets the church apart from all other merely human institutions.

APPLYING THIRD ARTICLE THEOLOGY

The rather simple exercise just worked through, where insights from the role of the Spirit in the life of Christ enabled parallels for the role of the Spirit in the life of the church to be determined, is a specific example of an approach that can be made much more general. As illustrated in the previous section, the Spirit can be used as a lens to look from Christology to ecclesiology, because it is the Spirit that forms the church as Christ's body. But the Spirit can also be used as a lens to look from the Trinity to ecclesiology, because it is by the Spirit that the church *participates* in God's Trinitarian life. Moreover, the Spirit can be used as a lens from which to look backward from eschatology to the church, for it is by the Spirit that the church is the proleptic anticipation of the coming kingdom. The common factor in each of these parallels is that the Spirit can be used as a lens through which we look to examine other doctrines.

The examples just outlined are three specific instances of utilising a theological methodology known as Third Article Theology.[16] This is an

---

16. As noted earlier, Third Article Theology coins its name from the third article of the Nicene Creed, which begins with reference to the Spirit. The key distinguishing

intentional methodological approach within systematic theology where rather than looking *at* the Spirit (which would simply be the theological doctrine of pneumatology) we look *through* the Spirit. The Spirit essentially becomes a lens through which other theological doctrines can be examined with great clarity and precision. And, as the examples above illustrate, one helpful way to use the Spirit as a lens is to look at one doctrine, from the vantage point of other doctrines, through the lens of the Spirit. So, taking the example of the church, using a Third Article Theology approach, we need to look *at* the church, *through* the Spirit, *from* a series of different theological perspectives—namely Christology, the Trinity, and eschatology. Imagine a surveyor driving around a vast and beautiful mountain and setting up a theodolite at different locations to examine the view of the mountain from several vantage points. In this illustration, the mountain being examined is the church. The different vantage points are various theological doctrines—Christology, the Trinity, eschatology—and the theodolite lens being looked through is the Spirit. The key recognition that emerges is that pneumatology works particularly well as a way of connecting different doctrines. As Bobrinskoy writes, "Pneumatology is not so much one specific chapter of Christian theology as an essential dimension of every theological view of the Church and of its spirituality and liturgical and sacramental life."[17] McDonnell argues similarly, "Pneumatology is to theology what epistemology is to philosophy. Pneumatology determines the 'rules' for speaking about God."[18]

Nicholas Wolterstorff's small but profound book *Reason within the Bounds of Religion* helps to unpack the approach being used here.[19] Wolterstorff argues that humans can approach a true understanding of an objective and independent reality through the interchange of background beliefs, data beliefs, and control beliefs. Wolterstorff uses the simple illustration of an astronomer measuring a star's position in the sky to illustrate. He labels the star's position as the data belief (the reality being determined), the telescope's features as the control belief (the basis on which the exploration

---

feature between the traditional loci of pneumatology and Third Article Theology is that pneumatology looks at the Spirit, while Third Article Theology looks through the Spirit in order to explore other theological doctrines. For a helpful introduction to Third Article Theology, see Habets, "Prolegomenon: On Starting with the Spirit," 1–20.

17. Bobrinskoy, "Holy Spirit," 470.

18. McDonnell, "A Response to D. Lyle Dabney," 264.

19. Wolterstorff, *Reason Within the Bounds of Religion*. A more detailed explanation of the application of Wolterstorff's work to Third Article Theology (as summarised briefly in the next several paragraphs) can be found in Liston, *The Anointed Church*, 68–81.

rests), and everything else that is not within the purview of the experiment (such as Newton's laws of motion) are labelled as background beliefs. The insightful simplicity of Wolterstorff's approach is that he recognises that what scientists and other scholars regularly do is to swap the positions of the data, control, and background beliefs. So, in another experiment, the astronomer will assume the workings of the telescope (background), and measure a star's position (control), in order to test Newton's laws of motion (data). By regularly swapping background, control, and data beliefs, a scholar can ensure that all their knowledge is coherent and consistently related to other knowledge. In this way, a true understanding of reality can be approached without any one aspect being considered as indisputable and foundational.

Consider the application of this dialogical approach to Third Article Theology, and (more specifically) to the development of a Third Article Ecclesiology. Applying the insights of Wolterstorff to our theological examination suggests that the way to get a truly coherent understanding of ecclesiology is to first choose ecclesiology as a data belief, and then set up Christology, or the Trinity, or eschatology as control beliefs. The next step uses the pneumatological links between each pair of doctrines to determine insights about Third Article Ecclesiology. Taking the pictures we gain from all three vantage points and combining them together enables insight to be gathered into a fully formed Third Article Ecclesiology, an understanding of what a truly Spiritual church looks like.

Wolterstorff's understanding suggests we do not even have to stop there, however, because the newly developed Third Article Ecclesiology should itself be used as a control belief, a vantage point from which to look at other doctrines. The rest of the paper will utilise precisely this approach. The next section will use the Trinity as a vantage point to explore the church through the lens of the Spirit. The following section will use the coming kingdom as a vantage point to explore the church through the lens of the Spirit. And the final section will utilise the newly developed data belief and use it as a control belief. In other words, the overarching understanding of Third Article Ecclesiology developed in the first sections of this paper will be used as a vantage point to explore the doctrine of missiology and how the church can and should go about acting in the world.

USING THE TRINITY AS A VANTAGE POINT

Using the Trinity as a vantage point from which to explore the church immediately raises two questions. The first is the question: which Trinity?

Not, of course, that there are many Trinities, but there are many different understandings of the Trinity. This paper will not go into detail justifying a particular understanding of the Trinity, except to note that Spirit Christology provides an excellent vantage point from which to explore the Trinity. Using Wolterstorff's terminology, Spirit Christology can be used as a control belief that provides almost unparalleled insight into the data belief of the Trinity. As Coffey argues, "Spirit Christology provides our best mode of access to the theology of the Trinity."[20] Further, using this approach leads to an understanding of the Trinity that is thoroughly orthodox and conciliar, but also has some interesting nuances similar to those outlined in Thomas Weinandy's reconceived Trinitarian understanding. Weinandy argues that the Father eternally begets the Son by the Spirit, and the Son returns the love of the Father by the same Spirit in which he was begotten.[21]

The second question that arises from using the Trinity as a vantage point to examine the church is whether you *can* draw parallels between the Trinity and the church. Many scholars have attempted to justify such a link. Perhaps the most well-known is Volf's reflective argument that the church should be an egalitarian, non-hierarchical community because the Trinity is an egalitarian, non-hierarchical community.[22] But there are also many scholars who debunk the efforts of those drawing such parallels. Kathryn Tanner, for example, fashioned a very convincing argument which concludes that "it would be better to steer attention away from Trinitarian relations when making judgments about the proper character of human ones in Christian terms."[23] Tanner's argument essentially boils down to the very trenchant recognition that we're not God, and so to try and say we can or should imitate him is ill-informed, naïve, and potentially dangerous.[24]

There is, however, one undeniable point of continuity between the Trinity and the church: the Spirit. The same Spirit who dwells in the Trinity also dwells in the church. Consequently, while a direct, logical comparison between the Trinity and the church is misguided, perhaps a pneumatologically enabled parallel between the two realities could work.[25] From

---

20. Coffey, "Spirit Christology and the Trinity," 315.

21. See Weinandy, *The Father's Spirit of Sonship*. For a detailed argument that Spirit Christology leads to this particular formulation of the Trinity, see Liston, *The Anointed Church*, 191–232.

22. Volf, *After Our Likeness*.

23. Tanner, *Christ the Key*, 207–8.

24. For Tanner's critique of such an approach, see Tanner, *Christ the Key*, 207–46.

25. For a detailed justification and discussion of this pneumatologically inspired alternative approach derived from Third Article Theology, and how it differs from the directly reflective approach of Volf, see Liston, *The Anointed Church*, 233–72. The

that crucial insight, the implications of such a pneumatologically inspired parallel between the Trinity and the church emerge quite naturally. Looking through a pneumatological perspective clearly illuminates how the Spirit repeats or reprises a similar kind of role again and again, on a series of expanding stages. So, throughout eternity, as mentioned above, the Father begets the Son by the Spirit. The Spirit is the person through whom the Son is empersoned. Expanding to consider the role of the Spirit in time, the Spirit repeats the same kind of action. In time, the Father incarnates the Son (in Christ) by the Spirit. The Spirit is the person through whom the Son is incarnated. Expanding again to consider humanity, the Father embodies the Son (in the church) by the Spirit. The Spirit is the person through whom the Son is embodied in the church. And then finally, expanding again (if expand is the right terminology) to each individual in the church, the pattern again repeats. For in the church, the Father forms the Son (in each individual) by the Spirit. The Spirit is the person through whom the Son is formed in each person. What the Spirit does within the Trinity in eternity, parallels in some way what the Spirit does in time, in humanity, in the church, and in each individual. Establishing the way the Spirit's role is reprised on a series of stages enables a Barthian type analysis to be performed, comparing the parallel roles the Spirit has in these different spheres, the contrasts that exist between them, and also the intrinsic asymmetry that exists between them. The detail of this analysis is once again not included in this paper due to its overarching nature.[26]

There are many valuable and important points that emerge from examining these parallels.[27] The one that has the most significance, however, in terms of understanding what it means to be a truly Spiritual church is the picture that emerges of what prayer can and should be. If the church reflects the Trinity, as in Volf's understanding, then the only way we can approach God is like a group of friends joining another group of friends.[28] If that is the case, then prayer is simply something that we offer to God as a community as we spend time with him. No doubt the Spirit helps us as we do this, but prayer is still fundamentally something that we do in and through our own initiative.

---

explanation in this reference argues that a pneumatologically driven link between the Trinity and the church not only does not contradict Tanner's argument, it is necessarily precursored by her work in the earlier chapters of *Christ the Key*.

26. For the detail of this analysis see Liston, *The Anointed Church*, 273–302.

27. For more detailed analysis of the implications of this understanding see Liston, *The Anointed Church*, 303–34.

28. Bauckham, "Jürgen Moltmann's The Trinity and the Kingdom of God," 160.

But the understanding that emerges from the analysis above, where the Spirit reprises his roles in eternity, in time, in humanity, in the church, and in individuals within the church leads to an understanding that prayer is not something that we do *with* the Trinity, but rather something we do *in* the Trinity. Prayer is nothing short of becoming part of the Trinity's ongoing life. Through the Spirit we are united with Christ, who takes our prayers and offers them to the Father as if they were his. Jesus prays, and we pray in him. In this understanding, it is only because the community in prayer is the body of the Son that it has, through the Spirit, access to the Fatherhood of the Father. Further, our very prayers are sourced from the Father, who directs us through the Spirit just as he directs Christ as we are in Christ and in the Spirit. In this understanding, prayer, as C.S. Lewis aptly puts it, is something of a soliloquy—it starts from and returns to Father. We get the privilege of joining in.[29]

Realising that in prayer I'm not just praying to God, but in God, has fundamentally changed the way I pray and worship. Instead of working up the enthusiasm and willpower to give God the praise he deserves, prayer and worship has become more like sinking into his life. Understood this way, prayer is not stressful but truly life giving. It is not about what we do but about joining in what is already happening—participating in the eternally ongoing love the Son gives to the Father by the Spirit. While there are many more implications of using a Trinitarian vantage point to explore the intrinsically Spiritual nature of the church, even this one small but important example of participatory prayer demonstrates the valuable insights that arise from exploring ecclesiology from the vantage point of the Trinity.

USING ESCHATOLOGY AS A VANTAGE POINT

Having utilised Spirit Christology and the Trinity as control beliefs to explore the data belief of ecclesiology through the lens of the Spirit, this fourth section uses eschatology as a control belief. What insights can be drawn from the recognition that the Spirit makes the church the proleptic anticipation of the coming kingdom? Using eschatology as a vantage point illuminates some significant insights regarding how the Spirit transforms the church, and how we can participate in what the Spirit is doing.

To explore the relationship between the church and the coming kingdom it is first necessary to understand the nature of time. While this is

---

29. Lewis, *Prayer*, 71. A more detailed explanation of the implications of this understanding for prayer, and a contrast with other understandings and their implications, can be found in Liston, *The Anointed Church*, 329–33.

neither a small nor a simple subject, these investigations can again leverage and extend the insights of people who have explored this topic, but perhaps neglected or paid insufficient attention to the pneumatological aspect. Once again, rather than going around the work of people like Barth and Torrance, this analysis deliberately and intentionally works through their understandings.

T. F. Torrance, for example, has argued that Christ has redeemed time, and so his experience of time is different from ours. Just as there was a union of divine and human natures in Jesus, so there is a union of the eternal and temporal. Understanding Jesus' divinity as analogically corresponding to eternity, and Jesus' humanity as analogically corresponding to time, Torrance says "we may think of there having taken place in the incarnation as it were a hypostatic union between the eternal and the temporal in the form of new time."[30] But the incarnation is not enough, says Torrance, "We must think of fallen time as having perfected itself through the Cross and the resurrection into the abiding triumph of a perfection in God."[31] The result is that for Torrance there are three times to be considered: old time (which is what humans currently experience in their fallen condition), eternity (which is God's time) and "new" time (which is the reconciliation of old time and eternity that occurs in Jesus). Represented diagrammatically, time for Torrance is essentially envisioned as two separate lines running in parallel, both positioned within the background and framework of eternity.

The question that naturally arises from this formulation is how does new time interact with and affect old time? Looking through the lens of the Spirit, and leaping over the necessary and important systematic and exegetical work needed to determine an appropriate answer, the only conclusion to draw is that all of new time impacts our present moment in old time.[32] Through the Spirit, all of Christ's past, present, and future—the entirety of his heavenly session—impacts us in our present moment of old time. So, Christ's past in new time impacts us by bringing forward the revelation of Christ's work. This aspect can be appropriated to Christ's prophetic role, and Barth explores this prophetic aspect of Christ's eschatological ministry in detail in the last volume of *Church Dogmatics*.[33] Christ's present in new time impacts us through our participation in Christ's ongoing vicarious

---

30. Torrance, "The Modern Eschatological Debate," 224. For Torrance's understanding of time, also see Torrance, *Incarnation*, 334–36; and Torrance, *Space, Time and Resurrection*, 98–99.

31. Torrance, "The Modern Eschatological Debate," 224–25.

32. For a full outline of the justification of this conclusion, see Liston, *Kingdom Come*, 43–58.

33. See particularly, Barth, *Church Dogmatics*, IV/1, 274–83.

humanity. This can be appropriated to Christ's priestly role. Torrance compellingly explores this priestly aspect of Christ's ongoing eschatological interaction with us.[34] Finally, Christ's future in new time impacts us by bringing back to us features of Christ's coming kingdom, a connection that can be appropriated to Christ's kingly role, and neither Barth nor Torrance has done a particularly detailed or extensive job of exploring this aspect in any depth.[35]

When this kingly aspect is investigated some helpful insights into the church's transformation emerge. Skipping over the detailed exegetical and systematic work to explore the unity, distinctions, and asymmetry that exist between the kingdom and the church,[36] the insight that emerges is the extraordinary truth that in bringing back Christ's kingly presence to the contemporary church, the Spirit also brings back characteristics of the coming kingdom that enrich, influence, and transform our churches in ways that prepare us for our ultimate destination. So, qualities like truth, life, justice, and love that characterise the coming kingdom because Christ is truly king there, do not just stay as future qualities. In bringing back the presence of Christ the king, the Spirit enables these qualities to be displayed in our present church communities, and even more than that the Spirit drives us on so that these kingdom qualities become increasingly apparent among us.

The immediate question that arises from this is how do we participate with the Spirit in this transforming work—how do we align ourselves with what the Spirit is doing? And again, jumping over the exegetical and systematic work to the answer, the insight that emerges through this analysis is that we participate with the Spirit through imagination, presence, and practice.[37] Talking about this abstractly is both challenging and unhelpful, so in the following paragraphs this participation will be illustrated through a specific example: the Eucharist. As the centre point of our worship, the

---

34. Torrance focuses particularly on this theme in his 1955 monograph, *Royal Priesthood*.

35. In *Atonement*, for example, Torrance's description of Christ as ascended king is less than one page (270–71) while his exploration of Christ's ascended role as priest (271–77) and as prophet (277–81) are at least 7 and 5 pages respectively. See 270–81. Eugenio concludes that "At least in comparison to his greater and more in-depth treatments of the prophetic and priestly offices of Christ, the kingly office in Christ's incarnate economy and its implications for Christian life are noticeably less discussed. In particular, he does not elaborate the important implications of Christ's vicarious victory over sin and death for Christians now." Eugenio, *Communion with the Triune God*, 139.

36. For further details see Liston, *Kingdom Come*, 59–76.

37. For a detailed justification and analysis of this conclusion, and particularly its application to the Eucharist and beyond, see Liston, *Kingdom Come*, 77–128.

Eucharist is the obvious example to choose. How does the Spirit transform the church when we celebrate the Eucharist together?

The first way the church partners with the Spirit's transformation in the Eucharist is through imagination. When taking the Eucharist we can and should picture our coming future. The Eucharist points us towards the future event of the wedding supper of the lamb, and in doing this it paints an image for us of reality as it will be—a place and time where Christ is truly and completely king, and we as the church are truly and completely united to him. In the Eucharist we intentionally imagine ourselves to be what we truly are—people of the kingdom. We remind ourselves that we are foreigners living in a strange world that is not our home. And as this truth fills our imaginations, we realise that this world is not like that world yet, and it makes us long for home. Imagining our future in this way inspires us to make our communities outposts or colonies of the coming kingdom.

Closely following this stretching of our imaginations is the recognition that any Eucharistic foretaste of heaven we experience, or any transformation we presently enjoy, is not of our own doing but is a gift from outside of ourselves. Transformation happens through the pneumatologically enabled presence of Christ among us. Debates about the exact manner of Christ's presence in the bread and the cup have raged in the church. While these debates are not unimportant, the significant insight emerging from this analysis is that it is not the specific manner but the genuine reality of Christ's presence in the Eucharist that ultimately matters. Christ's presence through the Spirit writes the laws of the king on our hearts and minds. He moves us to follow his kingly decrees.

But divine transformation does not happen intrinsically and automatically through taking the Eucharist, as if by divine magic. So, in the Eucharist, we do not merely *imagine* the coming kingdom, and we do not merely enjoy the *presence* of the coming king, we *practise* genuinely being part of the kingdom. Taking the Eucharist means doing the kinds of things that will happen in the coming kingdom. It means intentionally preparing ourselves for when we truly live there. We sing together with enthusiasm and passion during the Eucharist because singing is a core feature of the coming Kingdom, and we want to be ready. We listen intently to God's word together, hanging on every word, so we can practise hearing and responding to God speaking, which we will also do in the coming Kingdom. And perhaps most significantly, we practise enjoying being together, because heaven is a place where all are one in Christ Jesus through the Spirit, and the Eucharist is an anticipation of that.

Since completing this research on the pneumatological relationship between the church and the kingdom, it has been an immense privilege to visit several churches in my home country of New Zealand and take them through an extended communion service which intentionally and deliberately anticipates the coming kingdom. In this service, rather than squeezing the Eucharist in between the sermon and the notices like normally happens, we take the whole church service to celebrate together. It has been a joy to see people get excited as it gradually dawns on them as they take the Eucharist in this way: this is who we are, what we are doing here defines us. We are kingdom people. We are not defined by the world and what it thinks. We are defined by the future that God is preparing for us. There is genuine transformation happening, I believe, as we go about doing communion as an intentional anticipation of the coming kingdom. And communion does not have to be the only way this transformation occurs. Every activity we do together as the church of God on earth can be a tool through which we can partner with the Spirit through imagination, presence, and practice.[38] Thinking about church life as an intentional and ongoing anticipation of the coming kingdom gives an idea, perhaps, of what a truly Spiritual church could look like in our postmodern western culture.

IMPLICATIONS FOR MISSION

Having explored ecclesiology from the vantage points of Christology, the Trinity, and eschatology, this final section examines the important subject of mission. How should the church interact with the world? More specifically, what theological and practical understanding of mission emerges if we adopt an approach that intentionally prioritizes the Spirit?

The relationship between ecclesiology and missiology is not a small topic, and not an uncontroversial one. Much of the controversy is definitional though. Some people define mission very broadly, and consequently view mission as foundational to the church. If mission is everything and everything is mission, then it inevitably follows that the church's very being is missional. Alternatively, a narrow definition of mission (such as merely

---

38. Recognizing how we partner with the Spirit in and through our ecclesial practices does not intrinsically bind the Spirit to the church, as if the Spirit can only work in and through church practices. There is an equal recognition arising from this analysis that the Spirit can move outside of the church, and even more significantly, *against* the church, should the church's actioning of these practices become intrinsically sinful. This recognition contrasts the understanding of the Spirit's role in the church developed in a Third Article Ecclesiology with that of authors such as Hütter and Jenson. For a detailed discussion of this point, see Liston, *Kingdom Come*, 98–105. The recognition of the Spirit working both within, but also against the practices of the church is mentioned many times throughout chaps. 5 and 6 of *Kingdom Come*, but see particularly 101–2.

the winning of converts) clearly omits important ecclesial aspects. Such terminology-induced diversity means that clear definitions are important. This paper adopts a broad but not all-encompassing definition of ecclesial mission as what the church is and does for the world. Or to say the same thing in different words, ecclesial mission is the intentionally outward, world-facing part of the church.

Defined in this way, what is the appropriate relationship between the church and mission? How do these two doctrinal realities indwell, inform, and improve each other? There are five clear options. The first is that church and mission are distinct, with the two intersecting minimally. The second and opposite option is that church and mission are identical, so that the church is exactly equated with its outward focused missional activity, without any remainder. Without detailed justification, this paper regards these two simplistic and excessive options as inadequate.[39] Consequently, church and mission must be considered as partially overlapping realities. Illustrated as a Venn diagram, mission and church are overlapping sets, with ecclesial mission as the area of intersection between the two. The full breadth of the church is larger than just its missionary activity (as the church is more than just world-facing), and mission extends beyond ecclesial activity (for the Spirit is at work within, through, *and beyond* the church).

The question immediately arises from this recognition: which theological loci has priority? Does mission define the church, or does the church define mission. These are the third and fourth options for how church and mission could be related. The third option is that the church's ontological nature determines the church's missional activity, so that it is only once the intrinsic nature of the church is determined that the church's missionary activity can be considered. The fourth option is that mission determines the church's reality, so that it is only once an understanding of mission is determined that we can explore a church's nature. Many missional church authors argue for this fourth option, using the now ubiquitous catch phrase of the *missio Dei*.[40] While different authors use this phrase in different ways, most often the key point being made through it is that the mission is primarily God's and not just ours. For these authors, therefore, Trinity and Christology determine missiology, and missiology determines ecclesiology. (Ecclesial) structure follows (missional) strategy, in their understanding. While it cannot be denied that missiology (and the *missio Dei*) *informs*

---

39. Liston, "Spirit, Church and Mission," 24.

40. See for example Frost and Hirsch, *The Shaping of Things to Come*, 201–23. More specifically, Hirsch comments that "Christology determines missiology, and missiology determines ecclesiology." Hirsch, *The Forgotten Ways*, 142. For a more detailed analysis and critique of this option see Liston, "Spirit, Church and Mission," 25–26.

ecclesiology, it is overreaching to suggest missiology entirely determines ecclesiology, for the church extends beyond its world-facing mission. If we affirm the *missio Dei*, we must also affirm the *ecclesia Dei*. If it is primarily God's mission, it is also primarily God's church. Trinity and Christology can also be used as vantage points from which to determine what the church is, and this understanding of ecclesiology can and should inform the nature of missiology.

Exploring the pneumatological relationship between church and mission leads to a fifth understanding, where missiology informs ecclesiology, and ecclesiology informs mission. The concept of such mutually informing doctrines fits well with the Wolterstorffian approach adopted in this paper. Sometimes mission can be the control belief, and ecclesiology examined as the data belief. Other times the roles can be swapped, with ecclesiology as the control belief, examining mission as the data belief. It is through examining the coherence and consistency between both doctrines that the closest approximation to true reality can be approached. The question of how the insights of missiology can be applied to ecclesiology has been thoroughly examined by missional church authors, but what about the insights going in the other direction? How can the insights from ecclesiology be applied to missiology? This final section will take the ecclesiological insights gained earlier in the paper and use them as control beliefs to briefly explore the data belief of the church's mission in the world.

In the first section Spirit Christology was used as the vantage point, and it led to the affirmation that through the Spirit, the church in her obedient suffering reveals the person of Christ. This concept was illustrated through the term inscape, which is not just a theological truth but a practical skill. A truly Spiritual church becomes increasingly adept at seeing Christ when they look through the church. But extending this ecclesial understanding to mission leads to the recognition that the church doesn't just *reveal* Christ in and through her obedient suffering, she also *draws* the world to Christ through her obedient suffering. The reality of the resurrection means our story extends beyond suffering and death. And as we obediently suffer in the light of that bigger story, it both reveals Christ and draws people to him. Perhaps the most obvious illustration of this is the suffering of the martyrs. Holwerda argues that "Martyrdom is not what it appears to be. It appears to be the cruel cessation of witness, but actually it is its empowerment because martyrdom is the example par excellence of how God's kingdom of peace overcomes the violence of empires and ideologies opposed to Christ."[41] The disciples recognized Jesus and were drawn to him through his scars; the

---

41. Holwerda, "Suffering Witnesses," 131–32.

world will also recognize and be drawn to Jesus through our scars and how we bear them.

Using the vantage point of the Trinity illuminated the recognition that the Spirit repeats the same kind of role on a series of expanding stages. In eternity, the Father begets the Son by the Spirit. And the Son returns love to the Father through the Spirit he has been given. In time, the Father incarnates the Son by the Spirit, and the now human Son returns love to the Father by the very Spirit through whom he was incarnated. In humanity, the Father embodies the Son in the church by the Spirit. And the church, by the Spirit of Sonship given to them returns love to the Father. Finally, within individuals in the church, the Father forms the Son in each of us by the Spirit. And by the same Spirit given to us we return love to those who have shown it to us. The same pattern of breathing out and breathing in happens repeatedly.[42]

But having worked our way through the Spirit's repeating roles in eternity, time, the church, and individual believers, the same kind of pattern occurs in ecclesial mission, for God directs us to love others not just within the church, but beyond it. Just as the church exists wherever, by the Spirit, the love of Christ is offered and returned, mission occurs wherever by the Spirit the love of Christ is offered, and salvation comes wherever that love is returned. So, just as in eternity, in time, in humanity, and in individuals within the church there are two aspects, this breathing out of the Son by the Spirit, and the returning of love to the Father by the same Spirit (breathing in), so in our missional activity there are two aspects as well. We breathe out by showing love to the world and those around us, but then we gather again, breathing in and allowing Christ to be formed in us. And this repeated pattern, breathing out and in, does not just happen once, it happens constantly, again and again, over and over. The implications for mission of this repeated Trinitarian pattern are quite rich.

The third and final connection explored was eschatological. The intrinsically pneumatological connection between church and kingdom illuminated the church as the proleptic anticipation of the coming kingdom, and provided a nuanced picture of how the Spirit is transforming the church through time. In bringing back to us the presence of Christ the king, the Spirit draws back features of the coming kingdom to increasingly be part

---

42. Note that the term *breathing* is used here as an overarching phrase to refer to all the roles of the Spirit within all of the different stages. For each individual stage more technical terminology could be used. So, for eternity, the Son is *begotten* by the Father in or through the Spirit, in time, the Son is *incarnated* by the Father in or through the Spirit etc. But the term breathing is appropriated here as an overarching term across all of these stages as a collective term.

of our church communities. The Spirit makes our churches increasingly places of truth, justice, life, and love. But it is not enough to see the church as just an institution that is "being transformed" by the Spirit, it must be a "transforming" institution as well. Extending from ecclesiology to mission informs the insight that the Spirit works in the world *through* the church.[43] And what the Spirit brings to the world is an extension of what he brought to the church. The Spirit leads the church to speak public truth, the Spirit leads the church to liberate those who are oppressed, the Spirit leads the church to unite people and draw them together, and the Spirit leads the church to preserve life and bring healing. In this way the Holy Spirit leads the church and the world into truth, justice, love, and life. These are essential parts of the church's pneumatological mission because the church must act in the world in a way that is consistent with who the Spirit makes the church to be. The church's eschatological nature informs the church's mission.

CONCLUSION

This paper began by asking the question of what a truly Spiritual church looks like. Some constituent features of such a church have been revealed by examining ecclesiology through the lens of the Spirit from the vantage points of Christology, the Trinity, and eschatology. The ecclesiological understanding emerging has also been used as a control belief to examine the church's missional role in the world. The overarching ecclesiology developed from this approach is both theologically rich and practically relevant. While the theological and practical ideas outlined here give only a very narrow glimpse into the breadth of Third Article Ecclesiology, even this partial viewpoint amply illustrates its value. Prioritising the Spirit in our theology and practice leads to an understanding of the church that is both convincing and compelling. In conclusion, three overarching ecclesiological insights particularly stand out.

First, prioritizing the Spirit leads to making Christ central. There are recent examinations of the church that intentionally contrast a pneumatological focus with a Christological one.[44] They implicitly or explicitly argue that if you prioritize the Spirit, it intrinsically means downgrading or limiting the Son in some way. The possibility that Christ will be minimized by prioritizing the Spirit has been a prominent concern since the emergence of Third Article Theology. For example, writing in response to an early article

---

43. This is not to restrict the Spirit's work in the world to the church, but to recognize that one important way the Spirit works in the world is ecclesiologically.

44. See for example Studebaker, *From Pentecost to the Triune God.*

from Dabney introducing this theological methodology, Kärkkäinen writes "I am sure that Dabney doesn't want his Third Article Theology to be read as giving undue emphasis to the Spirit to the detriment of Christology, but I fear that this might be the case with the approach."[45] My experience of applying this methodology over the last decade is that this concern simply is not justified. In contrast, as amply illustrated in the preceding sections, adopting a theological methodology that prioritizes the Spirit leads seamlessly to making Christ ecclesiologically central both in our understanding and our practice.

Second, prioritizing the Spirit enables us to see the church as truly God's concern. Speaking personally, perhaps the biggest insight from this decade of research into Third Article Ecclesiology is the conviction that God is responsible for his church, and that he can be trusted with it. I have had two stints at being a senior pastor. The best word to describe my first stint would be stress, while the appropriate word to describe the second would be joy. Doing this research changed my attitude to church leadership. Through exploring a Third Article Ecclesiology, I realized that everything does not depend on the church leader, and God genuinely is in control. My role as a pastor is to relax and enjoy participating in what God is doing in our church through the Spirit. And I do that best when I see Christ in the church (inscape). Moreover, I have found that when I do relax in my role as senior pastor, everyone around me relaxes as well. The end result is that we get to enjoy together what it means to be a part of God's family, participating by the Spirit in both the Son's ongoing worship of the Father and his continuing mission to the world.

Third, and finally, I believe the church in the western world is in a *kairos* moment. It has an incredible opportunity to redefine itself. Over the last 50 years, the church in New Zealand, for example, has suffered an incredible loss of size, status, and significance. Statistics suggest the situation in most western countries is similar. I am firmly convinced, however, that this loss of size, status, and significance is not a tragedy but an opportunity. Through these losses, through our weakness, we can rediscover that at our core we are a profoundly and irreducibly supernatural entity. Not despite these challenges, but because of them, we can learn again what it means to walk by faith and not by sight, to understand ourselves not primarily as a key player in society, but as an institution that is fundamentally constituted by God's Spirit.

---

45. Kärkkäinen, "David's Sling," 151.

5

The Holy Spirit and the Apostolicity of the Unholy Church

Paul T. Nimmo

INTRODUCTION

THE PRESENTING ISSUE FOR this essay is a simple one, arising out of two features of the ecclesial landscape that sit uneasily together. On the one hand, the present era represents a time of mission for the Christian church. It is not simply the case that the church has a mission, as if mission were one aspect of its work alongside many other activities. In recent times, it has become more evident that the church is in its very essence a missional church, a church mandated to operate with mission in mind across its works in the world.[1] Indeed, given the ongoing retreat of the church in the ever more secularising west, the importance of this mission—no longer exclusively overseas, as once was the case, but now intensively at home as well—has become deeply evident. On the other hand, the present era sees the reputation of the church in that secularising west at a perilously low level. It is not simply the fact that the decline in the number of people who identify

---

1. For a paradigmatic expression of this view of the church, see Flett, *The Trinity*.

as Christian seems to continue inexorably. There have also been myriad scandals and abuses, some of the most harrowing sort, steadily diminishing the trustworthiness and esteem of the institution. Some of these scandals belong to former generations, their gravity only now being fully felt for the first time; others are from far more recent days—and are thus far fresher, far rawer. All this has contributed to a wider sense that the church is no longer (if it ever was) what it purports to be—a communion of saints. The result is that there arises an uneasy situation for the church: an ever-growing realisation of the significance of mission alongside an ever-growing recognition of its problematic history and present.

This essay seeks to consider this presenting issue further in a theological idiom. It does so by exploring two of the four notes of the church confessed in the Niceno-Constantinopolitan Creed—its holiness and its apostolicity. First, it considers the holiness of the church, offering an account of how this should be construed, while also recognising the force of the unholiness of the church. It turns, second, to the apostolicity of the church, that note of the church most intrinsically connected with mission, seeking at this point to find an appropriate contemporary hermeneutic for this note also. With these backdrops in view, it moves, third, to offer a particular focus upon the work of the Spirit in the church as a means to hold this complex picture together. It closes with some brief reflections upon the implications of this picture for the church today.

I THE HOLINESS OF THE CHURCH?

It is a core affirmation of both the creeds of the early Church and the confessions of the Reformation that the church is "holy," and it is a claim not absent from Scripture either.[2] Yet it is precisely in the context of a clear exposition of what it means for the church to be holy that light can be shed on its pervasive and perennial lack of holiness in practice. To understand the holiness of the church, it is essential first to consider the holiness of God. This section thus explores first the holiness of God and then the holiness of the church, before turning lastly to consider the unholiness of the church.[3]

To speak of holiness is to speak first, and last, of God, the One whose very nature it is to be holy. Scripture is replete with testimonies to the divine

---

2. See, for example, the Niceno-Constantinopolitan Creed and the Apostles' Creed, as well as the Augsburg Confession (Article VII), the Belgic Confession (Article 27), and the Second Helvetic Confession (Chapter XVII).

3. For a more detailed exposition of the material in this section, see Nimmo, "The Sanctification of the Church."

The Holy Spirit and the Apostolicity of the Unholy Church 75

holiness. The seraphs in the heavenly temple seen by Isaiah declare: "Holy, holy, holy is the LORD of hosts; the whole earth is full of his glory" (Isa 6:3). God is the One whose very name is holy. And more than this, God's holiness is *sui generis*—unique. In Revelation, the heavenly conquerors of the beast sing "Lord, who will not fear and glorify your name? For you alone are holy" (Rev 15:4). Holiness is thus not an accidental quality of deity, but pertains to its very substance. Emil Brunner captures the insight well: "To be holy ... is that which sets the Being of God apart from all other forms of being."[4] God is holy on God's own account, not from outwith, holy without reserve and without measure, holy in a way above and beyond anything else in all of creation.

There is a further specification of the holiness of God to register at this point, and that is the Trinitarian aspect of divine holiness as it is attested in the New Testament. Holiness is predicated here not only of the divine being—that is, of the divine nature or essence—but of each of the three persons of the Trinity, and in emphatic terms. Jesus himself prays to his "Holy Father" (John 17:11), while the unclean spirit in the Gospel of Mark cries out to Jesus: "What have you to do with us, Jesus of Nazareth? Have you come to destroy us? I know who you are, the Holy One of God" (Mark 1:14). Then there is the Holy Spirit: holy is the One who descends upon Jesus at his baptism and leads him to the wilderness, who teaches the disciples, fills them, inspires them, and assists them—there are many spirits, but one Holy Spirit.[5] This sanctifying work of the Spirit will be explored in greater detail later.

To this point, however, no material definition of holiness has yet been provided. As a starting point, one might adopt the definition of the Leiden Synopsis, which opines that "Holiness ... is the virtue whereby [God], being most pure, approves everything that is pure, and whereby [God] is repulsed by its opposite."[6] There is a twofold disposition that is thus in effect in the intrinsic holiness of God—towards purity and against sin. This holiness of the triune God with its double disposition is made known as God reveals Godself as holy, as majestic and sovereign Lord. Ezekiel reports the Word of the Lord thus: "I will display my greatness and my holiness and make myself known in the eyes of many nations. Then they shall know that I am the LORD" (Ezek 38:23). This making known of the holiness of God takes place in God's works within creation. Indeed, Petrus van Mastricht lists a

---

4. Brunner, *Dogmatics*, 1:158.

5. See respectively Luke 3:22; Luke 4:1; John 14:26; Acts 11:24; 1 Thess 1:15; and 2 Tim 1:14.

6. *Synopsis Purioris Theologiae*, vol. 1, *Disputations 1–23*, 6.40, 179.

catalogue of the works of God in which God reveals the divine holiness: from the decrees, through creation, providence, redemption, calling, and sanctification, to glorification.[7] At each point God is at work, overcoming sin, and advancing purity.

Precisely in the process of these holy divine works within creation, the holy God is revealed to be the God who covenants with people. Indeed, at the very heart of the purpose of the holy God in creation is the establishment of a holy community, in covenant relationship with God. It is here, then, that there is encountered the divinely intended holiness of the church. Thus Paul writes: "[God] chose us in Christ before the foundation of the world to be holy and blameless before him in love" (Eph 1:4). The reference to "choosing" indicates that the sphere of the divine election, that gracious and merciful decree of God, is in view here. The reference to "us" is to "the saints in Ephesus" (Eph 1:2) and—by extension—to the church everywhere. But this holy community of the church is itself grafted into the people of Israel, which, as Leviticus states, is similarly chosen for holiness: "You shall be holy to me; for I the LORD am holy, and I have separated you from the other peoples to be mine" (Lev 20:26). On this basis, it is little wonder that John Webster writes of holiness as "a mode of God's activity," that "identifies the manner of [God's] relation to us."[8]

However, holiness is also the mode of human activity that is called forth by this holy work of God. Thus, the Lord said to Moses and Aaron, and to all Israel: "I am the LORD your God; sanctify yourselves therefore, and be holy, for I am holy" (Lev 11:44). And this call and its ethical implication are reiterated in the new covenant: "as he who called you is holy, be holy yourselves in all your conduct; for it is written, 'You shall be holy, for I am holy'" (1 Pet 1:15–16). There is here an ethical imperative. The people of God are to be holy, just as the Lord their God is holy. In a distant analogy to the nature and acts of God, they too are to seek purity and to reject impurity; they too are to set themselves apart in creation without being separate from it. They are to be an echo on earth, however distantly, corresponding to God's original holiness.

At the same time, remarkably, there is also here an ontological indicative. Scripture relates that the sanctification of the people of God has happened already, has been effected already—in Jesus Christ. Paul writes, "To the church of God that is in Corinth, to those who *are sanctified* in Christ Jesus, called to be saints, together with all those who in every place call on the name of our Lord Jesus Christ, both their Lord and ours" (1 Cor 1:2).

---

7. Van Mastricht, *Theoretical-Practical Theology*, 2:411.
8. Webster, *Holiness*, 41.

The Holy Spirit and the Apostolicity of the Unholy Church 77

The recipients of these letters—and by implication all Christians—are called to be saints, to be holy, but are also *already* sanctified, *already* saints, *already* holy. The church is already now the *communio sanctorum*, the communion of the holy ones. Those chosen and called are already somehow set apart, not from the world, but in the world—and, it should be added, for the world, in a distant creaturely echo of the revealed holiness of God. And here too, the Trinitarian grammar of Scripture is in play: the gift of being rendered holy is from God (the Father), in Jesus Christ, and by the Holy Spirit.[9]

It is just here, however, where the miraculous significance of the scriptural indicative shines brightest, that there is the intrusion, the hellish intrusion, of sin, and the emergence of the brute reality of the unholiness of the church. The church as the covenant community of God exists in a sinful world. Though the church itself may be holy with reference to its calling and its cleansing, it is rather more difficult to speak of its holiness in practice. To say the very least, the church has not always fulfilled the high ethical imperatives that confront it in Scripture. Even within Scripture itself, the examples of the churches in Galatia and Corinth do not inspire admiration or imitation in regard to holiness.

One might wonder if the people of God has ever been holy in this sense. Francis Turretin defines a church as "true" when it is "said to be holy," and notes that this is so where "it contains nothing false as to doctrine of faith, nothing unjust as to doctrine of morals, [and] can be known from no other source than a comparison with the Scriptures."[10] Yet Turretin himself acknowledges that "every particular visible church can fall into deadly error, in faith as well as in practice . . . such errors are the proximate causes corrupting and destroying the church"—in other words, the church militant is vulnerable; it "creeps in the mire."[11] Of course, it is a consistent refrain across theology that the church as a whole will not fail: God will not be left without witness.[12] But this can be a very fragile witness: the church prior to the eschaton is not a holy place, and is at times the opposite: the community

---

9. See, respectively, 1 Thess 5:23, corresponding to the petition of Jesus at John 17:17; the offering of the body of Jesus Christ in death, Heb 10:10 and Col 1:22, and the Spirit as the agent of sanctification at, among other places, Rom 15:16.

10. Turretin, *Institutes of Elenctic Theology*, XVIII.xiii.8, Vol 3:113.

11. Turretin, *Institutes of Elenctic Theology*, III, XVIII.ix.5, 53 and XVIII.xi.26, 81.

12. For a typical statement of this belief, see the Second Helvetic Confession, chapter XVII: "Meanwhile God has in this world and in this darkness his true worshippers, and those not a few, but even seven thousand and more (I Kings 19:18; Rev. 7:3 ff.). For the apostle exclaims: 'God's firm foundation stands, bearing this seal, "The Lord knows those who are his," etc. (II Tim. 2:19)."

called by God has too often become "a den of robbers" (Jer 7:11), a "brood of vipers" (Matt 23:33).

In place of turning to purity and away from sin, the church has done the reverse. Far from being a light to the nations, the church has been at points an agent of darkness. And even where the church appears to be holy, there is a caution—again from Turretin—that "external holiness is deceitful and doubtful."[13] Turning from textbooks and treatises to the real world, there is little space among actual churches for the anticipated "lovely portraits" and "ideal paradigms."[14] It is more the case, as the Second Helvetic Confession observes, that "the church appears at times to be extinct."[15] In this way there can arise a disjunction between what Nicholas Healy described as "blueprint ecclesiologies" and the mixed ecclesiastical situation that is empirically confronted.[16] In a contemporary context, as Joseph Small writes, "church sin is evidenced in systemic ignoring of ecclesial racism, indifference to doctrine, sexual misconduct and abuse, . . . and a host of other grand and petty transgressions."[17] On this basis, it is easy to understand Job asking "How then can a mortal be righteous before God?" (Job 24:4). And perhaps even Martin Luther's bold claim that "There is no greater sinner than the Christian Church" comes into sharp perspective and becomes more understandable.[18]

The church itself thus appears to be at one and the same time both holy and sinful—one might even say, *simul sanctus et peccator*. This is no partial situation such that one group or congregation or denomination is holy and another is sinful. Rather one might better here think of a *totus–totus* dynamic, such that the church is entirely holy by way of its union with the holiness of Jesus Christ *and* entirely sinful on the basis of its failure to live in obedience to his commands. Of and in itself, as Karl Barth writes, "it is not holy, it is nothing out of the ordinary, indeed . . . it is just as unholy as [Adamic] humanity, sharing its sin and guilt and standing absolutely in need of its justification."[19] However, seen in Jesus Christ, and in light of his calling and redeeming work, the church is indeed holy.

The holiness of the church is thus an alien quality. It truly does belong to the church, but only improperly, that is—more precisely—by way

---

13. Turretin, *Institutes of Elenctic Theology*, III, XVIII.xiii.10, 113.
14. Small, *Flawed Church*, 3.
15. Second Helvetic Confession, chapter XVII.
16. Healy, *Church, World, and the Christian Life*, 25–51.
17. Small, *Flawed Church*, 117.
18. Martin Luther, cited in Webster, *Holiness*, 73.
19. Barth, *Church Dogmatics*, IV/1, 687.

of attribution or imputation. It is a quality extrinsic to it, passively received and recognised only in faith. And it is conceivable and recognisable only when the church is regarded in light of its union with Jesus Christ. Herman Bavinck alludes to this idea of the alien holiness of the church when he writes that Christians are "objectively counted as saints in Christ by virtue of God's imputation to them of the righteousness of Christ."[20] And Webster similarly opines, "to be a saint is to have one's holiness in Christ Jesus," and thus alludes to "the passivity which is at the heart of the Church as a creature of divine grace."[21] The holiness of the church is only to be grasped along such extrinsic, ec-centric lines: it is truly "holy," even in its problematic present, by virtue of its union with Jesus Christ.

Therefore church may indeed by holy, just as the creeds and the confessions claim; but it is also corrosively and rampantly unholy. To confess the former may broadly be an act of faith; but to observe the latter requires little skill in perception. The question that arises is: how does this affect its mission?

II THE APOSTOLICITY OF THE CHURCH

To turn to the apostolicity of the church is to turn to that mark of the church that speaks particularly of its mission. The basic meaning of the term itself pertains to the idea of sending, of mission. To be apostolic is to be sent. Hence Wolfhart Pannenberg observes that "the church's apostolicity means that the sending out of the apostles to all humanity is continued by the church."[22] This formal dimension of apostolicity has recently become hugely important in the ecumenical movement: it offers a way forward on which all can agree, for the idea that the covenant people are called and sent is at the heart of Scripture.

The term is not, however, merely formal. In material terms, there is a basic spiritual dimension to apostolicity. The one who sends the covenant people is God, who communicates by God's Word and animates by God's Spirit. This idea is memorably and clearly voiced by Paul himself, to the Galatians: "Paul an apostle—sent neither by human commission nor from human authorities, but through Jesus Christ and God the Father, who raised him from the dead" (Gal 1:1). Webster correspondingly comments that "talk of apostolicity is primarily talk of the church's Lord rather than of the Lord's

---

20. Bavinck, *Reformed Dogmatics*, 4:321.
21. Webster, *Holiness*, 83 and 55.
22. Pannenberg, *Systematic Theology*, 3:406.

servants."²³ Apostolicity is therefore from the outset not simply a human affair, but a dimension of the life of the church that depends for its truth and efficacy upon a divine commission and empowerment to ground its very reality. This divine impulse is the *terminus a quo* of this mark of the church.

There is thus, and perhaps uniquely among the four notes of the church, a correspondingly *concrete* dimension to the idea of apostolicity: it has, one might say, an intrinsic visibility. For the church stands or falls in its relation to the particular covenant people who were not only sent but also accorded the specific title of "apostles." There is thus a historical connection, a diachronic link, between whatever is deemed apostolic today and these individuals who were active during and immediately after the ministry of Jesus. Luke writes: "when day came, [Jesus] called his disciples and chose twelve of them, whom he also named apostles" (Luke 6:13). The apostles were not simply disciples in the wider sense, followers of Jesus who had chosen to walk with him; they were also specifically chosen by Jesus to be integral to his mission, as Mark writes: "to be with him, and to be sent out to proclaim the message" (Mark 3:14).²⁴ To equip them, Matthew notes, Jesus "gave them authority over unclean spirits, to cast them out, and to cure every disease and every sickness" (Matt 10:1). They were with him through most of his earthly ministry, ate a last meal with him, were among the first witnesses of the resurrection, and were the last people to whom he spoke before ascending to heaven.²⁵ They then carried forward the mission of Jesus in the early church, to Jews and Gentiles, as Acts so powerfully relates: offering teaching and fellowship, performing many wonders and signs, giving testimony with power, and deciding the strategy of the church.²⁶ And in the new earth to come, as Revelation notes, "the wall of the city has twelve foundations, and on them are the twelve names of the twelve apostles of the Lamb" (Rev 21:14). These, then, are the apostles, historical human beings with unique authority who are in some way connected to the *present* of the church, and in turn connect the present of the church directly back to the ministry of Jesus.

---

23. Webster, *Holy Scripture*, 50.

24. Together with the prophets, the apostles were sent by the Wisdom of God (Luke 11:49).

25. See Luke 22:14 ("When the hour came, he took his place at the table, and the apostles with him"), Matt 28:8–9 ("So they left the tomb quickly with fear and great joy, and ran to tell his disciples. Suddenly Jesus met them and said, 'Greetings!' And they came to him, took hold of his feet, and worshiped him"), and Acts 1:2 ("until the day when he was taken up to heaven, after giving instructions through the Holy Spirit to the apostles whom he had chosen").

26. The references here are Acts 2:42; 2:43; 4:33; 5:12; and 15:6.

Controversy, of course, has arisen over how this connection is secured across time. What it means to stand in diachronic connection, or—better—continuity with the apostles, and wherein that succession lies have been church-dividing issues. The perspective common to several churches that the apostolic succession is constituted by an unbroken historical series of intervening persons holding particular offices is not tenable from a Protestant perspective. Hendrikus Berkhof observes that it is "not a little strange" that the apostolic concept "rests completely on turning to the world" while "from the perspective of the apostolic succession, the apostles came to be regarded as static-hierarchical princes of the church."[27] Such an account can, at best, only testify to apostolicity; at worst, it relies neither upon the Spirit nor upon faith; it requires neither the presence of God nor the obedience of human beings; and it falls back instead only upon historical and ecclesiastical processes. The succession that exists between the apostles and later Christians is not of this sort. By contrast, Webster observes, apostolicity "is less to do with transmission and much more to do with identity and authenticity."[28] Specifically, this essay argues, apostolic continuity is to be found in *relationship*. More specifically, apostolic continuity is to be found in *covenant* relationship: in subsequent generations of believers existing under the same calling, teaching, and provisioning of God as did the original apostles, standing in the same dynamic of obedience to the Word of God, and seeking the same eschatological resurrection by the Spirit in the coming Kingdom of God. In this covenantal perspective, the apostolicity of the church is thus constituted extrinsically, from outwith, by the desire of God to be in covenant relationship. To describe the resultant continuity as a continuity of teaching is not incorrect, but nor is it adequate.[29] For one, the succession is relational and not simply paedagogical, and is so not only at the outset, but across the subsequent centuries of faith. Joseph Small correctly notes that "Christ's call to apostolicity . . . is personal, the beckoning of One who is with us now."[30] For another, the succession is enacted and not simply reflected, and again is so across the centuries of witness. Amy Plantinga Pauw rightly observes that "Church is called to be apostolic in its ordinary daily life, testifying to and enacting the apostolic teaching of Christ's love for

---

27. Berkhof, *An Introduction to the Study of the Christian Faith*, 412.

28. Webster, "The 'Self-Organizing' Power of the Gospel," 208.

29. Of course, continuity of apostolic teaching remains essential! See, for example, 2 John 9: "Everyone who does not abide in the teaching of Christ, but goes beyond it, does not have God; whoever abides in the teaching has both the Father and the Son," and cf. Titus 1:9.

30. Small, *Flawed Church*, 205.

the whole world."[31] Apostolicity is thus broader, deeper, and richer than any focus simply on dogmatic faithfulness.

This understanding of the apostolicity of the church has clear implications for the mission that is intrinsic to its work, the communication of the gospel that is the *terminus ad quem* of its apostolic nature. For in this view, the substance of apostolic confession that is to be communicated in mission is not to be found in a particular unbroken line of church personnel. It is also not to be found in a particular given form of church order. Indeed, and here care must be taken, it is not even to be found in a particular understanding of church structures, church liturgy, church architecture, church language, or church rituals. As John Flett has noted, the mission of the Word of God does not seek to impose a particular church culture, in quasi-imperialist fashion; rather, the Word of God in mission works to permeate and to transform cultures.[32] Hence Pannenberg observes:

> The church is authentically apostolic only when as a missionary church it remains ready to alter traditional ways of thinking and living, being renewed constantly on the basis of its origins, not for the sake of adjustment to the spirit of the times, but in order to be able to explicate . . . the eschatological truth of the revelation of God in Jesus Christ for each new generation and in each new world situation.[33]

The apostolic mission of the church is thus at heart a matter of standing in the line of the prophetic community of those who are caught up in the perennial movement of hearing and obeying the Word of God. This takes place under what Barth describes as the "normative authority, instruction and direction of the apostles," and seeks to catch others up in this movement in critical and liberating ways.[34] This can only take place under the divine command and with the divine empowerment: in this way, the church as an apostolic community and in its apostolic mission is a communion dependent at every point on grace.

Within this construal of apostolic succession, a narrow path is traversed with dangers on either side. On one side lies the danger of an overinflated view of the apostles, as if they were somehow ontically elevated

---

31. Plantinga Pauw, *Church in Ordinary Time*, 123. This fuller idea of apostolicity is evident in 1 Thess 4:1, where Paul writes, "Finally, brothers and sisters, we ask and urge you in the Lord Jesus that, as you learned from us how you ought to live and to please God (as, in fact, you are doing), you should do so more and more."

32. Flett, *Apostolicity*, passim.

33. Pannenberg, *Systematic Theology*, 3:407.

34. Barth, *Church Dogmatics*, IV/1, 714.

above ordinary Christians, somehow possessing an infallibility in and of themselves. On the other side lies the danger of an under-estimation of the apostles, which fails to recognise their particular calling and ministry, and—in particular—fails to appreciate the unique way in which their proximity to Jesus renders their testimony normative. The writer of Ephesians notes this connection clearly: "[the household of God is] built upon the foundation of the apostles and prophets, with Christ Jesus himself as the cornerstone" (Eph 2:20).[35] Close to hand here is the canonical import of the writings of the apostles, and thus the Scripture-principle that underlies work in Christian dogmatics.

To speak of the church as apostolic is thus to speak to both of these dimensions of the church: of the way in which created, fallen human beings are essential to the church and its history, and of the way in which they are made fit for the purposes of God by grace. That God accommodates the divine plan and the divine mission to creaturely servants in this way is a wonder in every sense . . . yet this truth lies at the heart of the gospel: that treasure is found in earthen jars, even jars that are cracked and broken. Among the followers of Jesus, there is no perfection: only creaturely and sinful beings. And the consequence of this for apostolicity is captured by Pannenberg, who notes that "We must . . . stress the church's apostolicity so strongly for the very reason that we detect so clearly that the church has broken away from its apostolic beginnings and is pushing on into an uncertain future."[36] For this reason, apostolicity remains a confession, not an observation.

In this way, the confession of apostolicity has two poles: the first in the sinfulness, the unholiness of the church; and the second in the purposes of God. The former has already been the subject of the first section; and so it is to the latter that the third section will now turn, as it moves to consider matters of pneumatology.

III THE WORK OF THE HOLY SPIRIT

The hinge which holds together the holiness of the unholy church on the one hand and the apostolicity of the church on the other hand is the work of the Holy Spirit. Without this, there would be no ascription of holiness and no visibility of apostolicity at all. In the ecclesial sphere there is thus a particular truth to the creedal confession of the Spirit as "the Lord, the Giver of Life."

---

35. See also 1 Cor 12:28: "God has appointed in the church first apostles, second prophets, third teachers."
36. Pannenberg, *Systematic Theology*, 3:409.

The work of the Spirit spans the whole economy, beginning with the creation of the world (Gen 1:2) and the creation and preservation of human beings: "The spirit of God has made me, and the breath of the Almighty gives me life" (Job 33:4). The Spirit is also at work throughout salvation history in particular, notably in the inspiration of the prophets, and above all in the incarnation.[37] But the focus in this section is on the work of the Spirit in the church, for the church of the apostles is a community vivified by the Spirit. Jesus himself prophesied: "But the Advocate, the Holy Spirit, whom the Father will send in my name, will teach you everything, and remind you of all that I have said to you" (John 14:26). And at the event of Pentecost, the Spirit does indeed descend upon the church: "suddenly from heaven there came a sound like the rush of a violent wind, and it filled the entire house ... Divided tongues, as of fire, appeared among them, and a tongue rested on each of them. All of them were filled with the Holy Spirit and began to speak in other languages, as the Spirit gave them ability" (Acts 2:2–4). The subsequent works of the Spirit on the regenerate community are manifold. According to Scripture, it is the Spirit who testifies, who dwells in Christians, who moves the hearts of Christians to call "Abba, Father!," who provides gifts of discipleship and guidance.[38] In theological idiom, Zacharius Ursinus remarks that "the office of the Holy [Spirit] is to produce sanctification in the people of God," and observes that this office "may be said to embrace the following things: to instruct, to regenerate, to unite to Christ and God, to rule, to comfort and strengthen us."[39] And Richard Muller draws attention just here to the Trinitarian background to this appropriated work, noting that the Spirit "confirm[s] with sanctification what the Father decrees and the Son has accomplished."[40] The Spirit is thus the agent of both the divine work and the human reception of illumination, regeneration, adoption, and sanctification. And it is the Spirit who impels and sustains the church in its acts of mission.

There are three particular aspects of this activity of the Spirit that deserve further attention here.

The first aspect is that this work of the Spirit relates specifically to human creatures just as they are, as fallen, and bestows truth and light and freedom upon them precisely in their currently benighted and imprisoned state. Thus the sinfulness, the corruption, the idolatry, the betrayal of fallen

---

37. See further on the Spirit and Jesus Christ: Mabry, "Christotelic Pneumatology," chap. 3; and Ford, *Christian Wisdom*, chap. 5.

38. References are to 1 John 5:6–7; Rom 8:9; Gal 4:6; 5:22–23, and 25.

39. Ursinus, *Commentary on the Heidelberg Catechism*, 277, cited by Muller, *Post-Reformation Reformed Dogmatics*, 4:380.

40. Muller, *Post-Reformation Reformed Dogmatics*, 4:381.

human beings is no obstacle to the Spirit. Not even the intransigence and wilfulness of human creatures can hinder the Spirit. Evocative of this power is the vision of the Valley of Dry Bones in Ezekiel, who records the Word of the Lord thus: "I will cause breath [or the Spirit] to enter you, and you shall live. I will lay sinews on you, and will cause flesh to come upon you, and cover you with skin, and put breath [or the Spirit] in you, and you shall live; and you shall know that I am the LORD" (Ezek 37:5–6). The Spirit is the Spirit of the resurrection, who can bring life out of death. So too the Spirit overcomes the pride of James and John, and the denial of Peter,[41] and is correspondingly able to work through and in the flaws of every person. Thus it is not the case that the Spirit can only work on holy ground; the Spirit is certainly able to work in the heights, but is equally able to work in the depths. The unholiness of the church is thus, by the Spirit, no obstacle to mission.

The second aspect is that this work of the Spirit is not an alien work of the Spirit, something which sits awkwardly or even at odds with some other work that the Spirit is purposed to undertake. The work of the Spirit in the economy, bringing knowledge and liberation and calling and empowering the church, is precisely that work for which the Spirit is eternally destined. Elsewhere the Spirit has been described as eternally *inecclesiandus*—destined from all eternity and sent in creaturely time to be the One who is at the heart of the life of the church.[42] And so the work of the Spirit in the midst of sinful humanity, and in the midst of the sinful community of the church, is no accident, but rather is constitutive of the Spirit's redemptive mission in the fallen creation. And its empowering of the mission of the church is a central constituent of that work.

The third aspect, however, is a note of caution. For all that mission is the proper work of the Spirit, and for all that the unholiness of the church is no obstacle to its prosecution, this work of the Spirit in all its breath-taking and manifold diversity is not a work that can ever be summoned by or appropriated to creaturely action. The Spirit is free, and cannot be domesticated by any creaturely word or practice. Jesus emphatically speaks of this to Nicodemus: "The Spirit blows where it chooses, and you hear the sound of it, but you do not know where it comes from or where it goes" (John 3:8). The Spirit thus cannot be instrumentalised, possessed, or canalised, whether by the apostles or by the church. G. C. Berkouwer notes the fear that "one ties down the life of the Spirit [such that] the Spirit blows where He will (John 3:8) becomes a past tense, and the Spirit has entered into the

---

41. The references are Mark 10:37 and 14:72.
42. Nimmo, "A Certain Unity of the Church."

firm structures of the Church."[43] The necessary refutation is instanced by Huldrych Zwingli, who observes on the basis of the same text that "the Spirit of grace is not conveyed by this immersion, not by this drinking, not by that anointing. For if it were thus, it would be known how, where, whence, and whither the Spirit is borne."[44] More comprehensively, Barth posits, "There can be no supposed human control over the Holy Spirit."[45] The Spirit works in the Spirit's way and the Spirit's time, and this is true also with regard to its enabling of the mission of the church.

This is not, of course, to deny the connection between the Word and the Spirit, to suggest that the Spirit is a divine person of arbitrariness or caprice, to yield to quasi-Montanist flights of enthusiasm. The Spirit remains the Spirit of the Word. But it is to suggest that the connection between Word and Spirit is not to be construed in such a way as to occlude the energetic and vivifying existence of the Spirit, whose presence and activity is not simply confined—for example—to the words of a text, however authoritative.[46] A pair of images might illuminate this point: the Spirit is not to be conceived as being bound to the Word after the fashion of a prisoner chained to an iron ball, able to move only with extreme difficulty by dragging their burden along behind them; perhaps instead the Spirit is to be visualised more in the manner of a kite, tethered to the ground that is the Word certainly, yet nonetheless flying with great freedom and spontaneity, in ways beautiful and patterned yet not entirely predictable. It is only in light of such a dynamic construal of this relation that the Spirit can be rightly recognised as possessing eschatological, critical, interruptive power, an ability to work both within and outwith the walls of the church, and an ability to surprise and shock—even as the Spirit is always irrevocably grounded in and witness to the Word.

43. Berkouwer, *The Church*, 219. Berkouwer continues slightly later: "it is impossible for the gift of salvation to be transferred to the command of men in such a way that the prayer *Veni Creator Spiritus!* would be superfluous because the Holy Spirit had come. No matter how many ways are cleared by the power of the Spirit, it is not possible to tie down and channel His work," *The Church*, 220.

44. Zwingli, "An Account of the Faith," in *The Latin Works of Huldreich Zwingli*, 46. Zwingli is quite clear on this: "grace comes from or is given by the Divine Spirit . . . so this gift pertains to the Spirit alone"; moreover, "a channel or vehicle is not necessary to the Spirit, for He Himself is the virtue and energy whereby all things are borne, and has no need of being borne," "An Account of the Faith," 46.

45. Barth, *Church Dogmatics*, IV/1, 720.

46. Locher writes, "To the end of his days Martin Luther marvelled that the Spirit should bind himself to the Word. In much the same way, Zwingli guarded most passionately the truth that the Word is bound to the Spirit. Thus our service of God is continually cast back, beyond all our liturgical ordinances, upon free grace," in *Zwingli's Thought: New Perspectives*, 13.

Bringing these three aspects of the work of the Spirit together, it is seen that the work of the sovereign free Spirit, willed from all eternity, is to establish the apostolicity of the church afresh in each generation and in each situation. It is by the grace of the Spirit alone that the witness of the flawed and unholy church can be lifted time and again up and out of the sinful mire of a fallen world to shine forth as a missional activity corresponding to the holy radiance of the divine Word. The activity of the church cannot become apostolic and faithful in this way independently, but only as—by the power of the Spirit—its "human work is totally directed, both dimensionally and correlatively, to God's work."[47] There is thus no grounds for self-righteousness or works-righteousness here in the realm of mission. Rather, as Paul commands: "Let the one who boasts, boast in the Lord" (2 Cor 10:17). The apostolic task of the church, fulfilled despite its sin in the work of the Spirit, is to point away from itself and towards its Lord. This decentring activity corresponds to its decentred existence.

CONCLUSION

This essay has sought to offer some reflections on a pressing issue facing the church today: how to make sense of its apostolic nature despite its holy calling being transmuted into an unholy spectacle. To achieve this, it has ventured to explore the relationship between the holiness and unholiness of the church and its apostolic nature. It has drawn attention to the work of the Spirit as the redeeming possibility in the life of the church, in so far as it is only by the grace of the Spirit that the church can accomplish its mission.

In drawing to a close, three of several possible practical lessons to be drawn from this ecclesiological perspective might be observed.

First, given that the starting-point of the visible church is always its humanity, and that humanity is never yet perfect, the church must always begin with repentance. It should do so not only before God, conscious of the way in which it falls short of its creaturely goodness and its covenantal calling. It should do so also as it engages in mission before the world and its people. It is called to repent for its false witness: its corrupted teachings, its oppressive dealings, and its faithless service. It has condoned the greatest of evils and persecuted the weakest of innocents. And it has behaved all too often as if it were the sole repository of truth in the world. There is no engaging with the apostolic calling and mission of the church today that does not involve confession and repentance, seeking the forgiveness of God and the understanding of the world.

47. Berkouwer, *The Church*, 204.

Second, given that the apostolic calling has at its heart the hearing and obeying of the Gospel, so too the church is time and again asked to renew its willingness to listen and to submit to the Word of God that is brought to it by the Spirit. And the corollary of this submission in the world is service, a mission in and for the world that is undertaken in humility. The church is inspired and empowered not for the purpose of having dominion, but for the purpose of exercising modesty as it serves God's purposes as the least of God's creatures. This is a matter, of course, of dominical imitation. But it also corresponds to the Spirit-led behaviour appropriate for those who are penitent. The church has no triumph of its own to secure and herald; it ought to be content to point in the world and for the world to the triumphant Lord ascended beyond the world. And it does so by tending to the least in the world in service of the Kingdom.

Finally, given that the Spirit who constitutes the apostolicity and, indeed, the holiness of the church is a free Spirit, the church should always consider afresh the foundational importance of prayer for its work of mission. The act of invocation is not an optional ecclesial extra. Instead, the heart-felt and perpetual prayer of the church must be *Veni, Creator Spiritus!*—come, Holy Spirit!—as it pleads and implores for God to come among the people of the church again, to bless, inspire, chasten, guide, and empower them as they witness to the Gospel in the world. This prayer is in itself no guarantee that the church will not err, that it will not remain mired in sin. It is no magic solution to the conundrums explored in this essay. But it is only as the Spirit comes that the grace of God can lift up the flawed acts of the unholy church, and transform them into events of apostolic witness to the glory of God.

6

The Eschatological Spirit and the Church
The Promise of an Ongoing Struggle

Cornelius Van der Kooi

In this contribution I want to elaborate on a metaphor that substantiates the church as participating in the eschatological reality. It is the metaphor of anointing as it is used by the Heidelberg Catechism to illuminate the participation of the followers of Christ in the outpouring of the Spirit. I will discuss the one office of Christ, prophet, priest and king as dimensions of the life of the church, dimensions that are a promise and cause of struggle.[1]

THE SPIRIT OF THE ESCHATON

Before entering into a discussion on the way this metaphor is used by this Catechism, first a few remarks on the biblical background. In the Old Testament the outpouring of the Spirit is promised as the act of God by which the presence of God with Israel is full and abundant. God will dwell among his people and will be on all flesh, even on the male and female servants (Joël 2.28). According to the New Testament the promise of the eschatological Spirit has begun to be fulfilled in the life of Jesus of Nazareth.

---

1. I have made use of parts of my book *This Incredibly Benevolent Force*, chap. 5.

The story of Jesus in the synagogue of Nazareth reflects the trumpet sound that proclaims the beginning of a new world. In reference to the promise of Isaiah 61:1 Jesus says: "Today this Scripture has been fulfilled in your hearing" (Luke 4:21). The promise of the eschaton seems to come to a dead end in the death of Jesus, but Easter marks a new initiative by the Father. Jesus is declared to be the Son of God in the power according to the Spirit of holiness (Romans 1:3). Jesus is exalted and partakes in the glory of the Father. The same Spirit, who was on Jesus in his earthly life, is now sent by the exalted Christ to guide them, to teach them, to comfort them, to transform the people of God from day to day. The new reality is that they are in communion with Christ. A clear example of this self-understanding can be found in the first letter to the Corinthians: "You were washed, you were sanctified, you were justified in the name of the Lord Jesus Christ and by the Spirit of our God" (1 Cor. 6:11), and "We are all baptized in the same Spirit, and all were made to drink from one Spirit"(1 Cor. 12:13). At the same time this letter exemplifies the tensions that this eschatological identity forms for the community of followers of Christ in Corinth.

HEIDELBERG CATECHISM AND ANOINTMENT

Remarkable in the Heidelberg Catechism is the fact that participation in Christ is expressed in terms of anointing or baptism with the Spirit. The relation between Jesus Christ and the Christians is pictured by means of the three functions according to which God had already been present among his people—prophet, priest, and king. It is this Spirit of Christ who is sent to draw us, to transform us and guide us. Questions 31 and 32 of this Catechism reads thus:

> *Question 31: Why is He called Christ, that is, Anointed?*
> *Answer: Because He has been ordained by God the Father, and anointed with the Holy Spirit, to be our chief Prophet and Teacher, who has fully revealed to us the secret counsel and will of God concerning our redemption; our only High Priest, who by the one sacrifice of His body has redeemed us, and who continually intercedes for us before the Father; and our eternal King, who governs us by His Word and Spirit, and who defends and preserves us in the redemption obtained for us.*
> *Question 32: Why are you called a Christian?*
> *Answer: Because I am a member of Christ by faith and thus share in His anointing, so that I may as prophet confess His Name, as priest present myself a living sacrifice of thankfulness to Him, and*

as king fight with a free and good conscience against sin and the devil in this life, and hereafter reign with Him eternally over all creation.

What is significant here is that the explanation applies the anointing to the individual person. However, in the New Testament the outpouring of the Spirit is also a communal experience. The resurrected Lord breathes on his disciples (John 20:21), in Acts 2 the outpouring of the Spirit is a communal fact, and Paul in his first letter to the Corinthians applies the metaphor of the temple as dwelling place of the Spirit of Christ first to the congregation, and secondly to the individual members of the church. As becomes clear in that letter, the Spirit of Christ has not seldom a hard time to find room in the congregation and in individual believers. It is a struggle.

SHARING IN HIS ANOINTING: THE ROYAL REGIMENT OF CHRIST THROUGH THE SPIRIT

Against the classic order of the one office of Christ, prophet, priest and king, I have chosen to begin with the kingly office. My argument for this change of order is the New Testament itself. Christ's kingship is manifested right at the start of his earthly life and does not only become effective at the ascension, as Calvin seems to suggest. Wherever Jesus came, the contours of God's final kingdom became visible. The work of the eschatological Spirit was palpable. Liberation of life took place, people were reunited with the God of Israel, they learned to do justice. People no longer belong to themselves or their past, but something more powerful is paving a way for itself and comes to overwhelm them. As the New Adam Christ took up the covenant with God and brought this life with God to fulfilment. His was a new regime which became visible in his appearance; he lived this new regime and it brought about beginnings of restoration. It was a regime in which union with the living God was realized.

Yet how does the Spirit of the eschaton work on the followers of Christ, on his church? By sharing in a new kingdom in which the powers of the old world no longer have the upper hand, and in which the Spirit of the end times is at work instead. The power of the Spirit is the pulling factor that draws people into the new reign of God. Recognition of Jesus' kingship means *first of all* that a congregation or church comes into existence whose members *confess that they have passed over from the kingdom of death into the kingdom of life*. It begins with a transition or transfer whose relevance does not just pertain to eternal life, but which is in a certain sense already active now. (1 Cor 1: 4–9). The church clings pertinaciously to this story.

We are no longer our own. The Heidelberg Catechism expresses this in terms of belonging. Those who place their hope in Christ no longer belong to the devil and his kingdom, to a social class or ethnic entity, or to modern powers like Google or Facebook, or the Stock Exchange. Rather, they are Christ's possession. This transition from death to life, this declaration of belonging receives its form and expression in the sign of baptism. Baptism is not, as Barth would have it, a human testimony as the counterpart to a Spirit baptism which has already taken place. Rather, the immersion in water makes one share in a certain way in effecting this transition. What happens physically in the water of baptism, in word and sign, is taken by God into his service. For that reason baptism is not in the first place a family event, nor should it be seen as a kind of baby shower. Christian baptism must be torn from the clutches of civil initiation rites and be restored to its dramatic significance.

The ritual of the baptism with water unites the human being with the dying and resurrection of Christ. It marks the transition from estrangement to the covenant of life. It proclaims in public that Christ is the legitimate Lord of this human and her life. The response to this from the human side is a life in which the human being as a disciple practices living in a way in which the God-estranged powers no longer dominate. Christian life therefore requires lifelong exercise. Paul uses the image of a fight, we are soldiers, who need armour. *Lifelong*, that means that in every phase of life new challenges appear. Youth, middle age, third and fourth phase, they all require response. Do we take this seriously in our churches?

A *second* characteristic that flows from the foregoing, is the *ec-centric* structure of this eschatological Christian identity. This identity is grounded on a promise, in baptism and in the eucharist we are addressed by the identifying Word and promise. It comes from outside us. Word and Spirit means that we are addressed by the Word and that the Spirit pulls us under that Word and promise. A new authority and source of life has appeared and interrupts. Due to this new constellation all leadership and authority is subordinated to God as the real sovereign. The only real king is Jesus of Nazareth, who was crucified in an allied action of politics, law, religion and socially correct people. It is a strange interruption of all earthly glittering images of power (cf. 1 Cor 1) Therefore it was right that king Charles at the occasion of his crowning in the Westminster Abbey was received by a boy, who welcomed him in the name of the King of Kings. The negative exposure of kingship forms a critical reminder for all forms of leadership. The desacralization of emperor, king, leader, president or CEO has deep roots in the confession of the church.

The Eschatological Spirit and the Church

I want to add to this a *third* highly significant element. Participation in this dimension of Christ's anointing implies renewal or *transformation*. In order to understand what this means we can refer again to the adoption metaphor. Adoption means that someone becomes part of a new family and has to try and feel at home in these new surroundings with their own rules and ambiance. He takes his seat at the table, which may aptly be called a 'welcome table', and becomes a part of that new environment. Adoption means the arrival of a new constellation, a new order—an order of love and justice, into which you are drawn. In that family the most important rule for life is however not self-preservation, but precedence is given to the experience of making and giving room: the new family member receives clothing, food, and a place to sleep. In short, the new constellation brings one in touch with a different experience, the experience of grace. Those who have tasted this new life and order have thereby access to a new reign, where a "creative, free self-withdrawal on behalf of others" is the new option.[2] This is the order that is operative in the kingdom of God.

This new experience of grace and love at the same time has wider transformative effects on culture and society. Depending on the context it is reasonable to assume that one's personal life, as well as the surroundings, culture, and moral order undergo influence from this story. Where the story of the Good Samaritan is told, there a greater receptivity is felt for notions of compassion, consideration, and justice. An 'agapic' revolution take place. "Transforming processes may take place—temporarily and with a certain fragility, indeed—in the fundamental notions according to which a society understands itself."[3]

It may have an effect on our use of natural resources, the way we try to diminish our ecological footprint personally and as a society. Again, I admit, it is an ongoing struggle.

What are signs of this new reign and future? In this context we have to speak of fruits and gifts. I will restrict myself now for reasons of time mainly to gifts.

What are these gifts? Gifts are functions of God's coming kingdom. The Spirit endows someone with his power, makes use of the human person in favor of his kingdom. Where God reigns, acts, manifestations of spirit and power will appear. The range of gifts of grace is much wider than the modern idea on charism. Paul mentions activities that we do not identify with charisms: such as utterance of wisdom, utterance of knowledge, helping, administering, comforting. Among these also the glossolalia and

---

2. Cf. Welker, *God the Revealed*, 224–25.
3. Buijs, *Tegenwind van Geest*, 35.

healing, and prophesying. It is clear that in history these last three gifts have drawn most attention. However, it must be emphasized that for Paul all the gifts he mentions are gifts of the eschatological Spirit to comfort the community of the church, to build up their community. It is also clear that in comparison with the New Testament the word charism has been subjected to a tremendous reduction and concentration. Charism became a concept that was restricted to glossolalia, healing and prophesying, with the sad result that other occasions where the Spirit has made use of people was seen as ordinary.[4] Paul rejects this separation of some gifts as particular signs of the work the Spirit. All the gifts come from the same Spirit. What we need is a fresh eye, a reparation of our theological tools identifying and perceiving the work of the Spirit of Christ.

A FEW WORDS ON HEALING

Let me say a few words on healing.

Several years ago there were fierce debates in the Netherlands over the phenomenon of healing services and faith healers. How were people and churches to respond? Were all these things to be rejected? I have criticized representatives of faith healing for their often defective theology. They do not give account of the fact that we live in the interim between resurrection, the mission of the Spirit and the consummation. They often adhere to a kind of realized eschatology, more or less like we find with the opponents of Paul in the first letter to the Corinthians. They think that they are already part of a fully realized kingdom. Some of these opponents may have considered glossolalia as proof of their very special spiritual existence. In the famous chapters 1 Cor 12—14 Paul teaches them that speaking in tongues and prophesy is part of this interim and will end when the fulfillment is there.

But this should not be the reason why we should dismiss it all. In the gospels we read how Jesus performed healings as a sign of the breakthrough of his kingdom. Reports of healing upon or after prayer similarly come to us from the world church. Reformed theology cannot afford simply to shrug off these sounds. In the modernist paradigm in which the churches of the northern hemisphere have by now lived for quite some time, miracles or healings are more or less excluded. Cessationism drove healing back behind the lines of the early church. This implied a near-complete acceptance of the modern division of life spheres, where we surrendered the sphere of health and illness to the medical sciences. Yet do the Bible and the experiences of the worldwide church really allow us to do so? I do not think so.

---

4. See Baumert, *Charisma—Taufe—Geisttaufe*, vols. 1 and 2.

What to think of Blumhardt, Stanger, the revivals in Wales, Korea, L.A., Toronto, Lourdes? Experiences of healing or recovering are rare, at least in western societies, but they are there, and probably even more in countries, where the medical circumstances are less available. They happen not only in the context of special faith healing ministries, but they occur in ordinary churches, after prayer.[5]

THE PRIESTLY DIMENSION

The second dimension of the threefold office is priestly. This makes us think back right away to the temple service, which was fulfilled in Jesus because he radically engaged himself for the sake of God's kingdom and in the process paid the ultimate sacrifice. Jesus Christ is at once priest and sacrifice. It is important here that the sacrificial ministry not be reduced to sin offerings and the burnt offering on the Day of Atonement. Daily sacrifices were brought in the temple: thank offerings for a variety of occasions marking the progress of life. The burnt offering and the sin offering served this progress in situations where life had met with serious obstacles.

Following the line of Rom 12:1, the catechism speaks about a 'living sacrifice of thankfulness'. This means that the sacrifice of thankfulness is not something lifeless, but the person herself, a subject who places her life actively and consciously in the service of God's compassion.[6] In this way Christ as head puts into action the powers in his body, whose members are the believers. The Spirit bears the care for a differentiated collusion of powers and possibilities through which Christ's mercy is given concrete shape in the world. Mercy and reconciliation between men, colleagues, husband and wife, and sometimes as a process of inner healing. In most cases it is a struggle. The examples of sin and need of a process of reconciliation and renewal have become visible and tangible. It suffices to point to our use of nature and natural resources. Climate change has made life hardly bearable around the equator. Or take modern forms of slavery in the clothing industry, our consumption of meat and the suffering of animals. The examples could be amplified easily.

The Eucharist or Lord's Supper is the place where paradigmatically the unity and collusion of Christ and his church is given shape. It is also a place of embarrassment and possible uneasiness. In 2 Cor 5:19–20 Paul speaks

---

5. See the doctoral thesis of Kruijthoff, "Healing after Prayer."

6. Welker, *God the Revealed*, 237, notices that in the Barmen Declaration all emphasis is laid upon Christ as Lord and the activity of the human being remains underexposed.

about the ministry of reconciliation and entreats his audience to *be* reconciled to God. But this is not easy. In the Eucharistic prayer we find a *dangerous* reminder, and a dark shadow passes in front of us when it refers to the "night on which he was betrayed." It is particularly at the Lord's Supper table that the participants are reminded that the betrayal of Jesus of Nazareth did not come from the outside but from within the very circle of his own followers. This is an important, unsettling lesson: among those who know Jesus and what he has done there may be exasperation and disappointment over the absence of visible results, until in the end they decide to leave that circle and quit.[7]

A second element of the priestly office is the progress it provides. The temple service was intended to serve the progression of society and human life. That progress pertained both to regular daily life and to situations of guilt and loss. That progression must be given a place in the restricted confines of the family, friends, and neighbourhood, but should also be translated to the broader sphere of politics and law. Where society is served in politics and government for the sake of the progress of human life and community, for the preservation of nature and the climate, there something appears of the priestly aspect for which we offer thanks to God.

THE PROPHETIC DIMENSION

Although in the tradition the prophetic dimension of Christ's one office comes first, I have chosen to treat it here as the third and final one. What is the prophetic element? The prophetic means that the light is turned on when we clearly see where we stand in the light of God's benevolence. This may happen in a worship service, but also elsewhere. It is necessary for us also to become familiar with the prophetic as something closer to home.

In the *Heidelberg Catechism* we read that Christ as prophet and teacher reveals the counsel of God to us. If we no longer interpret "counsel" as blueprint, but the revelation of his good will, his benevolence, the abstractive tone of the word in Reformed doctrine is left behind. God's counsel is in the end nothing else than the living God himself. In Christ and his life we see the *Deus decernens*, the God who turns himself toward his children and brings his grace about. His act and speech is the salvatory will of God, literally the *euaggelion*, good message. Thus he is the prophet, who mediates

---

7. Welker, *God the Revealed*, 298: Through announcing Christ's death in Holy Communion, the consciousness is renewed that we are "part of humankind that repeatedly, and with all possible means, tries to obscure and distort God's presence and the salvation and well-being for the world."

the Word of God and is the Word in person. Paradigmatically is the story of Jesus in the synagogue of Nazareth (Luke 4:14–30), where he quotes the words of Isaiah 61. He announces the "agreeable year of the Lord", the yobel year, which was to bring restoration for all and the whole society. Thus speaks Jesus' truth, God's truth, point black.

How and where do believers partake in this prophetic office? The reformation has located the prophetic office in the ministry of the Word, not in the actions of prophetic figures, who are said to have a word or vision of the Lord. The work of the Spirit was strictly bound to the given Word, the Scriptures, which were ministered to the people in proclamation. Against this background it is understandable that the weekly bible expositions, which were a custom in the Swiss reformation, were named *prophesije* or prophecy.[8] Preaching and exposition are indeed centres for the prophetic dimension of the church. When the preacher administers the Word as a concrete message addressed to people in their own context, then truth can be spoken, God's truth. It is here that distinction of the spirits—spirits working in society and in our own hearts—has its source.

Reformed theology and practice should learn a bit more to identify the prophetic dimension as part of the life of the church. At times it is necessary to learn to look with new eyes at existing practices. I mention two examples:

If prophecy is the announcement of how the world now looks in the light of God's appearance in Christ, we can already detect much more of prophecy going on in a traditional Presbyterian context than simply sermon and exposition alone. What I refer to here is the congregational singing. When the congregation sings psalms and songs the church takes up its function as "God's own people, in order to proclaim the mighty acts of him who called you out of darkness into his marvellous light." (1 Pet 2:9) When, following a meal, families sing a song together or read a Bible story with the children and the other guests, this is not just a 'song' or 'story' but proclamation of God's truth. Similarly, prayers before or after the meal form a part of prophetic and priestly activity as well. As faith practices, they might be assessed as possible avenues of the work of the Spirit.

Prophecy occurs in a broader and more diverse set of forms than the ministry of Word and Sacraments. There is a diversity and polyphony of the Spirit's work. This polyphony means that also our capacities may be engaged in order to praise God and to testify to the presence of the new life. Imagination, emotion, creativity, musical talents—the Spirit can use many different means as instruments in order to witness of Christ. In Pentecostal and free churches there is greater awareness for these avenues of the Spirit of Christ

---

8. De Boer, *The Genevan School of the Prophets*, 32–33.

than there has been in the traditional churches. If I am not mistaken, we currently find ourselves in a learning phase.

It is not the place here to enumerate and treat everything that is a part of this prophetic dimension (think of politics and public life), nor do I want to. Yet aside from music it is necessary to mention glossolalia as a gift that has been given to God's church and can suddenly manifest itself. In Acts 2:11 it is qualified as a token of prophesy: "we hear them telling in our own tongues the mighty works of God." Speaking in tongues is not normative, but is something that the church or individuals may receive. It bears pointing out that glossolalia ought not to be confused with ecstasy, in which someone's consciousness is turned off. Rather, speaking in tongues is a form of praise that has no propositional content. Compared to articulated speech it is a form of abstraction, but this does not mean that this abstraction is without meaning. It serves concentration and the praise of God (cf. 1 Cor 14:7). Speaking in tongues is a form of prayer and praise whereby a person's heart is with the Lord through the abstraction of clear concepts. It can be compared to a non-figurative painting: there is no concrete reality, and yet a reality is being mediated. Glossolalia ought further to be distinguished from xenolalia. The miracle described to us in Acts 2 is better qualified as xenolalia[9]: every person heard the apostles speak in their own language. This phenomenon cannot be relegated to the past, and is in fact easy to explain within a missional context.

The Holy Spirit is a bridge builder, the *pontifex maximus* who brings Christ and his gifts (charismata) to each person in his or her specific circumstances. The Spirit is the interpreter who brings Christ's salvation close to us, down to our own language. This is the missiological aspect of the gift of prophecy. It alone is reason enough for theology to have the task to translate into the vernacular and to speak the common tongue.

In the midst of this diversity one thing remains clear: if the Spirit takes from what belongs to Christ and gives it to us, various media or avenues may be used that Protestant theology has on the whole given very little, if any, attention to. These are the means of dreams, visions, words of wisdom, words from the Lord, even the architecture of a building and modern media may become an avenue of the work the Spirit of Christ to us. They can all become means of the Spirit of Christ to make us taste his grace, already now.

---

9. *Tegenwoordigheid van Geest*, 87.

7

Taking the History of the Church Seriously

Pneumatic Dissonance and Its Partial Resolution

Ephraim Radner

My discussion addresses a straightforward issue: our disappointment with the church, and the pneumatological significance of such disappointment. My answer will also be fairly obvious, although perhaps not in its more systematic implications, which have to do with the limitations of pneumatology—a theme I have dwelt upon in the past.[1] In an introductory section, I will lay out the issue of ecclesial unity and disunity as it has been viewed within certain broad confessional traditions. The next three parts of the essay will delve into and respond to the limitations of these views. First, I will take up the concept of "cognitive dissonance" as a tool for describing theological responses to ecclesial disappointment. I will then reflect on how the negative experience of "pneumatic dissonance" can be explained in terms of a positive understanding of the Holy Spirit's work as ever "partial" and limited. Finally, I will suggest what I consider a more adequate way of engaging the pneumatic unity of the church, in a manner that both takes seriously the experience of dissonance and the promises of God in Christ, a hope with which I will conclude.

1. Radner, *A Profound Ignorance*.

So let me begin with the issue unity and disunity, which will found my discussion of disappointment.

INTRODUCTION

By what do we measure the unity of the Church? How do we "know" if the Christian church is "at one"? Though we claim the church to *be* "one"—in the Nicene Creed—we are also able to identify quite concretely "division," "schism," and "heresy." Do these actually affect ecclesial unity, or are they only accidents that represent humanly subjective experiences, but in fact do nothing to touch the "thing itself"—just as looking at the sun may injure the eyes so that it can no longer see light, though the sun's light remains as full as ever?

Historically, Christians have not been consistent in their responses to these kinds of questions. They have tended, intellectually, to side with the "subjective misperception" thesis—experienced disunity does *not* affect the "actual" unity of the church. But in mutual practice Christians have in fact erected an array of shifting measures of unity that, as it were, have sought to assert objective correlations between human perception and divine reality.

To take, woefully broadly, the Reformed case as an example: sixteenth- and early seventeenth-century discussions of ecclesial unity applied the measure of doctrinal conformity to the evaluation of unity and disunity: the church can be *seen* as one insofar as doctrinal claims among Christians are one. By the latter seventeenth and into the eighteenth century, this shifted, in some Reformed circles (like Owen and Edwards) to a kind of affective measure, increasingly individual and, practically speaking, increasingly obscure: that is, while doctrinal conformity was a necessary condition for ecclesial unity, it was not sufficient (indeed, might prove deceptively insufficient) if not founded in a deeper affective condition of faith, often identified in terms of a certain kind of "love."[2] This love, furthermore, was often linked directly to the work or presence of the Holy Spirit. But identifying this pneumatic condition of love accurately became admittedly difficult. By the twentieth century, the larger drift of Reformed thinking has been both to reaffirm the givenness of ecclesial unity as well as to further muddy the subjective manifestations of such unity. A recent international Reformed-Anglican Dialogue statement on Koinonia (2020), speaks of *koinonia* as "fundamental," "complex," "multidimensional," "challenging," "eschatological," and an incorruptible divine "gift."[3] Unity, according to this agreed

---

2. Radner, "The Holy Spirit and Unity," 207–20.
3. Gregorgy and Welch, et al., *Koinonia: God's Gift and Calling*, par. 7.

statement, is lodged in the unchangeable integrity of "The Body of Christ," which is "received" variously, but never threatened. The end result is a kind of optimistic *laissez faire* approach to ecclesial division, which mirrors the general current of free-market toleration, seasoned by earnest moral concerns. As we know, however, this shift towards viewing ecclesial unity in terms of the communion of moral earnestness often pushes back towards a demand for a "praxis" oriented conformity, that leaves us back where we started: measuring who is in and who is out.

My own Anglican tradition, though it has its quite specific elements that, as we know, have pressed against the Reformed tradition that originally informed it—bishops and the three-fold ministry, dogmatic modesty (if not actual latitude), and so on—has followed a similar trajectory, literally joining the World Communion of Reformed churches in the statement just noted. Behind this drift is a long experience of struggles, buffetings, reassessments, and rearticulations in the midst of British history and social change, and now global demographic rearrangements. The basic question of the truth-value, in divine terms, of this process towards recognizing an always-present unity is important, however: have churches simply penetrated more deeply into the true character of Christian unity over time, such that older claims about unity founded cleanly in doctrine or structure have been unveiled as ignorant? And, if so (or not), what has God's providential purpose amounted to in the course of division, schism, and heresy and the conflicts these have given rise to over the centuries?

Part of my own sense is that this kind of question touches as much upon our conceptions of God's character as it does upon our refashioned ecclesial self-construals. Here, obviously, the question of the Holy Spirit arises immediately: what *kind* of God, and through what character of divine action is at work in this long tradition of antagonism, fracture, and sometimes violence? The venerable Christian press for identifiable and practical metrics of ecclesial unity have consistently assumed such unity as having either a stable or ideal nature, open both to human definition and itself invulnerable to human decisions. It is an assumption that itself presumes the Holy Spirit's presence as the agent of unity, and thus as itself a metric of ecclesial integrity. We (think we) know what unity is—or ought to be; we know its pneumatic foundation; and as a result, we know how to measure its demands. The fact, however, that this series of certainties is ever being destabilized is itself a bit of data requiring theological reflection. I would suggest we rethink the assumptions at work here.

1. DISSONANCE, CHURCH, AND SPIRIT

For the purposes of this reflection, I would single out the basic assumption we make about the Holy Spirit and the church which, again in traditional terms, has been mostly convergent among churches of varying stripes, including modern liberal ones: in Irenaeus' famous phrase, "For where the Church is, there is the Spirit of God; and where the Spirit of God is, there is the Church and every kind of grace."[4] Any church? In any place? Even if we have assumed this, we have also denied it in practice, ever rejigging the terms of "grace" itself according our sense of experiential contradiction. By "experience," in this essay, I simply mean taking history seriously, being somehow consciously—in a self-aware fashion—affected by the phenomena of the temporal world. There are obviously Scriptural examples where the phenomena of history, as it were, seem to challenge a set of theological assumptions: "if you are the Son of God, save yourself!" (Matt 27:40) or, from the disciples' side, "And we thought he was the one to redeem Israel" (Luke 24:21). One assumes that messiahship entails this or that; then, when something particular *happens* that does not cohere with these assumptions, one must readjust. More prosaically, if spectacularly, there is the so-called Children's Crusade of 1212, shrouded in uncertainty, but in the end giving rise to incredulity amongst both participants and historians; or the strange hopes placed on Sabbatai Zevi in the seventeenth century, a Jewish messianic expectation and judgment that crumbled in the face of his failures, and indeed pathetic final conversion to Islam. "We made a mistake about this," might be one reaction on the part of those who had originally put their faith in such movements or persons; or "there was never anything there in the first place, nor could there be," would be a more extreme response. There are various possible reorientations to be made in the middle.

In fact, though, much reaction to history is unconscious, though extraordinarily elaborate and even conceptually rich. We respond to experience, especially negative experience, by reconstructing its framework in our minds and judgments. The theory of "cognitive dissonance" is perhaps the most influential conceptual portal into this reality. Most of us take the motivating dynamics of cognitive dissonance for granted these days, but when, in 1956, Leon Festinger and his colleagues Henry Riecken and Stanley Schachter published *When Prophecy Fails* their claims basically settled a general perception that stands to the present.[5] Festinger and his

---

4. Irenaeus, *Adversus Haereses* 3.24.1.

5. Festinger, Riecken, and Schachter, *When Prophecy Fails*. For a stimulating assemblage of material that views "disappointment" as a major motor for American religious "evolution," in a positive sense, see Quillen, "The Great American Disappointment."

collaborators studied a small group of persons in Chicago who followed a woman who claimed to have special communications with extraordinarily intelligent planetary aliens. These communications included a predicted earthly catastrophe. The study focused on how the group responded to the failed prophecy. A major hypothesis that Festinger and colleagues upheld, was that the prophecy's failure—utterly "dissonant" with the groups expectations and now congealed identity—rather than dissolving their commitments, somehow "confirmed" them, and led the group to greater public self-assertion based on newly minted explications of reality. This was not true for all members of the group however, for some of whom the unfulfilled disaster simply subverted their previous convictions altogether and bred a much broader disillusion. Whatever the shortcomings of the experiment—and it has been criticized on a number of fronts—the basic arguments informing the notion of "cognitive dissonance" have stood firm and been developed into broader areas of rationalization and confirmation bias in a range of contexts.

That cognitive dissonance theory was first clearly formulated with religious convictions in mind is no accident. *When Prophecy Fails* opens with a long chapter on "Unfulfilled Prophecies and Disappointed Messiahs," moving from Montanus quickly through Anabaptist chiliasm, Jewish Sabbateanism, and the Baptist Adventism of nineteenth-century Millerites and their progeny. Dissonance, disconfirmation, rationalization, and adjustment. I was actually introduced to the book in graduate school by a Jewish social philosopher who wanted us to consider whether the scapegoating of Jews in the Middle Ages was a project of belief-adjustment in the face of unrealized Christian hopes of one kind or another. The point is not frivolous: much theological work of a certain kind, it seems to me, is indeed driven unconsciously by the dissonance of experience with religious claims. This comes with varied results of course, but they include those of elaborated rationalizations—that is, developing otherwise unobvious theological claims as a means of explicating dissonance—and of energized oppositions, that is, "blaming others."

The "theological work of a certain kind" that I have in mind is ecclesiology and pneumatology in particular. (This is something I am myself engaging here!) I suggest, in any case, that we pause to consider, given the topic on hand of "unity and the Holy Spirit," the pressures of what one might call "ecclesial dissonance" and its related category of "pneumatic dissonance."

So, for instance, we might reflect on certain common anecdotal observations, which seem to be backed up by unadorned behavioural statistics. Thus, it seems that many Christians treat the church with far less patience than they do their own families and civil polities. Not always of course!, but, arguably, in quotidian terms: that is, Christians seem far readier to leave their churches—whether congregations or denominations—than they are to abandon their families, or to emigrate or renounce their citizenship. Major religious research groups like the Pew Forum, or the Barna Group, back this up, at least for North America:[6] 35% of adult Americans have different religious affiliations now than that of their youth; over 40% are members of different denomination (Pew); 40% of Christians "church-hop" as their regular practice; and almost 20% change denominational affiliations every 4 years (Barna). Amongst Catholics and Protestants both, the major reason for adherence and membership instability has been disappointment with their given church's moral witness—something that takes in stands on social issues, as well as leadership behavior, including sexual abuse and financial impropriety. This filters, however, to a much wider net of vaguer dissatisfactions with official or local teaching.

One sees a related, if slightly different dynamic among older pastors and priests, whose disillusionment with ecclesial politics and related matters, often leads to their distance and indifference to ecclesial life more broadly, and sometimes even significantly limits their participation in the church altogether after retirement. It is not uncommon, among lay and ordained Christians, to hear the comment, associated with their peregrinations and estrangements, of "I was hurt by the church."[7] Those who enter the ministry, in this case, with high hopes and ideals, often discover something discordant with their expectations.[8]

Unity is one of the greatest foci of such felt dissonance: schism, division, and sometimes—in the past, rather often—outright violent conflict.[9] It is established that the rise of Deism and finally explicit atheism in the eighteenth century (a little, if not as much as often assumed) and certainly in the nineteenth century, is related to this. It is a complicated story, tied often obscurely to the disseminating sense of ecclesial complicity in a range of ills, for which division was a coalescing symbol: Christians killing other Christians and non-Christians. It took a while, but by the twentieth century, ecclesial disunity had become, almost axiomatically, a sign of moral corruption.

In one way, it is important to keep the categories of ecclesial and pneumatic dissonance separate. "The Church is not what we expected" is

---

6. See also *PRRI*, "Exodus: Why Americans are Leaving Religion"; Pew, "America's Changing Religious Landscape," 33–47; Pew, "Modeling the Future of Religion in America," 19–30; Barna, "Five Trends Defining Americans' Relationship to Churches"; Davis, Graham, and Burge, *The Great Dechurching*.

7. Slade, et al., "Percentage of U.S. Adults Suffering from Religious Trauma."

8. Carlson, "Going into the Laments."

9. Radner, *Brutal Unity*.

a judgment about human action, and its failures; "The Holy Spirit is not what we expected" is a judgment about our failure to understand the Holy Spirit, something that may prove yet more frightening than ecclesial corruption. But the two are practically conflated, leading to radical swings of commitment and relationship. Ironically, "blame the Holy Spirit [or its contradiction]" is easily (psychologically speaking) bound up with theologies of pneumatic unity. Convictions about the nature of ecclesial unity that are "disconfirmed" can be adjusted by a now refashioned evaluations of God and his pneumatic promises.

At this point, I simply want to mark out the deep directive energies of ecclesio-pneumatic dissonance in moving our judgments. Frankly, I do not think it is possible to judge dogmatic claims about the Church's pneumatic constitution, and thus its unity, without taking into account the way that all such claims, at least as made in human terms, are a farrago of adjustments, rationalizations, reactions, and nostalgic hopes. This won't work. At this point all I want to do is to suggest that apparent phenomenal qualities of e.g. the church's character, including its felt pneumatic dissonance, be measured by the truth of God's being.

And because that measure is, by definition, almost impossible to apply in human terms, "dissonance" itself may be an experience rightly cast aside.

2. PNEUMATIC DISSONANCE OR PNEUMATIC MEREOLOGY/PARTIALNESS?

Let me now turn explicitly, in this light, to the tradition of the church's pneumatic unity. Here, I will use an example founded on the breadth of "tradition," drawn from Eastern Orthodoxy. In a well-known contemporary and official American Orthodox catechism, the section on the Holy Spirit is repeatedly geared to what one might call the "pneumatic guarantee" thesis: "The Christian Church lives by the Holy Spirit. The Spirit alone is the guarantee of God's Kingdom on earth. He is the sole guarantee that God's life and truth and love are with men." And again, "The Holy Spirit is the personal presence of the new and everlasting covenant between God and man, the seal and guarantee of the Kingdom of God, the power of the divine indwelling of God in man." The unity of the church, in this catechism, is given in the character of the Church as pneumatic. Hence, that unity is itself guaranteed by the immovable "fact" of the Trinitarian God, of whom the Holy Spirit is the earthly, but also inevitable, instrument of establishment: "Orthodox Christians believe in the Church as they believe in God and Christ and the Holy Spirit. Faith in the Church is part of the creedal statement of Christian believers. The Church is herself an object of faith as the divine reality of the Kingdom of God."[10]

These kinds of statements, from a church that is herself associated with Orthodoxy in Eastern Europe, are today epitomes of, one might think, "dissonance." In those places of, we might think, the most demanding challenges—Russia and the Ukraine, for example—there is much that might raise questions for a believer. At least four separate Orthodox churches, bitterly arrayed on opposite sides of the battle lines, and in between, must offer their own account of pneumatic guarantee, along with the many non-Orthodox churches in the area. A recent survey in the Ukraine reports that "trust in the Church" more broadly has fallen from 51 to 44% in the last year.[11] There appears to be a good bit of denominational movement in the Ukraine, amidst the now fragmented Orthodox churches, with certain Protestant churches picking up attendance. The public picture, however, is arguably depressing: priests being tossed out of parishes, ecclesial leaders upholding alternative sides in a brutal war, civic legislation dismantling ecclesial life of one kind or another, and government security forces harassing and imprisoning leaders on different sides, often with the support of one church or the other. However this plays out in Eastern Europe, its witness has drawn clear negative commentary in the West.

While all of this is distressing—we are watching pneumatic dissonance unfold before our eyes, as in a movie theatre—we need to step back and pause. In the face of the guarantee thesis, after all, the coincidence of Holy Spirit and church is not in fact at all clear in Scripture. The Spirit is sent to the apostles; the Spirit moves those who confess Jesus as Lord; moves others to confess God as "Abba" and thus themselves as children of God with Jesus; and the Spirit gives gifts to the church. A key text like Eph 4:3—on "preserv[ing] the unity of the Spirit in the bond of peace"—is an "entreaty" not a phenomenological description, and it seems to render unity as a gift given—like faith—rather than as an identity-marker.

If there *is* a coincidence of Holy Spirit and Church, in scriptural terms, it is not the coincidence of fulfilment, or of fullness, in the sense of some of the Creedal affirmations of "catholicity" so picked up upon by theologians, and not just Orthodox ones. Rather, the coincidence is given in terms of a token. The English language of "guarantee" may itself prove misleading. A mostly modern English word, "guarantee" has quickly moved from a more

---

10. Hopko, *The Orthodox Faith*, vol. 1: *Doctrine and Scripture*.

11. See Ukrainian church loses trust among population (cne.news). For a discussion of the fragmented and conflicted nature of Christian ecclesial life during the war, see UN Security Council, "Over 115 Holy Sites Damaged in Ukraine"; and K. Shchotkina "War: How the Relationship of Ukrainians with God and the Church Has Changed."

strictly legal meaning or authorized (but not therefore certain) commitment, to a broader, almost moral-metaphysical meaning founded on "assurance": "I guarantee you that such action will cause the downfall of the institution!" someone might bellow at a committee meeting. Scripturally, however, the "guarantee" language related to the Holy Spirit is most clearly suggested in its "first fruits" or deposit connotations. The Holy Spirit is a given as a "guarantee" in the sense of a pledge, standing as security for a future full payment:

- He who has prepared us for this very thing is God, who has given us the Spirit as a guarantee. (2 Cor 5:5 RSV)
- He has put his seal upon us and given us his Spirit in our hearts as a guarantee. (2 Cor 1:22 RSV)
- And not only the creation, but we ourselves, who have the first fruits of the Spirit, groan inwardly as we wait for adoption as sons, the redemption of our bodies. (Rom 8:23 RSV)
- In him you also, who have heard the word of truth, the gospel of your salvation, and have believed in him, were sealed with the promised Holy Spirit, 14 which is the guarantee of our inheritance until we acquire possession of it, to the praise of his glory. (Eph 1:13–14 RSV)

All these are translations from the Revised Standard Version, three of a single Greek word, *arrabon*, and, in the Romans text, ("firstfruits") of the Greek *aparche*, the common term used in the Septuagint for such sacrifices. But they point to an otherwise odd notion: that the Holy Spirit is tied somewhat to what is "partial" in this life—a beginning, a first instalment, a representative token. And this stands in contrast to a mostly presumed semantic projection the tradition has tended to operate with that links the Spirit, as I mentioned above, with "fullness," as in the actual "Kingdom of God." Much quasi-Marcionite contrasts between the Old and New Testaments makes use of this partial-full dichotomy, as in the pneumatic King Saul vs. the fully "spiritual" St. Paul.

What I would suggest here is that the whole notion of the first fruits, from Cain on to Leviticus and into Romans, is, more fundamentally and consistently, founded on the conceptual logic of what philosophers might call "mereological" attitudes: that is, a sense of how the part—the *meros* in its Greek root—is related to the whole. In contemporary philosophy, "mereology" takes in a range of disciplines, from set theory to epistemic perspectivalism to social holism, in the fields of logic, science, and metaphysics.[12] When

---

12. Trogdon, "Full and Partial Grounding"; Cotnoir, *Mereology*.

applied to our particular biblical context, mereology engages especially epistemological concerns, from both human and divine directions: how do we know God, and how does God reveal himself? The answer to these questions is, "only partially." This is a broad claim that has a host of practical consequences in terms of action, but also deeper consequences in terms of our understanding of God's own nature and God's action. When Paul speaks of "knowing in part" in 1 Cor 13:9-12—contrasted with "knowing in full" or "perfectly"—he is explicitly using mereological terminology—*ek merous* vs. *to teleion*. The philosophical theologian Paul Gooch devoted a fine essay to 1 Corinthians 13 on just this topic, relating it to the contemporary topic of "partial knowledge."[13] The topic of "partial knowledge has engaged philosophers with respect to a variety of quotidian matters, from politics to economics to science, in which virtually all decisions are based on grasping only a "part" of what is true. The ethical implications of this common human dynamic are on display in 1 Corinthians 12, where being a "part" or "member" of the Body—that is, where one *cannot* be the "whole"—means that one can never make judgments based only on one's *own* character, nature, or function. Here, the "part"—the *melos* (not *meros*)—is contrasted to "the whole," or the *holos*—one of the few Scriptural texts that may root the non-Scriptural term "catholic" to the church.

Pneumatic deposit language indicates the relating of the part (active pneumatic agency) to the whole (viewed in terms of salvation, heaven, the *visio Dei*). That which is incomplete, and in its incompleteness distressing—dissonant—is stabilized in its assured relation to a whole not yet apprehended. We can note how mereological pneumatology, as it were, does not quite follow the same logic implied by the literary term "synecdoche," where the part *stands* for the whole—e.g. "the hand of God" for God himself. In a mereological case, the pneumatic partial *suggests* a whole, but does not reveal it as whole. We can trust in the whole, but we do not know really what a whole or "the whole" is like, except as related by its partial explication or experience. While the boundary between part and whole is porous, it is also essential. Yet our trust in a whole that is yet unseen, is given by a Spirit that is present as an orderer of the partial to the complete. What kind of experience is this?

3. THE MEREOLOGICAL RESOLUTION OF THE SPIRIT

Tying the Holy Spirit's existence, presence, or activity to the "partial" rather than to the whole, may be one way of reconceiving the pneumatic

---

13. Gooch, *Partial Knowledge*, 142–62.

dissonance deriving from ecclesial disunity, and the cascade of reactive responses that follow. Perhaps we should try to see the Spirit as stabilizing this disruptive dissonance—not resolving it, but rather ordering it in a certain way. Such pneumatic ordering might be understood as having human sin as its object, in such a way that sin is *navigated* (certainly not eliminated) within the Christian community so as to engage the church's own "partial" divine form and move it *towards* a fulfilment that is not yet in place. There is, of course, nothing odd in such a suggestion—in the Western tradition, the "church militant" was always viewed as distinct, and distinctively constrained in various ways, by its condition of being still *in via*, "on the way," perhaps even constituted by a "mixed" body of sinners and elect, sin and holiness sharing space. Such an approach to the church has usually and uneasily co-existed with claims to ecclesial—and pneumatic—"fulness" that have neither logically nor experientially cohered: "I believe in the one, holy, catholic, and apostolic church" has generally entailed "here it is!"; yet such a claim has almost always proven historically unstable.

So let me try to put some flesh on the idea. In Romans 8, the life of the Christian *in via* is transposed into a pneumatic movement of history as a whole, in which the church herself becomes the Spirit's mereological promise and direction—pneumatic partialness in action.

> We know that the whole creation has been groaning in travail together until now; and not only the creation, but we ourselves, who have the first fruits of the Spirit, groan inwardly as we wait for adoption as sons, the redemption of our bodies. For in this hope we were saved. Now hope that is seen is not hope. For who hopes for what he sees? But if we hope for what we do not see, we wait for it with patience. (Rom 8:22–25, RSV)

The experiential shape of this pneumatic movement by the church through the sufferings of time is described under the summary of "love," in 1 Corinthains 13. Love is a supreme pneumatic gift ("the greatest," Paul insists); but its form is given in endurance and suffering, commitment and stability, as Paul outlines in Rom 5:1–5. This sense of ecclesial giftedness and witness is paradoxical, certainly, because it comes in the face of the church's own failure and sin: the church is pneumatically ordered as she engages her own spiritual rebellion in a certain way, something Paul has been describing in 1 Corinthians 10 and 11—warnings, fallings, scandals, rebellions, shame, guilt, illness, death, damnation. In the face of the particular sins of division, we can perhaps be more concrete: how the Church engages its division actually *witnesses to* the mereological impetus of the Spirit, its "initial-ness," "first-fruitedness." In the context of division, the particular forms of love as endurance, suffering and stability—called forth precisely within a life torn asunder by sin and disunity—represent faith within the partialness that defines the church's pneumatic life. Actual disunity, that is, constitutes the locale wherein pneumatic partialness—essential somehow to the life we live—is granted visibility in particular gifts.

As literary religious example of this, we can consider the seventeenth-century poet Robert Herrick's "Litany to the Holy Spirit," a verse entreaty for comfort by a dying and penitent sinner. One might take the poem as a figure of the church, as much as of the individual:

> In the hour of my distress,
> When temptations me oppress,
> And when I my sins confess,
> > Sweet Spirit, comfort me!
>
> When, God knows, I'm toss'd about
> Either with despair or doubt;
> Yet before the glass be out,
> > Sweet Spirit, comfort me!
>
> When the tempter me pursu'th
> With the sins of all my youth,
> And half damns me with untruth,
> > Sweet Spirit, comfort me!
>
> When the Judgment is reveal'd,
> And that open'd which was seal'd,
> When to Thee I have appeal'd,
> > Sweet Spirit, comfort me![14]

These are just a few verses of the poem; and Herrick mentions various other things in the litany: the world's error and ignorance; the stupidity and heartlessness of doctors; fears, exhaustion, and the rest. It is an extended prayer. The church needs comforting in the midst of her own life and trials of such a kind. What are the forms of this comfort? Getting through the depletion of their burden with some degree of hope just as in a human life. In short, Herrick is calling upon the Spirit to provide the goods of *survival*; and in the case of the present discussion, the goods of ecclesial survival.

There is no sin in pursuing the goods of flourishing or even of perfection. These have, traditionally, been the focus of ecclesial self-identity, despite their repeated historical contradictions. But such goods are not in fact

---

14. Herrick, "His Letanie, To the Holy Spirit."

proper to the mereological scope of pneumatic ecclesial life, placed within the frame of partial apprehension. Identifying the proper goods of the church's *survival,* by contrast, is in fact not something that has consumed theological concern. Though it should. It is not the case, for instance, that the quite vigorous ecumenical project of determining "fundamentals" on the basis of which churches might recognize one another is the same as identifying the goods of ecclesial survival, the latter of which are defined largely by their capacity to sustain, in Jesus words, "endurance to the end" (Matt 24:13). There may be overlap; but the characters of survival and essence are distinct, and, furthermore, the goods of survival may themselves shift according to circumstance: surviving in the shadow of Tamerlane's vicious annihilation of whole peoples is not the same as surviving in today's cultural grip of materialism or biologism. Just that shifting difference of historical and cultural location is tied to the reality of partialness, at least as the category is parsed with philosophical care. (That is why doctrinal precision on the church's part may not always be a good measure of the church's pneumatic integrity. This is one of the open-ended topics of Endo's modern classic *Silence,* about seventeenth-century Japanese Christianity.[15])

The goods of ecclesial survival include words, acts, and signs. They would involve catechesis, practices of prayer and worship. Whether unity itself is such a good of survival is doubtful. While disunity may be a sin; and while active division may involve the character of murder, there is much evidence that fragmented Christianity, as in America and now Africa, can stoke competition, innovation, and exploration, and may even, in some circumstances, enhance the dynamics of propagation. Christian unity appears unrelated, essentially, to the church's survival through time, an endurance that seems to rely on other factors.

My point regarding the partial character of the goods of survival would, in any case, stress that these goods are discrete, denominated, and historically contingent realities, not patent to systematic metaphysical coherence (hence the impossibility of rationally persuasive dogmatic frameworks to maintain themselves in the face of experiential dissonance). The goods that uphold or derive from the partial character of our Christian apprehension are closer, thus, to the conceptual genre of Scripture itself than of logic: lots and lots, powerfully given, always in the process of being integrated. One might even go so far as to say that the "inconsistent" aspects of this integration are themselves signs of partialness, and thus, potentially, of pneumatic agency. The partial, once grasped as partial (rather than e.g. as a simple mistake; let alone as a perfection), has as its essence its own movement towards the whole.

15. Endo, *Silence.*

By reframing the church's pneumatic "guarantee" in mereological terms, I am not, however, trying to avoid the denotative power of the Holy Spirit's presence and work, the fact that we can actually "identify" this or that element as "his." There have been, traditionally, certain obvious elements that cannot be consigned to a realm of obscurity, such as the "fruit" of the Holy Spirit, "love, joy, peace, patience, kindness, goodness, faithfulness, gentleness, self-control" (Gal 5:23–23, RSV), by which Jesus insists the truth of a person or group is "known" (Matt 7:16, 20). But such fruit exist within disunity as much as in unity, a fact that has bedevilled Christian attempts to identify the true church, and has confused attempts at more systematic ecumenical efforts. If comprehensively exhibited—that is, if there were some great gathering of such fruitful Christians, and the outworking of their lives encompassed one another somehow—we might wonder if such fruit constitutes unity itself, at least in historical terms, the terms defined by the daily round of dissonance. But probably not. For such a gathering, while itself a certain good, is not intrinsically tied to the actual ecclesial life of the Spirit: comprehensiveness is not a pneumatic reality in this quotidian realm. Partialness is the character of all our "todays." In the case of the church's temporal life, the Spirit keeps us going; and survival does not constitute arrival.

CONCLUSION

Where, then, *does* unity—the bond of the Spirit—lie in this panoply of pneumatic and partial particulars that is the church's life impregnated by the great Gift breathed upon her? If my answer is "martyrdom," it is an answer aimed at the term's broadest sense of concentrated obedience. Whatever the nuances of one's Trinitarian theology, all Christians should agree on the Christic center of pneumatic movement. And within the perspective of a pneumatic mereology, partialness is fully resolved historically only in Jesus. From one perspective, Jesus' life, as a human being in history, is partial, one who, in Paul's terms, sees or understands "in part" and is himself but "a part" of a whole. That is, at least, the force of Hebrews' insistence on Jesus as "in every way" like us (Heb 4:15). But in fact, in human terms, he is also "perfect"—the *aner teleios* of Eph 4:13, "holy, blameless, pure, set apart, exalted" (Heb 7:26); and thus his life marks the coincidence of part and whole. *If* we wish to speak of the spiritual in terms of wholes, it can only be in terms of the bodily life of Jesus, that is given in the Gospels. This is another question—the nature of Scripture's referents, and the comprehensive character of scriptural figure as grounding wholly the partial phenomena of historical experience. I mention Scripture here only because it is not an accident that the major locus of pneumatic activity in the early church was the reading of Scripture and its redemptive character, as Origen described it: the movement of the soul from partialness to fullness. I still consider Scripture reading, in and of itself, to be the primary pneumatic good of the church, both in terms of survival as arrival.

In any case, Paul himself stresses the ordering towards unity that life in Christ entails, especially in Romans 5–8. But it is a life that is strikingly given in the register of partialness—"It is the Spirit himself bearing witness with our spirit that we are children of God, and if children, then heirs, heirs of God and fellow heirs with Christ, provided we suffer with him in order that we may also be glorified with him. I consider that the sufferings of this present time are not worth comparing with the glory that is to be revealed to us" (Rom 8:16–18). Paul "considers" the relation between part and whole to be incomparable in its fulfilment along an essential path from one to the other. He considers this, in the sense of "thinking it though," reasoning, counting. It is an almost philosophical term of the logical process. How? By the Spirit's own bearing witness, in a shared "martyrial" witness (*summartyrei*) that is given in the history of our sufferings with Christ—*sympaschomen*.

On this account, the church's spiritual unity is given in her experienced suffering—the burden of partialness—as joined to Christ Jesus. This is a traditional view. It is an attempt, I also admit, to solve the problem by having one's cake and eating it too: disunity as *both* horrendously real burden and as subjective misperception. Though "eating cake" hardly does justice to this reality as a metaphor. Pneumatic unity as something given in suffering together (including suffering *dis*unity) is more like "being baptized into the death of Christ" (Rom. 6:4) and living with him the life of the One God's survival on earth. None of this dismisses hopes, like those of the celebrated 1961 WCC New Delhi statement on ecclesial unity, expressed in terms of common apostolic faith and teaching, common prayer, common eucharist, common ministry, common witness "brought by the Holy Spirit into one fully committed fellowship" (par. 2).[16] But such unity is something, we are told, for which "we must pray and work." Today we are with Christ; tomorrow, God willing, with one another in a perfect way. Today, the partial is rendered tolerable, acceptable, even thanks-worthy, because of a God who bears and thus transfigures the often burdensome constraints of the partial. The Holy Spirit is given to survive ecclesial dissonance, a dissonance embodied in quite real disunity. Yet the Spirit is not given simply as a useful tool. Rather, the great pneumatic Gift is offered to reveal the fullness of

---

16. Visser 't Hooft, ed., *New Delhi Statement*.

grace in a space that is ever so small and often conflicted. Frankly, I reckon we understand little of these things. Augustine writes, in the manner of a great question wrapped up in a yet larger prayer:

> But, as You fill all things, fill them with Your whole self, or, as even all things cannot altogether contain You, do they contain a part, and do all at once contain the same part? Or has each its own proper part—the greater more, the smaller less? Is, then, one part of You greater, another less? [*An quia non possunt te totum capere omnia, partem tui capiunt et eamdem partem simul omnia capiunt? An singulas singula et maiores maiora, minores minora capiunt ?*] Or is it that You are wholly everywhere while nothing altogether contains You?[17]

---

17. Augustine, *Confessions* I.3.46.

8

Ecclesiological Pneumatology over the Last 50 Years

Mark W. Elliott

INTRODUCTION

THIS ESSAY IS INTENDED to take stock of and review the recent (post-1965) history of attempts to do ecclesiology in light of the doctrine of the Holy Spirit, or more precisely, to consider how the Holy Spirit is the Holy Spirit of the Church, as well as the Spirit of Christ or God as third person. In doing this I want to come right up to date and consider some new attempts at Ecclesiology. Admittedly, there might well be something unsatisfactory, pre- if not sub-dogmatic about doing modern theology as historical theology over the last half-century; yet one advantage of the approach is to see things "genealogically," or in terms of an awareness of the traditions out of which recent and contemporary theologians are writing. One *disadvantage* is that one cannot do justice to the volume and richness of that history, if one is to hope to be able to give both a comprehensive and analytical account. Historical theologians are not really allowed to "cherry-pick" in the way that systematic theologians may, but they may have to, in order to say anything at all that spans the period.

There might be another problem. For, connected with the question of the proper place of Ecclesiology among the theological subdisciplines, is an objection to Ecclesiology's claim to be a dogmatic (whether historical or systematic) enterprise at all. It could be that "the church" is more fittingly treated within the remit of practical theology. This would mean that 'the church' belongs more to projects like 'Ecclesiology and Ethnography', reflections on the current state of the church and wisdom-driven practice arising out of empirical observation and ethical considerations. As one might gather from the 2012 volume edited by Peter Ward, *Perspectives on Ecclesiology and Ethnography*, ethnographic research includes qualitative research into the actual practice and social context of the church. Yet it is at least arguable that while doctrinal theology could do with being mindful of its church setting, so too projects such as the one mentioned could afford to enlist more biblical and dogmatic theologians to assist in their deliberations.

When one approaches the Church from below, as part of the Practical Theological task, the question of believing the Church given all its scandals and mediocrity may seem hard enough.[1] But what if as would-be dogmaticians we affirm that we believe *in* the Church (εἰς μίαν ἁγίαν καθολικὴν καὶ ἀποστολικὴν ἐκκλησίαν·)? While she is some way down the line in the order of being, the Church has a good case to be *prima inter pares* (along with Scripture) in the order of knowing. 'For my part, I should not believe the gospel except as moved by the authority of the Catholic Church.' (*Against the title of the epistle of Manichaeus*, 6). Or even more boldly: 'no one can have God for Father who does not have the church as mother' (Cyprian, *On the Unity of the Church*, 6). Yet perhaps a better approach is to consider that, whatever these Latin fathers might have thought, in the ecumenical Nicene-Constantinopolitan creed it isn't a question of how much authority the church has. We are called to believe in not so much the church *per se*, but rather in the *properties* of the church as *unam, sanctam, catholicam, apostolicam*, just as when in the first line of the creed we are not so much saying we believe in God but believe in him *as* The Father, the Almighty, Maker of Heaven and earth. So here we are called not so much to believe *in* the church and her authority as to believe in her being she is one, holy, catholic and apostolic. Yet how to conceive of these things?

---

1. This seems to be the chief criticism made by Brittain of theoretical and theological ecclesiologies, that they tend to airbrush the evils perpetrated by the actual church; see Brittain, "Why Ecclesiology Cannot Live by Doctrine Alone," 5–30. And yet the church, despite all this, can still be called 'holy', even as an ideal to live up to in the power of God: see von Balthasar, "Casta Meretrix," 143–92.

The typical Protestant way has been to downgrade the church somewhat, to keep ourselves who are the church humble, so as to avoid the temptation of deifying it and ourselves, and doing this through emphasizing the Word of God, The Kingdom of God or the Spirit of God. "He must increase, but I must decrease" (Jn 3:30), might well be the motto. So the four marks of the unity, sanctity, catholicity and apostolicity of the church are deprecated. Moreover, these easily become four impossible ideals without much purchase on reality or capacity to inspire.

Recently Simeon Zahl has used pneumatology to supplement or even correct the prevailing drift to 'participatory ontology', which privileges a somewhat static emphasis on 'being' over experience in conceptions of the Christian life and prefers a 'being in Christ' Ecclesiology to an actualism of the Spirit's power and impact. He writes of the need for theology to do justice to embodied existence, or perhaps to the realm of spiritual experience, bodies included.[2] He is wary of the discourse of 'participation', but prefers to focus on Pneumatology, where it encounters affective psychology. This pneumatology is accordingly one not of presence but is more about the facilitating of experiential action, realising that the phenomenon of Christian mediocrity is a challenge to virtue ethics and 'transformation'.[3] Hence what he calls the critical and realistic account needs supplementing by the Pentecostal emphasis on the Holy Spirit's power.[4] However not a lot is said about the church since that would obscure the light that needs to be shone on mediocre Christian existence of individuals.

One might think of this emphasis on the Spirit as characteristically (Eastern) Orthodox, where a pneumatological ecclesiology steps forward to balance a 'Christological' ecclesiology, as seemingly favoured by the Western church. Yet when one looks at Orthodox examples this 'characteristic' does not seem to stand out quite so clearly. Conversely, when one looks at Catholic developments of Ecclesiology within my lifetime, there is more than a little room for the language of pneumatological ecclesiology. But what about ecclesiological pneumatology? Can the influence of Spirit on the Church not work both ways, meaning can the church's experience give shape to the forms the work of the Holy Spirit takes? In this 'giving the church due respect', the least we can do is listen to the Catholics.

Before I return to the heart of this paper, where I will consider the Protestant ecclesiologies by Moltmann, Pannenberg and Greggs, I want first

---

2. Zahl, *The Holy Spirit*, 234.
3. Zahl, *The Holy Spirit*, 237.
4. Zahl, *The Holy Spirit*, 242.

to tune into the strengths and weaknesses of Catholic ecclesiology in the wake of the Second Vatican Council.

CATHOLIC ECCLESIOLOGY: THE CHURCH AND THE SPIRIT

This side of Vatican II it is easy to lose sight of just how much preparation went on not only in the sense of explicit and intentional preparation in the period between 1961 and the Council's opening in 1963 but also and more significantly in many earlier decades of the twentieth century, "the century of the church."[5] And then out the other side especially in the 1960s and 70s when de Lubac, Küng, Schillebeeckx, Rahner, Balthasar, Dulles (he of the famous textbook, *Models of the Church*) and others set about interpreting and applying the theory in the conciliar document *Lumen Gentium*. Behind this there was a history of ecclesiological reflection from at least the Conciliar period onwards (thus 1400), in contradistinction to Protestantism, for which Ecclesiology often seemed to be an afterthought, and often written in reaction to Catholic first moves. Perhaps one of the first books on the Church I read was that eponymous book by Edmund Clowney, published by IVP (UK) in 1995. What struck me was how much it seemed like a Protestant version of Avery Dulles' *Models*. John Webster's famous article, "On Evangelical Ecclesiology," first published in 2004,[6] is another example although less of imitation but of qualification and even refutation of Catholic hegemony in the field, with perhaps a fear that the likes of Miroslav Volf had too readily borrowed the Catholic clothes (in Volf's appreciation of Ratzinger's ecclesiology).[7] As Webster reported, de Lubac had influentially promoted a dislike of ecclesiologies where "Christ as supernature and the church as nature are placed in a purely extrinsic relation."[8] However, this integration of spirit and nature "compromises the imparticipible perfection of God's triune life, and so disturbs the fundamental assymetry of Christ and the church."[9] Webster concludes with what seems a rather odd reading of Calvin here (*Inst*. III.xi.10), where the Reformer actually seems closer to de Lubac, except that Calvin's emphasis on union is not union in *God* as such, since IV.i.3 admittedly has "fellowship with *Christ*."[10] The concept of

5. Mulder, *The Turn to The Church*.
6. Webster, "On Evangelical Ecclesiology," 153–93.
7. Volf, *After Our Likeness*.
8. Webster, 'On Evangelical Ecclesiology," 162.
9. "On Evangelical Ecclesiology," 163.
10. "On Evangelical Ecclesiology," 170.

'fellowship' is preferable since it is neither extrinsicist, given that Christians are 'in Christ' yet nor is it monist, and this might avoid Webster's implied criticism in lines like: "The Church is risen with Christ, but it is not risen as Christ," while we remain creatures of his mercy.[11] But have Protestants paid enough attention to what it means for the Church to be risen with Christ, in the way that the likes of de Lubac have? Whether right or wrong in its details and results, de Lubac's major work *Catholicism* has a range of imagination and a systematic scope which Protestant works can hardly rival. And this applies to recent Orthodox versions of ecclesiology as in those by Loudovikos. In offering resistance to the fashionable Schellingite-Solovyev mystical, anti-institutional panentheism, which needs correcting through the patristic tradition.[12] For Loudovikos there is a *created Sophia* that draws on uncreated grace, denying any autonomy to nature (as in the 'scholastic' West). But this is just de Lubac in Orthodox clothes.

Actually, if one stands within the Catholic tradition, there is little such sense of unanimity of view and purpose, hence much less of a monolith than implied by Webster. In fact the extent of polarisation and division on just what the church was meant to be was lamented in M. Kehl's book.[13] Some Catholic theologians thought that *Lumen Gentium* spelled a democratisation, others (with some justification) that the appeal in *Lumen Gentium* 12 to the sense of faith of all believers, a *vox populi*, tended towards reinforcing the more conservative theology of the magisterium, with the *lex orandi* as indefectible, traditional and somehow determinative of future dogma in Augustine's terms. Hence the Liberation Theologian Jose Comblin: "Besides this, *Lumen Gentium* took up an idea derived from the Fathers, in particular St Augustine, emphasized by St Thomas and already put forward in *Mystici Corporis*: that of the Holy Spirit as the soul of the church."[14] Against this, unfortunately in Comblin's view, *Dominum et vivificantem*, the third in the Trinitarian trilogy of John Paul II's encyclicals, returned to Bellarmine's "church as a society of baptised believers" submitting to the Hierarchy. This Comblin regards as a backward step. In an analogous way Richard McBrien criticised Hans Küng for too Lutheran a view of the kingdom which reduces "church" to a community of proclamation rather than of socio-political diakonia.[15]

---

11. "On Evangelical Ecclesiology," 173.
12. See Loudovikos, *Church in the Making*, 210.
13. Kehl, *Die Kirche*, 77–79.
14. Comblin, *The Holy Spirit and Liberation*, 83.
15. McBrien, *Church: The Continuing Quest*, 58.

But this is unfair to John Paul II. In his Encyclical the Polish Pope quoted Paul VI's insistence on Vatican II's ecclesiology needing to be supplemented by pneumatology:

> The Holy Spirit is the 'fire from heaven' which works in the depth of the mystery of the Cross. [He] comes down, in a certain sense, into the very heart of the sacrifice which is offered on the Cross . . . He consumes this sacrifice with the fire of the love which unites the Son with the Father in the Trinitarian communion.[16]

The Spirit confronts each person with this 'burning coal', and as Balthasar comments, this occurs via the sacraments and into the human heart.[17] Hence, again, in the words of *D&V*:

> The Holy Spirit, in his mysterious bond of divine communion with the Redeemer of man, is the one who brings about the continuity of his work: he takes from Christ and transmits to all, unceasingly entering into the history of the world through the heart of man . . . It is the Spirit that makes the body of Christ: In this reality, Christ, who has gone away in his visible humanity, comes, is present and acts in the Church in such an intimate way as to make it his own Body.[18]

However, it would appear that the Church itself is made the body of Christ but once that has happened, the Spirit's work is done with the Church and from that point onwards the object of the Spirit's mission is the individual heart, such that we cannot speak of a pneumatological ecclesiology. For even as the church as made the body of Christ exists through the presence and action of the Spirit, in the Papal vision here, the Church is the broker or the instrument of grace, a channel for the Spirit to flow so that the Trinity can work on the individual soul. "True the church is sacrament in the sense that it is sign and instrument of the Spirit's power."[19] A few pages earlier the Pope had laid the foundations for this claim:

> True, the great Jubilee of the year 2000 thus contains a message of liberation by the power of the Spirit, who alone can help individuals and communities to free themselves from the old and new determinisms, by guiding them with the "law of the Spirit, which gives life in Christ Jesus," and thereby discovering and

---

16. John Paul II, *Dominum et vivificantem*, 22–25.
17. Von Balthasar, "Retrieving the Tradition."
18. John Paul II, *Dominum et vivificantem*, 67.
19. John Paul II, *Dominum et vivificantem*, 64.

accomplishing the full measure of man's true freedom. For, as St. Paul writes, "Where the Spirit of the Lord is, there is freedom."[20]

There is a passing reference to 'communities' but notice how it is not said that the Church in the sense of the Catholic church is the object or beneficiary of liberation or renewal in the way that 'communities' and individuals are. The idea seems to be that the Spirit uses the Church as a place from which to reach individuals and communities, which are something other than or distinct from the church. There is little in the way of pneumatological *ecclesiology*, and hence little chance for ecclesiological pneumatology.

And yet, to linger a few moments longer with the Encyclical, where it emphasises that the church is born on the cross and is only revealed at Pentecost with the coming of the Spirit, this seems like a little inconsistent:

> And thus he the firstborn of all creation becomes firstborn among many brothers, and thus also becomes the head of the Body, which is the Church, *which will be born* [has been born?] on the Cross and revealed on the day of Pentecost-and in the Church, he becomes the head of humanity: of the people of every nation, every race, every country and culture, every language and continent, all called to salvation.[21]

The purifying goes on in individual hearts. "The church embracing sinners in her own bosom is at the same time holy and always to be purified, she pursues penance and renewal at all times . . . She has the dignity and freedom of the sons of God in whose hearts the Holy Spirit indwells like in a temple."[22] Any chance that the *purificans* of *Lumen Gentium* 8–9 might be an ecclesial one does seem lost in *Dominum et Vivificantem*, since according to the latter the church is "already" holy.

So, the problem with *Dominum et Vivificantem* is less what Comblin complains, that it marks a return to the 'societal' model. No, it is very much a dynamic one, about the church as the expansive and expanding body of Christ and is thereby somewhat triumphalist: "*in the Church* he becomes the head of humanity." This might arguably have scriptural warrant. Indeed, Rudolf Schnackenburg identifies the church according to the Epistle to the Ephesians with weak and fallible believers under the cross, yet he then adds: "Theologically the Epistle to the Ephesians pushes towards the consideration

---

20. John Paul II, *Dominum et vivificantem*, 60.

21. John Paul II, *Dominum et vivificantem*, 52.

22. Lumen Gentium I, 8: *Ecclesia in proprio sinu peccatores complectens, sancta simul et semper purificanda, poenitentiam et renovationem continuo prosequitur . . . Habet pro conditione dignitatem libertatemque filiorum Dei, in quorum cordibus Spiritus Sanctus sicut in templo inhabitat.*

of the rôle of the church in God's plan of salvation, her mediatory function in the atoning work of Christ, its being taken hold/ penetrated/ effected with the Holy Spirit despite all the depressing experiences in the reality of this world."[23] Further: "Christ as head of both church and cosmos holds both these entities in tension, yet through the church he will make the area of his Lordship and blessing expand."[24] This might well be where a Protestant account of matters in Ephesians begs to differ, preferring to see God's filling the church and filling the world as two related but discrete operations. Schnackenburg views the Church as a missionary saving unit created by God in Christ, which otherwise includes and sums up the empirical ecclesial communities and is in that sense earthed, for the church realises itself in these communities, and through them the church meets the world. Yet, *contra* Schnackenburg, when examined carefully Ephesians does not seem to describe the church growing into the fullness of Christ who/ which [?] grows to fill the universe; rather God does the filling of the latter anyway, and if anything the Church is a launchpad or prototype for that. What the Pneumatology of Ephesians really offers to post-Vatican II ecclesiologies is a strong hope of being led into unity, especially that between congregations and hierarchies/offices (Eph 1:22–23; 3:10, 21).

In his mission to get behind the centuries-accretion of traditional ecclesiology and to locate in the New Testament writings a purer Christianity of an unsullied fountain, E. Schillebeeckx, in his book *Church* sets out his stall with the title of Chapter 4: "Towards Democratic Rule in the Church as a Community of God."[25] He argues that the Church's "indefectibility" really means self-correction, with a constantly renewed *metanoia*. Progress involves a questioning of authority, and of the assumption that common believers and church hierarchy do always agree, such that dissent means sin, and those dissenting are not the church. No, contends Schillebeeckx, Galatians 3:28 puts paid to this, he maintains, with its call to inclusion and

---

23. Schnackenburg, *Der Brief an die Epheser*, 357: 'Theologisch zwingt der Epheserbrief zum Nachdenken über die Rolle der Kirche im Heilsplan Gottes, ihre mittlerische Funktion im Versöhnungswek Christi, ihre Durchdringung mit dem heiligen Geist trotz aller deprimierenden Erfahrungen in der Wirklichkeit dieser Welt."

24. Schnackenburg, *Der Brief an die Epheser*, 306: "Diese kosmische Ausweitung der Konzeption bewirkt eine umfassendere ekklesiologische Sicht, insofern die Kirche auch in ihrem Verhältnis zur Welt und in ihrer von Gott bestimmten Aufgabe in der Welt und an der Welt gesehen wird. Christus ist Haupt der Kirche und Haupt der Welt und halt so in seiner Person beides zusammen und zugleich in Spannung. Er will durch die Kirche den Bereich seiner Segensherrschaft ausweiten und damit auch den Einfluß der in der Welt noch immer—trotz der Unterwerfung durch den Kreuzessieg Christi (vgl. Kol 2,115; Eph 1,20f)—agierenden Unheilsgewalten zurückdrängen."

25. Schillebeeckx, *Church*.

tolerance. The *oekumene* is not that of Christians or the Christian church but of the world, that is the *oekumene* of suffering mankind (with a nod to J.-B. Metz).[26]

We could get round difficulties of defining the *ekklesia* by using "kingdom of God," adds Schillebeeckx. *Lumen Gentium* managed a compromise which tends in the direction of "kingdom of God" in its employing the Lordship of Christ theme. The church is to be "the nucleus and beginning of the kingdom," so there is not a total identification of church and kingdom (*Lumen Gentium*'s *subsistit in* is glossed by Schillebeeckx as meaning that the true catholic church is to be found buried under rubbish), plus one should not forget that "ecclesial elements exist outside it."[27] One here might want to contrast the traditionalist vision of B. D. de la Soujeole, who is bold enough to assert "We do not say that the Church is *like* the kingdom of God, but that she *is* the kingdom of God."[28] Then continuing in this vein, Soujeole feels content to conclude: "We can actually say that the RCC *actually* is the one, unique Church of Christ . . . we have treated the question dogmatically, dealing with the ecclesial being as such, in its ontology."[29]

Here we see theologians of opposing parties spending most of their efforts on the question of power, jurisdiction, and authority. Schillebeeckx went a step further than Küng[30] (who was content to remain within the inner-churchly discourse of power), in order to open a challenge to all political pretensions to power, in the spirit of Critical Theory, with some amount of debt to the Frankfurt School. Interim conclusion: even if the Catholic Church is not divided, then its Ecclesiology certainly is, with a great polarisation between maximalist (Soujeole and others) and minimalist (Schillebeeckx and others) views.

PROTESTANT PARALLELS: THE SPIRIT AND THE CHURCH

Of course a Protestant can recognize a similar, if not quite as radical agenda to that of Schillebeeckx in Jürgen Moltmann's *Church in the Power of the Holy Spirit*. As usual, Moltmann is extremely helpful in offering the gist and often some detail (quotation and paraphrase) from the tradition. The Church is best understood as moving from below and the vision here might

26. Schillebeeckx, *Church*, 189.
27. See especially Schillebeeckx, *Church*, 216–17.
28. De la Soujeole, *Introduction to the Mystery of the Church*, 58.
29. De la Soujeole, *Introduction to the Mystery of the Church*, 128.
30. Küng, *The Church*.

well be refreshing, even over half a century later. And of course there was encouragement not only from Vatican II, but also and especially from the liberationist readings of Vatican II, according to which *Lumen Gentium* based its doctrine of the Church on the Holy Spirit's mission.

Right away Moltmann is clear that the Spirit is that of Christ, but also that the Spirit is given to the Church for the sake of mission, to help the church look outwards, to undo or at least offset its *incurvatus in se* tendency. Ecclesiology is predicated on Pneumatology, Moltmann believes, as when he writes: "It is the doctrine of the Holy Spirit in particular that depicts the processes and experiences in which and through which the church becomes comprehensible to itself as the messianic fellowship in the world and for the world."[31] Yet this is an unusual Pneumatology of a very Hegelian-like tone, as seems also the case when he agrees with Rahner against Barth that the Church can indeed be a sacrament. "If sacrament means 'the theological concept of a mediation which does not merely mediate something, but mediates itself as well' then we must certainly accept other mediations in addition to the one and only mediation of God in and through Jesus Christ."[32]

Yet one might ask: what is the logic of the implication that God's self-mediating through Christ means that the church mediates itself, and that there are mediations other than that of the Incarnation? Roughly speaking, what matters and what in effect gets mediated by the church is "the kingdom," itself in turn served by the church in mission. "Not Christ for himself but Christ in the Holy Spirit, not the church for itself but Christ's church in the Holy Spirit, must be called the mystery or 'sacrament' whose actions are always pointing towards the kingdom."[33] The Church's "own existence, fellowship and activity springs from that story of liberation," which for Moltmann means a spontaneous existence and is not about checking up on each other or ourselves.[34] Heaven forfend that the church be accused of being insular and anything other than continuing Christ's kenoticism and self-effacement for the sake of the kingdom!

One might conceivably retort to Moltmann that the Western church has suffered from too much of this model of the church, whereby the church is a channel for the Spirit's effects of the kingdom in the world without the church much repenting, changing or growing herself. As for Schillebeeckx, "He must decrease and I must decrease" is to be the Church's 'kenotic' motto,

---

31. Moltmann, *Church in the Power of the Holy Spirit*, 198.

32. Moltmann, *Church in the Power of the Spirit*, 201, the reference is to Jüngel, *Unterwegs zur Sache*, 41.

33. Moltmann, *Church in the Power of the Spirit*, 205.

34. Moltmann, *Church in the Power of the Spirit*, 226.

but that can too easily mean the church getting out of the way and hiding from the action, looking to see the change happen outside itself.

Another major theologian's understanding of the church under the Word and open to the Word's directing alone seems at first glance more promising. In his book *The Church* Wolfhart Pannenberg seems to claim that a Christianity outside the church might have more of a claim to be universal than Christianity within the church, which is too often split through striving after power. On the other hand, he believes that an ecumenical council is urgent necessity, allowing for certain differences of belief as consistent with a church on the way to eschatological perfection: "there can be genuine alterations of traditional doctrine without endangering the truth."[35] He is aware that Otto Semmelroth coined the phrase *Kirche als Ursakrament*, even if O. H. Pesch preferred to speak of it as *Grund-* not *Ur-Sakrament*.

Against such Catholic inclinations, Moltmann too wanted to reaffirm the Barthian insistence "to let God perform his work—this and this alone is the function of the church's action."[36] The word (divine) brings to speech what has already taken place, so that there is nothing to complete. Our work is mere passive repetition, and only as hearing is it speaking. The Church is no more than a great sacramental sign (sacramental in a derived way, not a sacrament as such), which represents Jesus. " 'Mother church' does not stand over the individual Christian; rather 'mother church' *is* Christians as they belong together through the Word of God and derive from the Word of God."[37] The church is daughter of the Word, or in marked and firm response to *Lumen Gentium* 8 which, as we have seen above, states "the church is at once holy and in need of purification"(*sancta simul et semper purificanda*), Moltmann cites Luther's phrase: "the church, which knows itself to be a sinner" (from a sermon on Matthew 28; 9 April 1531.)[38] Viewed positively, she is clean by the Word God has spoken to her.

This Lutheran accent on 'development' as a function of the church's passivity before the Word in Pannenberg's ecclesiology seemed to intensify when he came to write the third volume of his *Systematic Theology* in 1993. Here, not only the Word, but the "Spirit making all things new" is invoked, and parsed as an *eschatological* pneumatology, that makes for freedom, since the Spirit's effect not being truly causal is itself less likely to be the product of impure influences. If one starts at the very opening lines of Volume 3 (1993) of the *Systematic Theology*, one reads about the Holy Spirit of

---

35. Pannenberg, *The Church*, 66–68.
36. Moltmann, *Church in the Power of the Spirit*, 203.
37. Moltmann, *Church in the Power of the Spirit*, 213.
38. Luther, *LW* 2.101.

God, who is given to believers in a totally specific way. He "dwells'"in them (Rom 8:9; 1 Cor 3:16), he "who is no other than the creator of all life in the whole range of events in nature, as well as in the new creation of the resurrection of the dead." Pannenberg clarifies: "This has to do with much more than only a divine help to knowledge or understanding of an otherwise remaining incomprehensible event of Revelation. The effect of the Holy Spirit in his church and in believers serves the fulfilment of his effect in the world of creation."[39]

Pannenberg's exegetical solution to the theological problem was to work with the Lucan alternative to the Johannine-Pauline preference for a close identification of the Spirit with Christ, that sees the Spirit's work in the Church as the half-way, bridging point between creation and the fulfilment of all things. The method on display here is actually quite different from Pannenberg's usual style, or that in the earlier two volumes of the *Systematic Theology*. The argument is founded on biblical exegesis informed by biblical scholarship. The Spirit of God operates on believers less as an invisible and ungraspable force-field from outside-in (as per the conception of the Spirit which made Pannenberg famous), but rather the Spirit is given to believers as gift for their own keeping and therein consists the particularity of His function. The gift of the Spirit as a soteriological, and ecclesiological function is anticipation of the eschatological pouring out of the Spirit, which is the Holy Spirit in full-blooded missionary and transformative mode! The Church is the prototype for what the Spirit will finally and consummately do with the cosmos.[40]

Hence, for Pannenberg, the Spirit's own role is played out in such a way that creatures have that life and movement in them even if before and beyond them. The church should not "encapsulate" the Spirit but be a house through which he comes, from creation to eschaton. The Spirit has significance for life and preaching only when creation and eschatology are taken into account, along with a realization that Spirit works also outside the community. This work of the Spirit happens thoroughly in continuous connection with his operation in the world of nature and source of life and especially in human beings as the source of the spontaneity of their spiritual activity, which raises human beings ecstatically over their own particularity, so they can grasp what is beyond them. Pannenberg starts with New Testament texts but ends with a form of natural theology, as the general absorbs the particular and exemplary.

---

39. Pannenberg, *Systematic Theology*, 3:2.
40. Pannenberg, *Systematic Theology*, 3:4–9.

Last but not least, I want to consider Tom Greggs' ambitious and impressive recent project (*Dogmatic Ecclesiology*), one that wants to ensure any identification of Christ with the Church is only plausible through an appeal to the Holy Spirit's constant input. The Spirit thus acts as qualifier to the substantive "Church," which is to affirm a participation in Christ's humanity as mediated by the Spirit. The emphasis is on a church that exists for God and those outside the church or not-yet the church. The Church does not exist for itself.

On this interpretation then, Acts 1 describes a human society not yet the church: One has to wait for Acts 2. As per Paul Nimmo, the Spirit is essentially *inecclesiandus*.[41] "Theologically speaking, the church begins in chapter 2 of Acts since here we have an account of the cause of the church in the divine economy through the work of the Holy Spirit . . . the form of the church subsists within the event of the act of the Spirit"[42] In other words, no Spirit, no Church, and Greggs thinks this helps to avoid Institutionalism, in keeping with Calvin (*Inst* 4.1.17). Divine gracious action is prior even to faithful disposition. However, one might add this rejoinder: is to pray for revival merely action of "piety," assuming that prayer is moved by grace in the first place? What were the disciples doing in Acts 1 if not waiting in prayer?

"This work of the Holy Spirit fulfils the mediating work of Christ on the vertical and horizontal planes of ongoing creaturely existence: Christ, who mediates God to humanity and humanity to God, is made present in the community of believers by an event of the Spirit's act . . . The principal activity of ecclesiology is to describe this work of God the Holy Spirit."[43] One problem might be that it is God the Holy Spirit who mediates Christ's humanity to God's people. How does that work?

Greggs muses: is church just a place for knowing saving doctrine? No, not only, for the church is part of the economy of salvation. For all that Ecclesiology is a derivative doctrine, the church itself as an act of God is an object of the faith in its own right. It is to be understood as "an event of the act of the eternal God in history through the presence of God's faithful and eternal Spirit in the contingent contemporaneity of every present-day life."[44] It is about God's doing, and hence not reducible to postliberal present practices. The church is "the location of the theater of divine-creaturely relationship in the time between the creation and the eschaton."[45] In true Wesleyan fashion,

---

41. Greggs, *Dogmatic Ecclesiology*, 17n61.
42. Greggs, *Dogmatic Ecclesiology*, liii.
43. Greggs, *Dogmatic Ecclesiology*, 1.
44. Greggs, *Dogmatic Ecclesiology*, xxxiv.
45. Greggs, *Dogmatic Ecclesiology*, xl.

Greggs adds that the Reformation was as much about re-configuring divine and human agency as it was about a theology of the Word.

There is invisible church: what there is there is God's invisible activity. The visible church subsists in the invisible church, not vice versa (contra *Lumen Gentium* 8). Greggs wants to qualify that: "The visible church, we might say, subsists therefore in the invisible act of God revealed in the event of the church."[46] Since there is this invisibility, God's action can only be seen in faith. This would strike a blow against those who think ecclesiology should be approached empirically, or that one can run models that would guarantee success.

As early as Chapter One Greggs frames the doctrine of the church. "Ecclesiology, as a derivative doctrine of pneumatology, describes a salvific event of the act of the Spirit in the context of creation in its spatiotemporal contingency . . . Ecclesiology concerns, therefore, simultaneously the hidden and the visible church, which can never be spoken of separately, since the church (as an object of faith) is (a) a creation of the Spirit *ex nihilo* (b) in the visibility of the space and time of history."[47] There is always a danger then of overidentifying the Church with God. Calvin was concerned not to believe *in* the church.[48] No, "The church is an *event* of the act of the Holy Spirit." The Spirit's act is always 'more' than the church.[49] And hence one may and must believe in the Church. So one can believe *in* the church because it is divine work. The influence of Barthian actualism is acknowledged by Greggs, the reservations of his mentor Webster's *zum Trotz*.

Greggs wants to qualify these spiritualizing and actualizing tendencies by adding: "But the church needs form to be corporally . . . the particular form of Christ we now turn to is that of the priesthood of Christ . . . as the priest simultaneously orientates and mediates the other towards God and God towards the other."[50] Noting that *en Christô* is used 83 times in the Pauline epistles, and *en kuriô* 47 times, Greggs' particular emphasis is to view this shared priesthood as something carried out with reference to the world. "The church actively participates in Christ and in this participation is its existence as a priesthood." This connection and life is made possible by the Holy Spirit. He is clear that "body of Christ" is a "metonymy," i.e. "the closest possible association but not the identity of one thing and another."[51]

---

46. Greggs, *Dogmatic Ecclesiology*, li.
47. Greggs, *Dogmatic Ecclesiology*, 1.
48. Calvin, *Institutes* 4.1.2.
49. Greggs, *Dogmatic Ecclesiology*, 10.
50. Greggs, *Dogmatic Ecclesiology*, 47.
51. Greggs, *Dogmatic Ecclesiology*, 87.

There is no sense of the continuity of Christ's work in the ongoing work of the church, for Christ has ascended while we await him (so, Bonhoeffer). And so, to repeat: "There is an interruption between the life, death and resurrection and ascension of Christ and the church—an interruption which exists before the coming of the Spirit at Pentecost . . . this is an intimacy [with Christ] mediated by the Holy Spirit."[52] The church has a continued need for epiclesis, i.e., for orientation and being drawn up, as we grow into Christ, our humanity enhanced, drawing substance from His humanity. So one should think not in terms of deification, but rather in terms of a constant drawing back up of that which keeps falling.

Right at the end of the book Greggs offers this summary:

> In order of being, ecclesiology (the doctrine of the church) is derivative of economic pneumatology (the doctrine of the works of the Holy Spirit), which is itself derivative of. The doctrines of appropriations (the attribution of specific economic works to the individual persons of the Trinity) and of ontological pneumatology (the doctrine of the Holy Spirit). The doctrine of appropriations is derivative of the doctrine of the economic Trinity. The doctrines of the economic Trinity and of ontological pneumatology are derivative of the doctrine of the immanent Trinity and the principle *opera trinitatis ad extra indivisa sunt*. But in the experienced doctrine of knowing, the reverse is the case: we know of the Holy Spirit through the Spirit's act in creation in illuminating the Word of God in the church. Through the event of the act of the Spirit, we receive the revealedness of the divine life—the life of the Holy Trinity.[53]

Greggs wants, in the manner of theological theology—a dogmatic ecclesiology that provides no less than help towards the contemplation of the Trinity. This might well help to keep ecclesiology spiritual and Spirit-filled, even if one has questions about what can be known of ontological pneumatology as opposed to economic pneumatology, and why this is preferred as the object of knowledge to, say, the immanent Trinity.

However, my main reservation is that this could be to move in the wrong direction. Rather the church needs to glimpse what it means in concrete and storied terms for the Spirit to work in the church ('pneumatological ecclesiology'), and that requires wisdom to discern what is going on in its sphere of operation. It may well be no coincidence that the Reformation abandoned "one, holy, catholic and apostolic" as distinguishing marks of

---

52. Greggs, *Dogmatic Ecclesiology*, 88.
53. Greggs, *Dogmatic Ecclesiology*, 459.

the church. Perhaps its churches need to look at where those things are to be discerned, and hence be able to offer an account of ecclesiological pneumatology? This means to have standards for itself before God, rather than seeing its task as prophetic to the world.[54]

CONCLUSION

Given the way the creed works, it is the church that is part of the third article, with the further mention of baptism in connection with the forgiveness of sins as fairly crucial: one could say that this along with the mention of the resurrection and the life of the world to come is the climax of the third article and the creed as a whole, and not an afterthought or footnote to the confession of the Holy Spirit. There is some encouragement in the accounts of baptism and the imparting of the Spirit in Acts 8 and Acts 19 and the seeming requirement for an apostle to be present for that to happen, to see that the church might be best considered as more than a channel but also as a co-worker with God the Spirit, while no means a co-redemptrix. Further, if the church is taken more seriously in terms of its "'properties" (*one, holy, catholic and apostolic*), this has implications for our pneumatology, as what we know of an invisible cause, which is an efficient and hence present cause is to be gleaned from the visible effect: just how and in what way is the church one, or holy or catholic or apostolic? What are the ideals, the principles and standards for behaviour and operation, the visions and the goals which align with those four marks? Sticking with the Reformational marks of preaching and due administration of the sacraments will only get the church so far and will run too much the risk of clericalism. As we look at how the Spirit gifts these properties to the church, this will allow us to speak to or with the practical theologians (see the contributions by Fiddes and Avis).[55] However, in tracing the direction of flow our eyes should follow that which begins and ends in the work of God, resisting the tendency to reduce scripture, theology and practice to "story" or "data."

---

54. An attractive but finally unconvincing argument for a smaller, more marginal church as by necessity a more outward-looking is made by Mulder in the conclusion of his *The Turn to the Church*.

55. Fiddes, "Ecclesiology and Ethnography"; Avis, "Ecclesiology and Ethnography." Also Brittain, 'Why Ecclesiology Cannot Live by Doctrine Alone.'

Bibliography

Addo, Giuseppina. "Join the Holy Spirit on Zoom: African Pentecostal Churches and their Liturgical Practices during COVID-19." *Approaching Religion* 11 (2021) 45–61.
Allen, Michael. *The Fear of the Lord: Essays on Theological Method*. London: T. & T. Clark, 2022.
———, ed. *The New Cambridge Companion to Christian Doctrine*. Cambridge Companions to Religion. Cambridge: Cambridge University Press, 2022.
Allison, Gregg R. *Sojourners and Strangers: The Doctrine of the Church*. Wheaton, IL: Crossway, 2012.
Allison, Gregg R., and Andreas J. Köstenberger. *The Holy Spirit*. Nashville: B&H Academic, 2020.
Althouse, Peter, and Michael Wilkinson. "Musical Bodies in the Charismatic Renewal: The Case of Catch the Fire and Soaking Prayer." In *The Spirit of Praise: Music and Worship in Global Pentecostal-Charismatic Christianity*, edited by Monique M. Ingalls and Amos Yong, 29–44. University Park: Pennsylvania State University Press, 2015.
Augustine. *The Confessions: Saint Augustine*. Edited by John E. Rotelle. Translated by Maria Boulding. Green Bay, WI: Aquinas Institute, 2023.
Avis, Paul. "Ecclesiology and Ethnography: An Unresolved Relationship." *Ecclesiology* 14 (2018) 322–337.
Badcock, Francis John. *The History of the Creeds*. New York: Macmillan, 1938.
Balthasar, Hans Urs von. "Casta Meretrix." In *Explorations in Theology* vol. 2, *Spouse of the Word*, 143–92. Translated by John Saward. San Francisco: Ignatius.
———. "Retrieving the Tradition: A Commentary on John Paul II's Dominum et Vivificantem." Republished in *Communio* 47 (2020) 839–61.
Barna Group. "Five Trends Defining Americans' Relationship to Churches." n.d. https://www.barna.com/research/current-perceptions/.
Barth, Karl. *Church Dogmatics*. Edited by G. W. Bromiley and T. F. Torrance. Translated by G. W. Bromiley et al. Edinburgh: T. & T. Clark, 1956–1975.
Bauckham, Richard. "James and the Jerusalem Council." In *The Book of Acts in Its Palestinian Setting*, 415–40. The Book of Acts in Its First Century Setting 4. Grand Rapids: Eerdmans, 1995.

———. "Jürgen Moltmann's The Trinity and the Kingdom of God and the Question of Pluralism." In *The Trinity in a Pluralistic Age*, edited by Kevin J. Vanhoozer, 155–64. Grand Rapids: Eerdmans, 1997.

Baumert, Norbert. *Charisma—Taufe—Geisttaufe*. Vol. 1: *Entflechtung einer semantischen Verwirrung*. Würzburg: Echter 2001.

———. *Charisma—Taufe—Geisttaufe*. Vol. 2: *Normativität und persönliche* Berufung. Würzburg: Echter 2001.

Bavinck, Herman. *Reformed Dogmatics*. 4 vols. Edited by J. Bolt. Translated by J. Vriend. Grand Rapids: Baker Academic, 2008.

Beale, G. K. *The Book of Revelation: A Commentary on the Greek Text*. Grand Rapids: Eerdmans, 1999.

Bekkering, Denis J. "From 'Televangelist' to 'Intervangelist': The Emergence of the Streaming Video Preacher." *Journal of Religion and Popular Culture* 23 (2011) 101–7.

Bender Kimlyn J., and D. Stephen Long, eds. *T&T Clark Handbook of Ecclesiology*. London: T. & T. Clark, 2020.

Bender, Kimlyn J. *Karl Barth's Christological Ecclesiology*. Aldershot, UK: Ashgate, 2005.

Berkhof, Hendrikus. *An Introduction to the Study of the Christian Faith*. Translated by Sierd Woudstra. Grand Rapids: Eerdmans, 1979.

Berkouwer, G. C. *The Church*. Translated by James E. Davison. Grand Rapids: Eerdmans, 1976.

Betsy Cooper, Daniel Cox, Rachel Lienesch, and Robert P. Jones. "Exodus: Why Americans Are Leaving Religion—and Why They're Unlikely to Come Back." *PRRI*. 2016. https://www.prri.org/research/prri-rns-poll-nones-atheist-leaving-religion/.

Billings, J. Todd. *Union with Christ: Reframing Theology and Ministry for the Church*. Grand Rapids: Baker, 2011.

Bobrinskoy, Boris. "Holy Spirit." In *Dictionary of the Ecumenical Movement*. Edited by Nicholas Lossky, et al., 470–73. Grand Rapids: Eerdmans, 1991.

Bonhoeffer, Dietrich. *The Communion of Saints: A Dogmatic Inquiry Into the Sociology of the Church*. New York: Harper & Row, 1963.

Bray, G. L. "Communion of Saints." In *New Dictionary of Theology: Historical and Systematic*, edited by Martin Davie et al., 195–96. Downers Grove, IL: IVP, 2016.

Brittain, Christopher. "Why Ecclesiology Cannot Live by Doctrine Alone." *Ecclesial Prac-tices* 1.1 (2014) 5–30.

Bruce, F. F. *The Book of the Acts*. Rev. ed. New International Commentary on the New Testament. Grand Rapids: Eerdmans, 1988.

Brunner, Emil. *Dogmatics*. Vol. 1: *The Christian Doctrine of God*. Translated by Olive Wyon. London: Lutterworth, 1949.

Buijs, Govert. "Tegenwind van Geest." In *De werking van de Heilige Geest in de Europese cultuur en traditie*, 21–43. Kampen: Kok, 2008.

Burridge, Richard A. *Holy Communion in Contagious Times: Celebrating the Eucharist in the Everyday and Online Worlds*. Eugene, OR: Cascade Books, 2022.

Calvin, John. *The Acts of the Apostles 1–13*. Translated by John W. Fraser and W. J. G. McDonald. Edited by David W. Torrance and Thomas F. Torrance. Edinburgh: Oliver & Boyd, 1965.

———. *Institutes of the Christian Religion*. Translated by Ford Lewis Battles. Edited by John T. McNeill. Library of Christian Classics 21. Philadelphia: Westminster, 1960.

———. "The Manner of Celebrating the Lord's Supper." In *John Calvin: Tracts and Treatises on the Doctrine and Worship of the Church*, vol. 2, edited by Thomas F. Torrance, 119–22. Translated by Henry Beveridge. Grand Rapids: Eerdmans, 1956.

Campbell, Constantine R. *Paul and Union with Christ: An Exegetical and Theological Study*. Grand Rapids: Zondervan, 2012.

Campbell, Heidi A., and John Dyer, eds. *Ecclesiology for a Digital Church: Theological Reflections on a New Normal*. London: SCM, 2022.

Campbell, Heidi. "When Churches Discovered the Digital Divide: Overcoming Technological Inaccessibility, Hesitancy & Digital Reluctance During the COVID-19 Pandemic." *Ecclesial Practices* 10 (2023) 36–61.

Campbell, Heidi. *Exploring Religious Communities Online: We are One in the Network*. New York: Lang, 2005.

Carlson, Sandra. "Going into the Laments: The Effects of Church Conflict on Clergy and Their Families." Phd diss., Northern Illinois University, 2010.

Cartledge, Mark J. *Charismatic Glossolalia: An Empirical-Theological Study*. Aldershot, UK: Ashgate, 2002.

———. "Digital Pentecostal Sacramentality: A Theological Reflection on Benny Hinn's 'Zoompartation.'" *Journal of Pentecostal Theology* 34 (2024) 1–19.

———. "Empirical Theology as Theological Netnography: Methodological Considerations." *Journal of Empirical Theology* 35 (2023) 187–204.

———. *Encountering the Spirit: The Charismatic Tradition*. London: Darton, Longman & Todd, 2006.

———. *The Holy Spirit and Public Life: Empowering Ecclesial Praxis*. Lanham, MD: Lexington Books / Fortress Academic, 2022.

———. *The Mediation of the Spirit: Interventions in Practical Theology*. Grand Rapids: Eerdmans, 2015.

———. "Pentecostalism and the Eucharist in a Digital Age: A Theological Reflection on Bill Johnson's Praxis." *Journal of Pentecostal and Charismatic Christianity* 44 (2024): 93–109.

———. "Studying Digital Pentecostalism: Empirical-Theological Hermeneutics, Ethnography, and the Internet." *Pneuma: the Journal of the Society for Pentecostal Studies* 44 (2022) 479–96.

———. "Virtual Mediation of the Holy Spirit: Prospects for Digital Pentecostalism." *PentecoStudies: An Interdisciplinary Journal for Research on the Pentecostal and Charismatic Movements* 21 (2022) 30–50.

Cartledge, Mark J., and Mark A. Jumper, eds. *The Holy Spirit and the Reformation Legacy*. Eugene, OR: Pickwick Publications, 2020.

The Catechism of the Catholic Church for the United States of America. Washington, DC: United States Catholic Conference, 1994.

Chow, Alexander, and Jonas Kurlberg. "Two or Three Gathered Online: Asian and European Responses to COVID-19 and the Digital Church." *Studies in World Christianity* 26 (2020) 298–318.

Clowney, Edmund. *The Church*. Leicester, UK: IVP, 1995.

Coffey, David. "Spirit Christology and the Trinity." In *Advents of the Spirit: An Introduction to the Current Study of Pneumatology*, edited by Bradford E. Hinze and D. Lyle Dabney, 315–38. Milwaukee: Marquette University Press, 2005.

Bibliography

Cole, Graham A. "The Doctrine of the Church: Towards Conceptual Clarification." In *Church, Worship and the Local Congregation*, edited by B. G. Webb, 3–17. Homebush West, NSW: Lancer, 1987.

———. *He Who Gives Life: The Doctrine of the Holy Spirit*. Wheaton, IL: Crossway, 2007.

Comblin, José. *The Holy Spirit and Liberation*. London: Burns & Oates, 1989.

Cotnoir, A. J., and Achille C. Varzi. *Mereology*. Oxford: Oxford University Press, 2021.

Davis, Jim, et al. *The Great Dechurching: Who's Leaving, Why Are They Going, and What Will It Take to Bring Them Back?* Grand Rapids: Zondervan, 2023.

De Boer, Erik. *The Genevan School of the Prophets: The Congregations of the Company of Pastors and Their Influence in 16th Century Europe*. Geneva: Droz, 2012.

Del Colle, Ralph. "Spirit Christology: Dogmatic Issues." In *A Man of the Church: Honoring the Theology, Life, and Witness of Ralph Del Colle*, edited by Michel René Barnes, 3–19. Eugene, OR: Pickwick Publications, 2013.

Delorenzo, L. J. *Work of Love: A Theological Reconstruction of the Communion of Saints*. Notre Dame: University of Notre Dame Press, 2017.

Drescher, Elizabeth. *Tweet if You [Heart] Jesus: Practicing Church in the Digital Reformation*. New York: Morehouse, 2011.

Dulles, Avery. *Models of the Church*. New York: Image Books, 1974.

Dunn, James D. G. *The Epistles to the Colossians and to Philemon: A Commentary on the Greek Text*. Grand Rapids: Eerdmans, 1996.

Emry, P-Y. *L'unite des croyants au cei et sur la terre*. Verbum Caro—Supplement 16 (1962) 1–240.

Endo, Shusaku, and Martin Scorsese. *Silence*. London: Picador, 2016.

Estes, Douglas. *SimChurch: Being the Church in the Virtual World*. Grand Rapids: Zondervan, 2009.

Eugenio, Dick O. *Communion with the Triune God: The Trinitarian Soteriology of T. F. Torrance*. Eugene: Wipf & Stock, 2014.

Farwell, James W., and Martha Moore-Keish, "Sacramental Theology and Worship Technology in Wake of a Pandemic." Pages 478–88 in *T & T Clark Handbook of Sacraments and Sacramentality*. Martha Moore-Keish and James W. Farwell, eds. London: T&T Clark, 2022.

Festinger, Riecken, and Schachter, *When Prophecy Fails. When Prophecy Fails : A Social and Psychological Study of a Modern Group That Predicted the Destruction of the World*. New York: Harper Torchbooks, 1956.

Fiddes, P., B. Haymes, and R. Kidd. *Baptists and the Communion of Saints*. Houston: Baylor University Press, 2014.

Fiddes, Paul S. "Ecclesiology and Ethnography: Two Disciplines, Two Worlds?" In Perspectives on Ecclesiology and Ethnography, edited by Peter Ward, 13–35. Grand Rapids: Eerdmans, 2012.

Fields, C. Ryan. "Ecclesia as Gathering Only? Evaluating the Use of Scripture in Proposals of the 'Knox-Robinson Ecclesiology'" *ATR* 102.1 (2020):49–69.

Flannery, Austin ed. *Vatican Council II: The Basic Sixteen Documents : Constitutions Decrees Declarations : A Completely Revised Translation in Inclusive Language*. Collegeville: Liturgical Press, 2014.

Flett, John G. *Apostolicity: The Ecumenical Question in World Christian Perspective*. Downers Grove: IVP Academic, 2016.

Flett, John G. *The Trinity, Missio Dei, Karl Barth, and the Nature of Christian Community.* Grand Rapids: Eerdmans, 2010.

Foord, M. "We Meet Again! In Heaven or on Earth? Donald Robinson's Ecclesiology." In Donald Robinson. Vol. 3: Appreciation, edited by P. Bolt and M. Thompson, 225–34. Camperdown: Australian Church Record, 2008.

Ford, David F. *Christian Wisdom: Desiring God and Learning in Love.* Cambridge: Cambridge University Press, 2007.

Fowl, Stephen E. *Engaging Scripture: A Model for Theological Interpretation.* Challenges in Contemporary Theology. Oxford University Press: Blackwell, 1998.

Francis, Leslie J. and Andrew Village. "'This Blessed Sacrament of Unity'? Holy Communion, the Pandemic, and the Church of England." *Journal of Empirical Theology* 34 (2021) 87–101.

Frost, Michael, and Alan Hirsch. *The Shaping of Things to Come: Innovation and Mission for the 21st-Century Church.* Grand Rapids: Baker, 2013.

Fung, Ronald Y. K. "Body of Christ." In Dictionary of Paul and His Letters, edited by Gerald F. Hawthorne, et al., 77–78. Downers Grove, IL: IVP, 1993.

Gaurdini, Romano. *The Saints in Christian Life.* Philadelphia: Chilton, 1966.

Gerald F. Hawthorne, Ralph P. Martin, and Daniel G. Reid, eds. *Dictionary of Paul and His Letters.* Downers Grove, IL: IVP, 1993.

Gooch, Paul W. *Partial Knowledge: Philosophical Studies in Paul.* Chicago: Notre Dame University Press, 1987.

Gorman, M. *Participating in Christ: Explorations in Paul's Theology and Spirituality.* Grand Rapids: Baker Academic, 2019.

Green, Chris E. W. *Toward a Pentecostal Theology of the Lord's Supper: Foretasting the Kingdom.* Cleveland: CPT, 2012.

Green, Clifford. "Human Sociality and Christian Community." In *The Cambridge Companion to Dietrich Bonhoeffer*, edited by John W. De Gruchy, 113–33. Cambridge Companions to Religion. Cambridge: Cambridge University Press, 1999.

Greggs, Tom. *Dogmatic Ecclesiology.* Vol. 1: *The Priestly Catholicity of the Church.* Grand Rapids: Baker Academic, 2019.

Gregory, Howard and Elizabeth Welch, et al, *Koinonia: God's Gift and Calling, The Hiroshima Report of the International Reformed–Anglican Dialogue (IRAD).* London, 2020. IRAD-Koinonia-Gods-Gift-and-Calling.pdf (wcrc.ch).

Habets, Myk. *The Anointed Son: A Trinitarian Spirit Christology.* Eugene: Pickwick Publications, 2010.

———. "Prolegomenon: On Starting with the Spirit." In *Third Article Theology: A Pneumatological Dogmatics*, edited by Myk Habets, 1–19. Minneapolis: Fortress, 2016.

Hawthorne, Gerald F. *The Presence and the Power: The Significance of the Holy Spirit in the Life and Ministry of Jesus.* Dallas: Word, 1991.

Hays, Richard B. *The Moral Vision of the New Testament: A Contemporary Introduction to New Testament Ethics.* New York: Harper Collins, 1996.

Healy, Nicholas. *Church, World, and the Christian Life: Practical-Prophetic Ecclesiology.* Cambridge Studies in Christian Doctrine 7. Cambridge: Cambridge University Press, 2000.

Heppe, Heinrich. *Reformed Dogmatics.* Edited by Ernst Bizer. Translated by G. T. Thomson. Eugene, OR: Wipf & Stock, 2007.

Herrick, Robert. "His Letanie, to the Holy Spirit." *ATR* 88.2 (2006) 241–42.

———. "Litany to the Holy Spirit." English Verse. https://englishverse.com/poems/litany_to_the_holy_spirit.

Higton, Mike. *Christian Doctrine*. London: SCM, 2008.

Hill, Wesley. "Apocalyptic Theology." In *The New Cambridge Companion to Christian Doctrine*, edited by Michael Allen, 315–29. Cambridge Companions to Religion. Cambridge: Cambridge University Press, 2022.

Hirsch, Alan. *The Forgotten Ways: Reactivating Apostolic Movements*. Grand Rapids: Baker, 2016.

Holwerda, David E. "Suffering Witnesses—to What End? A Sermon on Revelation 11:1–14." *Calvin Theological Journal* 41 (2006) 127–32.

Hopko, Thomas. "The Orthodox Faith." Orthodox Church in America. 1981. https://www.oca.org/orthodoxy/the-orthodox-faith.

Horton, Michael. *Rediscovering the Holy Spirit: God's Perfecting Presence in Creation, Redemption, and Everyday Life*. Grand Rapids: Zondervan, 2017.

Hunsinger, George. *How to Read Karl Barth: The Shape of His Theology*. Oxford: Oxford University Press, 1991.

Hutchings, Tim. *Creating Church Online: Ritual, Community and New Media*. London: Routledge, 2017.

Irenaeus. *Against Heresies*. https://www.newadvent.org/fathers/0103.htm.

Irenaeus. *Demonstration of the Apostolic Preaching*. Translated by John Behr. Popular Patristics 17. Crestwood, NY: St. Vladimir's Seminary Press, 1997.

John Paul II, Pope. *Dominum et vivificantem* (18 May 1986). https://www.vatican.va/content/john-paul-ii/en/encyclicals/documents/hf_jp-ii_enc_18051986_dominum-et-vivificantem.html#-7A.

Johnson, Elizabeth A. *Friends of God and Prophets*. New York: Continuum, 1998.

Johnson, Luke Timothy. *The Acts of the Apostles*. Sacra Pagina 5. Collegeville, MN: Liturgical, 1992.

———. *Living Jesus: Learning the Heart of the Gospel*. San Francisco: HarperSanFrancisco, 1998.

———. *Scripture & Discernment: Decision-Making in the Church*. Nashville: Abingdon, 1996.

Johnson, M. P. *One with Christ: An Evangelical Theology of Salvation*. Wheaton, IL: Crossway, 2013

Jüngel, Eberhard. *Unterwegs Zur Sache: Theologische Erorterungen I*. Tübingen: Mohr Siebeck, 1972.

Kaiser, Christopher B. "Climbing Jacob's Ladder: John Calvin and the Early Church on our Eucharistic Ascent to Heaven." *SJT* 56 (2003) 247–67.

Kärkkäinen, Veli-Matti. "David's Sling: The Promise and the Problem of Pentecostal Theology Today: A Response to D. Lyle Dabney." *Pneuma* 23 (2001) 147–52.

———. *Toward a Pneumatological Theology: Pentecostal and Ecumenical Perspectives on Ecclesiology, Soteriology, and Theology of Mission*. Lanham: University Press of America, 2002.

Keesmat, Sylvia. "Welcoming in the Gentiles: A Biblical Model for Decision Making." In *Living Together in the Church: Including Our Differences*, edited by Greig S. Dunn and Chris Ambidge, 30–48. Toronto: Anglican Book Centre, 2004.

Kehl, Medard. *Die Kirche: Eine katholische Ekklesiologie*. Würzburg, Echter, 1992/2001.

Knox, D. B. "The Church and the Denominations." *RTR* 23.2 (1964) 44–53.

———. "The Church and the People of God in the Old Testament." *RTR* 10.1 (1951) 12–20.

———. "The Church, the Churches and the Denominations of the Churches." *RTR* 48.1 (1989) 15–25.

———. "Demythologising the Church." *RTR* 32.2 (1973) 48–55.

Kristanto, Billy. *Ecclesiology in Reformed Perspective*. Eugene, OR: Pickwick Publications, 2022.

Kruijthoff, Dirk. "Healing after Prayer: An Interdisciplinary Case Study." PhD diss., Vrije Universiteit Amsterdam, 2023.

Kuhn, Chase R. *The Ecclesiology of Donald Robinson and D. Broughton Knox: Exposition, Analysis, and Theological Evaluation*. Eugene, OR: Wipf & Stock, 2017.

Küng, Hans. *The Church*. Translated Ray and Rosaleen Ockenden. London: Sheed & Ward, 1967.

Lamirande, Emilien. "The History of a Formula." In *The Communion of Saints*, 15–38. Translated by A. Manson. New York: Hawthorn, 1963.

Lane, Anthony N. S. "Was Calvin a Crypto-Zwinglian?" In *Adaptations of Calvinism in Reformation Europe: Essays in Honour of Brian G. Armstrong*, edited by Mack P. Hodt, 21–41. Aldershot, UK: Ashgate, 2007.

Levering, Matthew. *Engaging the Doctrine of the Holy Spirit: Love and Gift in the Trinity and the Church*. Grand Rapids: Baker Academic, 2016.

Lewis, C. S. *Prayer: Letters to Malcolm*. London: Fount Paperbacks, 1964.

Liston, Gregory J. *The Anointed Church: Toward a Third Article Ecclesiology*. Minneapolis: Fortress, 2015.

———. "A 'Chalcedonian' Spirit Christology." *Irish Theological Quarterly* 81 (2016) 74–93.

———. *Kingdom Come: An Eschatological Third Article Ecclesiology*. London: T. & T. Clark, 2022.

———. "Spirit, Church and Mission: Toward a Third Article Theology of Ecclesial Mission." *Evangelical Quarterly* 92 (2021) 21–38.

Locher, Gottfried W. *Zwingli's Thought: New Perspectives*. Translated by Milton Aylor and Stuart Casson. Studies in the History of Christian Thought 25. Leiden: Brill, 1981.

Lord, Andy A. "Theology of Sung Worship." In *Scripting Pentecost: A Study of Pentecostals, Worship and Liturgy*, edited by Mark J. Cartledge and A. J. Swoboda, 84–93. Explorations in Practical, Pastoral, and Empirical Theology. London: Routledge, 2017.

Loudovikos, Nikolaos. *Church in the Making: An Apophatic Ecclesiology of Consubstantiality*. Translated by Norman Russell. St. Vladimir's Seminary Press, 2015.

Lubac, Henri de. *Catholicism: Christ and the Common Destiny of Man*. Translated by Lancelot C. Sheppard and Elizabeth Englund. San Franciso: Ignatius, 1988.

Luther, Martin. *Luther's Works*. Vol. 2: *Lectures on Genesis, Chapters 6–14*. Edited by Jaroslav Pelikan and Daniel E. Poellot. Translated by George V. Schick. St. Louis: Concordia, 1960.

Mabry, M. Adam. "Christotelic Pneumatology." PhD diss., University of Aberdeen, 2023.

Macchia, Frank D. "Spirit Baptism: Initiation in the Fullness of God's Promises." In *The Routledge Handbook of Pentecostal Theology*, edited by Wolfgang Vondey, 247–56. Routledge Handbooks in Theology. London: Routledge, 2020.

———. *The Spirit-Baptized Church: A Dogmatic Inquiry*. T&T Clark Systematic Pentecostal and Charismatic Theology. London: T. & T. Clark, 2020.

Marthaler, Berard. *The Creed: The Apostolic Faith in Contemporary Theology*, 3rd rev. ed. New London: Twenty-Third, 2007.

Martin, Lee Roy. "Introduction." In *Toward a Pentecostal Theology of Preaching*, edited by Lee Roy Martin, 1–16. Cleveland: CPT, 2015.

Maruyama, Tadataka. *Calvin's Ecclesiology: A Study in the History of Doctrine*. Grand Rapids: Eerdmans, 2022.

McBrien, Richard. *Church: the Continuing Quest*. Mahwah, NJ: Paulist, 1970.

McDonnell, Kilian, OSB. *John Calvin, the Church, and the Eucharist*. Princeton: Princeton University Press, 1967.

———. "A Response to D. Lyle Dabney." In *Advents of the Spirit: An Introduction to the Current Study of Pneumatology*, edited by Bradford E. Hinze and D. Lyle Dabney, 262–64. Milwaukee: Marquette University Press, 2005.

Moltmann, Jürgen. *Church in the Power of the Holy Spirit*. Translated by Margaret Kohl. London: SCM, 1975.

Mulder, Sjoerd. *The Turn to The Church in The Twentieth and Twenty-First Centuries: A Promising Ecclesiology*. London: Routledge, 2022.

Muller, Richard A. *Post-Reformation Reformed Dogmatics*. Vol. 4: *The Triunity of God*. Grand Rapids: Baker Academic, 2003.

Murray, John. *Redemption: Accomplished and Applied*. Rev ed. Grand Rapids: Eerdmans, 2015,

Niesel, Wilhelm. *The Theology of Calvin*. Translated by Harold Knight. Grand Rapids: Baker, 1980. Originally published as *Die Theologie Calvins*. Munich: Kaiser, 1938.

Nimmo, Paul T. "A Certain Unity of the Church." *Journal of Biblical and Theological Studies* 10.1 (2025).

———. "The Sanctification of the Church: Contemplating the Progress of the People of God." In *Confessing the Church*, edited by Oliver D. Crisp and Fred Sanders, 21–40. Grand Rapids: Zondervan Academic, 2024.

Pannenberg, Wolfhart. *The Church*. Louisville: Westminster John Knox, 1983.

———. *Systematic Theology*. Volume III. Geoffrey W. Bromiley, trans. Grand Rapids: Eerdmans, 1998.

Parker, T.H.L. *Calvin: An Introduction to His Thought*. London: Continuum, 1995.

Pauw, Amy Plantinga. *Church in Ordinary Time: A Wisdom Ecclesiology*. Grand Rapids: Eerdmans, 2017.

Peterson, David. *The Acts of the Apostles*. Pillar New Testament Commentary. Grand Rapids: Eerdmans, 2009.

Peterson, Eugene. *Practise Resurrection*. London: Hodder & Stoughton, 2010.

Pew Research Center. "America's Changing Religious Landscape." May 12, 2015 https://www.pewresearch.org/wp-content/uploads/sites/20/2015/05/RLS-08-26-full-report.pdf.

Pew Research Center. "Modeling the Future of Religion in America." September, 2022. https://www.pewresearch.org/wp-content/uploads/sites/20/2022/09/US-Religious-Projections_FOR-PRODUCTION-9.13.22.pdf.

Bibliography

Quillen, Ethan Gjerset. "The Great American Disappointment: An Introduction to the Great Disappointment Theory as a Way to Explain the Unique Evolutionary Processes of Socially-Guided Religion by Means of American Civil Religion." PhD diss., Baylor University, 2010. http://hdl.handle.net/2104/7944.

Rabens, Volker. *The Holy Spirit and Ethics in Paul: Transformation and Empowering for Religious-Ethical Life.* 2nd ed. Minneapolis: Fortress, 2103.

Radner, Ephraim. *A Brutal Unity: The Spiritual Politics of the Christian Church.* Waco: Baylor University Press, 2012.

———. "The Holy Spirit and Unity." *IJST* 16 (2014) 207–220.

———. *A Profound Ignorance: Modern Pneumatology and Its Anti-Modern Redemption.* Waco: Baylor University Press, 2019.

Ralston, Joshua. "Preaching Makes the Church: Recovering a Missing Ecclesial Mark." In *John Calvin's Ecclesiology: Ecumenical Perspectives,* edited by Gerard Mannion and Eduardus Van der Borght, 124–42. London: T. & T. Clark, 2011.

Ridderbos, Herman N. *Paul: An Outline of His Theology.* Translated by John Richard de Witt. Grand Rapids: Eerdmans, 1975.

Robinson, Donald. "The Church in the New Testament." *St Mark's Review* 17 (1959) 4–14.

———. *The Church of God: Its Form and Unity.* Punchbowl: Jordan Books, 1965.

———. "The Church Revisited: An Autobiographical Fragment." *RTR* 48.1 (1989) 4–14.

———. *Donald Robinson: Selected Works.* Vol. 1. Edited by P. G. Bolt and M. Thompson. Camperdown: Australian Church Record, 2008.

Rogers, Eugene F. *Sexuality and the Christian Body: Their Way into the Triune God.* Challenges in Contemporary Theology. Oxford: Blackwell, 1999.

Sánchez M., Leopoldo A. *T&T Clark Introduction to Spirit Christology.* London: T. & T. Clark, 2021.

Schillebeeckx, Edward. *Church: The Human Story of God.* Translated by John Bowden. London: SCM, 1993.

Schmidt, Katherine G. *Virtual Communion: Theology of the Internet and the Catholic Sacramental Imagination.* Lanham, MD: Lexington / Fortress Academic, 2020.

Schnackenburg, Rudolf. *Der Brief an die Epheser.* Evangelisch-katholischer Kommentar zum Neuen Testament. Neukirchen-Vluyn: Neukirchener, 1982.

Schwöbel, Christoph. "The Creature of the Word: Recovering the Ecclesiology of the Reformers." In *On Being the Church: Essays on the Christian Community,* edited by Colin E. Gunton and Daniel W. Hardy, 110–55. London: T. & T. Clark, 1989.

Shchotkina, Kateryna. "War: How the Relationship of Ukrainians with God and the Church Has Changed." RISU (June 2023). https://risu.ua/en/war-how-the-relationship-of-ukrainians-with-god-and-the-church-has-changed_n139943.

Slade, Darren, et al. "Percentage of U.S. Adults Suffering from Religious Trauma: A Sociological Study." *Socio-Historical Examination of Religion and Ministry* 15.1 (2023) 1–26.

Small, Joseph. *Flawed Church, Faithful God: A Reformed Ecclesiology for the Real World.* Grand Rapids: Eerdmans, 2018.

Soujeole, Benoit-Dominique de la. *Introduction to the Mystery of the Church.* Thomistic Ressourcement Series. Washington, DC: Catholic University of America Press, 2016.

Bibliography

Spadaro, Antonio. *Cybertheology: Thinking Christianity in the Era of the Internet.* New York: Fordham University Press, 2014.

Studebaker, Steven M. *From Pentecost to the Triune God: A Pentecostal Trinitarian Theology.* Grand Rapids: Eerdmans, 2012.

Synopsis Purioris Theologiae. Vol. 1: *Disputations 1–23.* Edited by Roelf te Velde, translated by Riemer A. Faber. Studies in Medieval and Reformation Traditions 187. Leiden: Brill, 2015.

Tanner, Kathryn. *Christ the Key.* Current Issues in Theology. Cambridge: Cambridge University Press, 2010.

Teer, T. J. S. "Inseparable Operation, Trinitarian Missions and the Necessity of a Christological Pneumatology." *JTS* n.s. 72 (2021) 337–61.

Thompson, Deanna A. *The Virtual Body of Christ in a Suffering World.* Nashville: Abingdon, 2016.

Tomberlin, Daniel. *Pentecostal Sacraments: Encountering God at the Altar.* Cleveland: Center for Pentecostal Leadership and Care, Pentecostal Theological Seminary, 2010.

Torrance, Thomas F. "Atonement and the Oneness of the Church." *SJT* 7 (1954) 245–69.

———. *Atonement: The Person and Work of Christ.* Downers Grove, IL: IVP, 2009.

———. *Incarnation: The Person and Life of Christ.* Downers Grove, IL: IVP, 2008.

———. "The Modern Eschatological Debate." *Evangelical Quarterly* 25 (1953) 45–54, 94–106, 167–78, 224–32.

———. *Royal Priesthood: A Theology of Ordained Ministry.* Edinburgh: T. & T. Clark, 1993.

———. *Space, Time and Resurrection.* Edinburgh: T. & T. Clark, 1976.

Trogdon, Kelly; D. Gene Witmer. "Full and Partial Grounding." *JAPA* 7 (2021) 252–271.

Trozzo, Eric, et al., eds. *Communion of Saints in Context.* Oxford: Regnum, 2020.

Turner, Max. *Power from on High: The Spirit in Israel's Restoration and Witness in Luke-Acts.* Journal of Pentecostal Theology Supplement Series 9. Sheffield: Sheffield Academic, 1996.

Turretin, Francis. *Institutes of Elenctic Theology.* 3 vols. Edited by James T. Dennison Jr. Translated by George Musgrave Giger. Phillipsburg, NJ: P&R, 1992–1997.

Tylenda, Joseph N. "Calvin and Christ's Presence in the Supper—True or Real." *SJT* 27 (1974) 65–75.

United Nation Security Council Meeting Coverage. "Over 115 Holy Sites Damaged in Ukraine Since Start of Russian Invasion, Top UN Official Tells Security Council, Urging Respect for Religious Freedom." SC/15366, 26 July 2023. https://press.un.org/en/2023/sc15366.doc.htm.

Ursinus, Zacharias. *Commentary on the Heidelberg Catechism.* Translated by G. W. Williard. Cincinnati: Bucher, 1851.

Van der Kooi, Cornelis. *This Incredibly Benevolent Force: The Holy Spirit in Reformed Theology and Spirituality.* Grand Rapids: Eerdmans, 2018.

———. *Tegenwoordigheid van Geest: Verkenningen op het gebied van de leer van de Heilige Geest.* Kampen: Kok, 2006.

Van der Kooi, Cornelis, and Gijsbert van den Brink. *Christian Dogmatics: An Introduction.* Translated by Reinder Bruinsma with James D. Bratt. Grand Rapids: Eerdmans, 2017.

Bibliography

van Mastricht, Petrus. *Theoretical-Practical Theology*. Vol. 2: *Faith in the Triune God*. Edited by Joel R. Beeke. Translated by Todd M. Rester. Grand Rapids: Reformation Heritage Books, 2019.

Van Oorschot, Frederike. "Public Theology Facing Digital Spaces: Public Theology, Digital Theology and Changing Spaces for Theological Reasoning." *International Journal of Public Theology* 16 (2022) 55–73.

Venema, Cornelius. *The Promise of the Future*. Edinburgh: Banner of Truth, 2000.

Village, Andrew. "Attitude toward Virtual Communion in Relation to Church Tradition during the COVID-19 Pandemic in the United Kingdom." *Journal of Empirical Theology* 35 (2022) 95–117.

Visser 't Hooft, W. A., ed. *The New Delhi Report: The Third Assembly of The World Council of Churches 1961*. London: SCM, 1962. https://www.oikoumene.org/resources/documents/new-delhi-statement-on-unity.

Volf, Miroslav. *After Our Likeness: The Church as the Image of the Trinity*. Grand Rapids: Eerdmans, 1998.

Vondey, Wolfgang. "Pentecostal Sacramentality and the Theology of the Altar." In *Scripting Pentecost: A Study of Pentecostals, Worship and Liturgy*, edited by Mark J. Cartledge and A. J. Swoboda, 94–107. London: Routledge, 2017. Republished in Vondy, *The Liturgy of the Gospel: Theological Hermeneutics in Pentecostal Perspective*, 144–59. Word and Spirit. Eugene, OR: Cascade Books, 2025.

Ward, Peter, ed. *Perspectives on Ecclesiology and Ethnography*. Grand Rapids: Eerdmans, 2016.

Webster, John. *Holiness*. London: SCM, 2003.

———. *Holy Scripture: A Dogmatic Sketch*. Cambridge: Cambridge University Press, 2003.

———. "On Evangelical Ecclesiology." *Ecclesiology* 1.1 (2004) 9–35.

———. "The 'Self-Organizing' Power of the Gospel: Episcopacy and Community Formation." In *Word and Church: Essays in Church Dogmatics*, edited by Richard Longenecker, 191–210. New York: T. & T. Clark, 2001.

Weinandy, Thomas. *The Father's Spirit of Sonship: Reconceiving the Trinity*. Edinburgh: T. & T. Clark, 1995.

Welker, Michael. *God the Revealed: Christology*. Translated by Douglas W. Stott. Grand Rapids: Eerdmans, 2013.

White, A. W. "Gathered Together: The Grammar of 'Church' from Acts." *Presbyterion* 45.2 (2019) 60–79.

Wilson, Walter P. *The Internet Church*. Nashville: Word, 2000.

Wise, Justin. *The Social Church: A Theology of Digital Communication*. Chicago: Moody, 2014.

Wolterstorff, Nicholas. *Reason Within the Bounds of Religion*. Grand Rapids: Eerdmans, 1976.

Wood, S. "Sanctam Ecclesiam Catholicam." In *Exploring and Proclaiming the Apostles' Creed*, edited by Roger Van Harn, 219–32. Grand Rapids: Eerdmans, 2004.

Zahl, Simeon. *The Holy Spirit and Christian Experience*. Oxford: Oxford University Press, 2020.

Zizioulas, John D. *Being as Communion: Studies in Personhood and the Church*. Crestwood, NY: St. Vladimir's Seminary Press, 1985.

Zwingli, Huldreich. "An Account of the Faith." In *The Latin Works of Huldreich Zwingli*, edited by William John Hinke, 2:33–61. Translated by Henry Preble. Philadelphia: Heidelberg, 1922.

Index

Abraham's offspring, 27
Acts, 13, 80
Acts 15, viii, 24
adoption, 93
adoptionism, 54–55
agapic revolution, 93
agent of darkness, the church as, 78
"agreeable year of the Lord," Jesus announcing, 97
Allen, Michael, viii
American Orthodox catechism, 105
Amos, prophecy of, viii
Anglican Church of Australia, 2
Anglican tradition, on unity, 101
anointing, 89, 91–94
apostles, x, 80, 81, 82–83
Apostles' Creed, on holiness, 74n2
apostolic teaching, continuity of, 81n29
apostolic witness, xi
apostolicity, of the church, 73–88
appropriations, doctrine of, 129
ascension of Christ, the church and, 129
atheism, rise of, 104
Augsburg Confession (Article VII), on holiness, 74n2
Augustine, 37, 114
authority, of the apostles, 80
Avis, as a practical theologian, 130

baptism, 92, 130
Baptism of the Holy Spirit, Pentecostal doctrine of, 40

Barmen Declaration, 95n6
Barth, Karl
  on the apostles, 82
  on baptism, 92
  on a Christological Ecclesiology, 55
  on Christ's eschatological ministry, 64
  on the church as holy and unholy, 78
  on the correlation between Christ and the church, 56
  on no human control over the Holy Spirit, 86
  on the work of the Spirit in the church, ix
Bavinck, Herman, 8–9, 79
Beale, G. K., 17
"bearing fruit," language found in Calvin explicitly, 43
"being in Christ" Ecclesiology, preferring, 117
being together, enjoying in the Eucharist, 66
Belgic Confession (Article 27), on holiness, 74n2
beliefs, background, 60
believers
  access to God in the heavenly temple, 16
  bound to one another in one body of Christ, 12
  common membership in the people of God, 4n13

believers (continued)
    different gifts to, 14
    transformed by the Spirit, 9n34
Berkhof, Hendrikus, 81
Berkouwer, G. C., 11, 12–13, 85–86, 86n43
biblical prophecy, pouring out of the Holy Spirit as, 41
blaming others, 103
Bobrinskoy, Boris, 59
"body," metaphor of, 4
body of Christ, xiii, 12, 14, 101, 120
Bonhoeffer, Dietrich, 13
bread and wine, consecration of, 48n62
breathing, referring to all the roles of the Spirit, 70, 70n42
Brittain, Christopher, 116n1
broadcast church, 44
"brood of vipers," church as, 78
Brunner, Emil, 75

Calvin, John
    on avoiding Institutionalism, 127
    on Christ's kingship, 91
    on the church, 35, 44–45, 128
    ecclesiology of, viii, 35, 50
    on the Holy Spirit, 38
    referencing affectivity in relation to the sacraments, 46
    on the sacraments, 37
    on the Trinity, 8n30
    on union, 118
Campbell, Heidi, 43–44
Cartledge, Mark J., viii
Catholic Catechism, 6
Catholic Church, gospel moved by the authority of, 116
Catholic developments, of ecclesiology, 117
Catholic ecclesiology, in the wake of the Second Vatican Council, 118–23
catholic marks, of the church, 41n45
Catholic view, on fellowship, 16
Catholicism (De Lubac), 119
"catholicity," Creedal affirmations of, 106
celebration, in Pentecostal and charismatic worship, 45

cessationism, 94
Chalcedonian Christology, ix
charism, 94
Charismatic Renewal movement, 33–34
Children's Crusade of 1212, 102
Christ. *See also* Jesus; the Son
    created unity in himself, 11
    as head of both church and cosmos, 122
    Holy Spirit fulfilling the mediating work of, 127
    minimizing by prioritizing the Spirit, 71
    mission of/, 29
    ordained by God the Father, and anointed with the Holy Spirit, 90
    presence of, 66
    reigning by his Word alone, 36
    role of the Spirit in, 54–58
    union with, 7
Christian unity, 11, 101, 111
Christianity, digital expressions of, 34
Christians
    called to be holy as already sanctified, 77
    counted as saints in Christ, 79
    as ready to leave churches, 103–4
    requiring lifelong exercise, 92
    sharing in Christ's anointing, 90–91
Christological ecclesiology, 117
Christotelic impetus, marking the Church, ix
the church
    as an act of God, 127
    apostolicity of, x, 79–83
    approaching from below, 116
    around the world, 36
    beginning in chapter 2 of Acts, 127
    believing given all its scandals and mediocrity, 116
    as both holy and sinful, 78
    as broker or the instrument of grace, 120
    as Christ's body, 55
    as communion of the saints, vii
    as a community vivified by the Spirit, 84
    considering eschatologically, x

Index

COVID-19 pandemic and, 34, 44, 49
as a co-worker with God, xiii, 130
described, 36n13, 57
as distinct and identical from mission, 68
drawing the world to Christ, x, 69
enacted by God through the Spirit, xiii–xiv
existing for God and the world, xiii
existing in a sinful world, 77
failure and sinfulness of, xiv
history of taken seriously, 99–114
holiness and apostolicity of, xi
holiness of, 74–79, 116n1
as humans united by the Spirit to Christ, 57
judging between false and true, 36
looking at through the Spirit, 59
looking through and seeing Christ there, 58
measuring the unity of, 100–101
members of, 3, 36
and mission, 68
nature of, 57
needing comforting, 110
as one, holy, catholic and apostolic, xii
open to the Word's directing, 125
as part of the third article, 130
as people gathered to and by Christ, 2
pointing towards the kingdom, xiii, 124
practicing scriptural discernment, 31
prioritising the Spirit in, 52–72
pursuing penance and renewal at all times, 121
receiving the Spirit, xi
as referred to by Calvin, 39
referring to assembling and fellowship, 3n7
revealing Christ to the world, 58
as risen with Christ, 119
as a rubric for analysis, 22
as a sacrament, 124
as a sacramental sign representing Jesus, 125
scandals and abuses in, 74
shared worship of the earthly and heavenly, 16
sharing in heavenly worship, 17
as a society of baptised believers, 119
the Son embodied in, ix
as the Spirit enabled union of the incarnate Christ, ix
the Spirit guiding, viii
the Spirit speaking to, 10
as the Spirit's mereological promise and direction, 109
as where Christ is, 2
will not fail, 77
The Church (Pannenberg), 125
Church Dogmatics (Barth), 64
Church in the Power of the Holy Spirit (Moltmann), 123
church leadership, attitude on, 72
church life, experiences of creating unity in Christ, 13
church membership, Knox's comments on, 3
church militant, 16, 109
Church of England in Australia, 3n6
church services and meetings, online, 34
circumcision, viii, 25
climate change, 95
Clowney, Edmund, 118
coffee, post-service, 45
Coffey, David, 61
cognitive dissonance, 99, 102, 103
Comblin, Jose, 119
comfort, forms of for the church, 110
coming kingdom, 54, 70–71
communio sanctorum, 5–6, 77
communion of the saints, vii, 1–19, 74
communion service, 67
community
  access to the Fatherhood of the Father, 63
  characteristics of, 42
  church as, 4, 57
  participation in the Spirit creating, 14
  of praise, 43
  progress of, 96

Index

complementarity, of *Logos* and Spirit Christologies, 55n8
confession, 83, 87
confirmation, as a devaluation of baptism, 39
congregational singing, proclaiming the mighty acts of God, 97
congregationalism of the Robinson-Knox view, 18
congregations, 2, 18
consulting, as similar to pastoring, 52–53
control belief
  defined, 59–60
  ecclesiological understanding as, 71
  eschatology as, 63
  mission as, 69
conversion practices, in Evangelicalism and Pentecostalism, 47
corporeal presence, Calvin not believing in, 48n63
cosmic renewal, church as the prototype of, xiii
Council. *See* Jerusalem Council
counsel, of God, 96
covenant community, of the new covenant, 4n11
covenant loyalty, repetition of the old nature of, 28
covenant relationship, apostolic continuity in, 81
covenants, of the holy God with people, 76
COVID-19 pandemic, changes to church life, 34
Cranmer, Thomas, 33
creation and re-creation, relationship of, 26–28
creation of the world, work of the Spirit and, 84
Critical Theory, spirit of, 123
the cross, 64, 121
cultural conditions, impacting the church, 20
Cyprian, 116

Dabney, on Third Article Theology, 72
data belief, 59, 60, 69
Day of Pentecost. *See* Pentecost
de la Soujeole, B. D., 123
de Lubac, Henri, dislike of ecclesiologies with Christ as supernature, 118
decisions
  attention to in Acts 15, 21
  based on grasping only a "part" of what is true, 108
Deism, rise of, 104
democratisation, *Lumen Gentium* as, 119
Demonstration of the Apostolic Preaching (Irenaeus), 24
"a den of robbers," church as, 78
denominations
  assisting fellowship between congregations, 2
  Christians changing, 104
  Robinson-Knox claims about, 3
  in Ukraine, 106
desacralization, of all forms of leadership, 92
Deus decernens, in Christ and his life, 96
dialogical approach, to Third Article Theology, 60
digital church, ix, 33–51
digital ecclesial expression, 43–49
digital platform, ix
disappointment
  with the church, 99
  as major for American religious "evolution," 102n5
discernment, 21, 28, 30, 31
disciples, at Pentecost, 40
disruptive dissonance, the Spirit stabilizing, 109
dissent, meaning sin, 122
distinctiveness, relative to cultures, 22n15
disunity, 110, 113
divinity, of Jesus, 64
division
  Church engaging its, 109–10
  as a coalescing symbol, 104
doctrinal conformity, 100
Dogmatic Ecclesiology (Greggs), xiii, 127
Dominum et vivificantem (John Paul II), xii, 119, 121

Index

doxological mission, expression of, 42
doxology, 42n51, 43
drunkenness, glossolalic speech not associated with, 41
Dyer, John, 44

earthly church, as "multiform" and "intermittent," 3
Easter, marking a new initiative by the Father, 90
Eastern Orthodoxy, 105, 117
ecclesia, study of the word, 2
ecclesia Dei, affirming with *missio Dei*, 69
ecclesial discernment, 20–23, 31–32
ecclesial dissonance, pressures of, 103
ecclesial division, *laissez faire* approach to, 101
ecclesial mission, 68
ecclesial occasionalism, 3, 18
ecclesial politics, disillusionment with, 104
ecclesial survival, goods of, 110, 111
ecclesial unity, 100, 105, 113
ecclesiological gaze, on the Pentecostal narrative, 40
ecclesiological pneumatology, 115–30
ecclesiology
 connection between Pentecost and the church in Calvin's, 39
 getting a truly coherent understanding of, 60
 informing mission, 69
 in light of the doctrine of the Holy Spirit, 115–30
 relationship with missiology, 67
 Robinson-Knox, 1–5
ecclesio-pneumatic dissonance, 105
economic Trinity, doctrine of, 129
ecstasy, 98
ecumenical movement, at its zenith, 2
Edinburgh Dogmatics Conference 2023, vii
ekklesia, defining using "kingdom of God," 123
the elect, united to Christ, 35
elements, of the Holy Spirit, 112
Elliot, Mark W., xii
Emmaus Road, Luke's account of, 26

end to be beginning, Old and New Testaments relating, 23
endurance, the Spirit enabling, xii
"endurance to the end," capacity to sustain, 111
Ephesians (Epistle to), 121–22
epiclesis, continued need for, 129
eschatological aspect, of the Spirit, xiv
eschatological Christian identity, xi, 92
eschatological community, church as, 4n11
eschatological orientation, of participation in the Spirit, 17–18
eschatological pneumatology, 125
eschatological Spirit, the church and, 89–98
eschatology, as a vantage point, 63–67
eschaton, 77–78, 89–90, 91
eternity, for Torrance, 64
ethical imperative, for the people of God to be holy, 76
ethical teaching, in biblical writings, 25
ethnographic research, into the church, 116
euaggelion, good message, will of God as, 96
Eucharist (Lord's Supper), x, 5, 65–67, 95. *See also* Lord's Supper
Eugenio, Dick O., 65n35
Evangelicals, online home communion and, 48n65
experience, 24, 102
explicit membership, 3
external holiness, as deceitful and doubtful, 78
Ezekiel, 75

faith, xiii, 37, 105–6, 128
faith healers, 94–95
fallen creation, xi, 26
fallen human beings, as essential, 83
families, proclaiming God's truth, 97
the Father. *See also* God
 believing in God as, 116
 forming the Son by the Spirit, 61, 62, 70
 illumining our minds, 38
 presence of, 7

fellowship
  with believers broadly, viii
  of Christ's people, 3, 6n26
  constituting the Christian life, 13
  global, 14–15
  as neither extrinsicist nor monist, 119
  with others gathered online, 49
  with the Spirit, 7
  of the Spirit, 8, 12
  through the online environment, 45
  in words grounded on the Word of God, 18
Festinger, Leon, 102–3
Fiddes, as a practical theologian, 130
filioque, as essential, 29–30
first fruits, notion of founded on "mereological" attitudes, 107
firstborn
  of all creation, 121
  ecclesia of, 2
Flett, John, 82
followers of Jesus, as sinful beings, 83
Fowl, Stephen E., 21, 24
fruits, of the Holy Spirit, 112
fruits and gifts of the Spirit, xi
fullness, claims to ecclesial and pneumatic, 109
fundamentals, determining, 111

gathering
  church marked by, 43
  from dispersed places, 44
Gentiles
  ethical instruction for, viii
  as Gentile believers rather than Israelites, 25
  inclusion of, viii, 24, 29
  redeemed in a new manner, 27
  as unclean by nature, 26
gift(s)
  as functions of God's coming kingdom, 93–94
  of the Holy Spirit, 41, 126
  of love, 9
  as people serving with God's word, 12
  of prophecy, 98

glory, intermediate state of, 16
glossolalia, 40, 94, 98
God. *See also* the Father; Triune God
  directing us to love others, 70
  gave us the Spirit as a guarantee, 107
  holiness of, 74–75
  overidentifying the Church with, 128
  praising in unity and diversity, 40
  as responsible for his church, 72
Gooch, Paul, 108
Good Samaritan, story of, 93
goods of survival, 111
gospel, 26, 88, 116
grace
  acting contrary to nature, 27
  advancing upon nature, viii
  diversity of in one community, 35
  experience of, 93
  of God lifting up the unholy church, 88
  recasting nature as the Spirit illumines, 31
  rejigging, 102
  relating continuously with nature, 28
  of the Spirit, 87
Greggs, Tom
  on the church, xiii, 17–18, 127
  on the communion of saints, 15
  framing the doctrine of the church, 128
  on the Spirit bringing people into fellowship, 14
  wanting a dogmatic ecclesiology, 129
Gregory of Nazianzus, on the Trinity, 8n30
"guarantee," as a mostly modern English word, 106–7

healing, 94–95
Healy, Nicholas, 78
hearers, "cut to the heart" by Peter's Word, 41
hearing of the Word, preached online, 47
hearts and minds, Holy Spirit moving, 46
heavenly assembly, 2
heavenly church, 3
Heidelberg Catechism, xi, 89, 90–91, 92, 96

Index

Heppe, Heinrich, 7
Herrick, Robert, 110
High Priest, Jesus as, 90
Hirsch, Alan, 68n40
historical continuity, participation in the Spirit giving, 15
history, reaction to as unconscious, 102
holiness
    of the church, 74–79
    identifying the true Church, x
Holwerda, David E., 69
holy assemblies, of the church, 35–36
Holy Communion, announcing Christ's death in, 96n7
holy community, of the church, 76
Holy One of God, Jesus as, 75
Holy Spirit
    for all people in many places, 43
    as the basis for evangelism and incorporation, 42
    as a bridge builder, 98
    Calvin's ecclesiology and, 35–39
    came upon all at Pentecost, 40
    on the church as the eucharistic community, 41n46
    considered by Calvin as a kind of instrument, 39
    descending upon Jesus at his baptism, 75
    digital church and, 33–51
    discerning, 20–32
    dwelling in believers, 125–26
    enabling the church to cross physical-digital boundaries, 49
    enabling the church to live in sin and fracture, xii
    enlightening believers' minds, 36
    failure to understand, 105
    as the "fire from heaven," 120
    first fruits or deposit connotations, 107
    functions of, 39
    given to survive ecclesial dissonance, 113
    holding together the holiness of the unholy Church, x
    as Holy Spirit of the Church and the Spirit of Christ or God as third person, 29, 115–30
    indwelling in hearts, 121
    inner grace of, 38
    intense experience of by worshippers, 45
    leading the church and the world, 71
    as a missionary and transformative mode, 126
    Pentecostal emphasis on the power of, 117
    presence of as the agent of unity, 101
    receiving the gift of, 42
    representing different languages, cultures, and people, 40
    sustaining and maturing believers, viii
    teaching everything, and reminding of all that Jesus has said, 84
    tied to what is "partial" in this life, 107
    uniting the triune God in covenant with his people, 41
    visible mission of, 29
    work of, 39, 83–87
home experience, of preaching, 46
home meetings, including the Lord's Supper, 42
How to Read Karl Barth (Hunsinger), 56n11
human life, progress of, 96
humanity
    of Jesus analogically corresponding to time, 64
    Spirit relating to just as they are, 84–85
    as the starting-point of the visible church, 87
Hunsinger, George, 56
hybrid service, ix, 44, 49

idolatry, Reformation critique of, 6
"illumination of minds," as language found in Calvin, 43
illumination work, of the Spirit, 9
immanent Trinity, doctrine of, 129
Incarnate Son, 28, 29

incarnation, offering an encounter, 10
incompleteness, stabilized in its assured relation to a whole, 108
the indicative, imperative not existing apart from, 13
"indissoluble bond," between the preaching of the Word and the inward illumination of the Spirit, 38
indwelling, of the Spirit, 7
inhabitation
    corporate dimension of, 11n37
    of the Spirit as a unique personal communion, 10
inheritance, Holy Spirit as the guarantee of our, 107
in-person worship event, 45
in-person/digital discontinuities, 49
inscape artists, capturing genuine inner essence, 57–58
inscaping, as a practical skill, 69
inseparable operations, principle of, 8
Institutes (Calvin), 33, 39
institutional church, keeping the machinery running, 53
institutionalism, avoiding, 127
interactive church, described, 44
intertextual exegesis, relationship of old and new, 23–26
inviolable volitional unity, of the Godhead, 30
invisible cause, gleaned from the visible effect, 130
invisible church, 11n37, 128
Irenaeus of Lyons, 24, 102
issues, the church facing a host of, 20

James, viii, 24, 25, 28
Jerusalem Council, 20–23, 25
Jesus. *See also* Christ; the Son
    betrayal of, 96
    healings performed by, 94
    life as a human being, 112
    as only a human or as God himself, 58
    as the only real king, 92
    praying to his "Holy Father," 75
    quoting the words of Isaiah, 97
    on Scripture being fulfilled, 90
    sending the Spirit, 30
    as the Son of God, 90
    on the Spirit, 30, 85
Jews
    fulfilling the Law and the Prophets, 23
    scapegoating of in the Middle Ages, 103
Job, 78
John Paul II, 120
Johnson, Elizabeth A., 5
Johnson, Luke Timothy, viii, 21–23, 25, 28

kairos moment, of the church in the western world, 72
Kärkkäinen, Veli-Matti, 54, 72
kata physin, Gentiles grafted in, 27
Keesmat, Sylvia, 21, 24, 24n19
the kingdom, 65, 66
kingdom of death, passing into the kingdom of life, 91
Kingdom of God, emphasizing, 117
kingdom people, 67
kingly role, of Christ, 65, 91
kite, visualising the Spirit as a, 86
knowing, doctrine of, 129
"knowing in full," 108
Knox, Broughton, 1–5, 1n2
koinonia, as an incorruptible divine "gift," 100–101
koinonia ton agion, in the Greek speaking church, 5
Kooi, Cornelius van der, xi
Küng, Hans, 119, 123

Leiden Synopsis, definition of holiness in, 75
lens, using the Spirit as, 59
Lewis, C. S., on prayer, 63
lex orandi, in Augustine's terms, 119
life of the church, prophetic dimension of, 97
life of worship, affirming a continued shared, 16
Liston, Gregory J., ix
"Litany to the Holy Spirit" (Herrick), 110

Index

lives of others, genuine participation in, 42
"living sacrifice of thankfulness," catechism on, 95
Logos, replacing with the Spirit, 55
Logos Christology, compared to the church, 55–56
Lord's Supper, ix, 48n66. *See also* Eucharist
Lordship of Christ theme, in *Lumen Gentium*, 123
Loudovikos, on ecclesiology, 119
love, as a supreme pneumatic gift, 109
Luke
　on the church, 42–43
　on the selection of apostles, 80
Lumen Gentium, 5, 118, 123, 124
Luther, Martin, 78, 86n46, 125

magisterium, conservative theology of, 119
management consultant, similarities of a senior pastor to, 52–53
marks of the church, 36, 41n45, 50, 129–30
martyrdom, 69, 112
"martyrial" witness (*summartyrei*), of the Spirit, 113
Mastricht, Petrus van, 75–76
maximalists, on the church as pure, xii
McBrien, Richard, 119
McClean, John, vii
McDonnell, Kilian, 59
mediations, other than the Incarnation, 124
medical sciences, sphere of health and illness surrendered to, 94
members of the church
　instability of, 104
　keeping a roll of, 3
　recognising, 36
　unity and diversity of, 43
mercy, of Christ, 95
mereological resolution, of the Spirit, 108–12
mereological work of the Spirit, recognising, xii

mereology, taking in a range of disciplines, 107–8
messiahship, assumptions about, 102
metonymy, "body of Christ" as, 128
minimalists, on the Church in constant repentance, xii–xiii
ministry of the Word, prophetic office in, 97
missio Dei, 68–69
mission
　of the church, 79–83
　at home and overseas, 73
　implications for, 67–71
　mattering to the Spirit, xiv
　pattern of, x
　pneumatological focus on, 54
Models of the Church (Dulles), 118
modesty, the church exercising, 88
Moltmann, Jürgen, xiii, 123, 124, 125
mother, the church functioning as, 35
Mount Zion, 16
Muller, Richard A., 84
Murray, John, 11n36
mystery, participation in the Spirit as, 8–9
mystical union with and participation in Christ, 48

natural theology, of Pannenberg, xiii
nature
　God's grace rebuilding and restoring, viii
　integration of spirit and, 118
New Adam, Christ as, 91
new creation, vii, xiv, 28
new humanity, formed in Christ, 14
New Testament
　as analogous to the Talmud, 21
　attention to the shared life of churches, 14
　on fellowship between congregations, 15
　outpouring of the Spirit as a communal experience, 91
　promise of the eschatological Spirit, 89–90
　as a purer Christianity of an unsullied fountain, 122
　on the visible church, 4

new time, x, 64
new wine, glossolalic speech as the result of, 41
New Zealand, church in suffering, 72
Niceno-Constantinopolitan Creed
   as the basis for assessment of the church, xiii
   the Church in, x
   claiming the church to be "one," 100
   following, xii
   on holiness, 74n2
   holiness and apostolicity confessed in, 74
Nimmo, Paul T., x, 127

occasionalism. *See* ecclesial occasionalism
Old Testament
   foretold a later fulfillment, 23
   on the outpouring of the Spirit, 89
old time, for Torrance, 64
olive tree, metaphor of, 27
online church, 44
online participants, 46, 47
ontological nature, of the church, 68
ontological pneumatology, doctrine of, 129
"opening of hearts," language found in Calvin, 43
ordo salutis, 11, 11n37
Origen, 113
Orthodox Christians, believing in the Church, 105
Orthodox churches, on opposite sides of battle lines, 106
outpouring of the Spirit, 89, 91

pandemic, thrust us into digital interface around worship, 34
Pannenberg, Wolfhart
   on allowing for differences of belief, 125
   on the church's apostolicity, 79, 82, 83
   ecclesiology of focused on the Word, xiii
   on the Spirit's role, 126

para physin ("contrary to nature"), God acting, 27
parallels
   between Christ and the church, 56
   for the role of the Spirit in the life of the church, 58
   between a Spirit Christology and a pneumato-ecclesiology, 57
   between the Trinity and the church, 61
the "part" (*melos*)
   contrasted to "the whole" (*holos*), 108
   suggesting a whole, xii
the partial, movement towards the whole, 111
partialness, fully resolved only in Jesus, 112
participation in the Spirit, 11–12, 17
"participatory ontology," 117
pastoral role, similarity to consulting, 52n1
patience, the Spirit enabling, xii
Paul
   on all gifts coming from the same Spirit, 94
   on death and resurrection, 23
   on God choosing us, 76
   on God demonstrating his own justice, 26
   on the image of a fight, 92
   on the Jew/Gentile issue, 27
   on "knowing in part," 108
   on the ministry of reconciliation, 95–96
   ordering towards unity, 113
   on the relation between part and whole, 113
   on sanctification in Christ Jesus, 76
   sent through Jesus Christ and God the Father, 79
   on the unity of the Spirit, 12
   on "where the Spirit of the Lord is, there is freedom," 121
peace, Christ has proclaimed, 11
Pentecost
   coming of the Spirit on, 11, 121
   event of, 84

as key in the establishment of the
    church, 39–43
  widening focus from, viii
Pentecostal perspectives, Calvinian
    view augmenting, ix
Pentecostalism, study of contemporary,
    33
Pentecostals, on the work of the Holy
    Spirit through digital means, 47
people of God, reconstituted in
    covenantal union, 42
perfecting cause, Spirit as, 16
personal communion, participation in
    the Spirit as, 9–10
*Perspectives on Ecclesiology and
    Ethnography* (Ward), 116
Pesch, O. H., 125
Peter, 22, 42n50
Peterson, Eugene, 57
physical-digital hybridity, life now lived
    in, ix
planetary aliens, communications with
    intelligent, 103
Plantinga Pauw, Amy, 81–82
pneumatic dissonance
  deriving from ecclesial disunity,
    108–9
  negative experience of, 99
  pressures of, 103
  separating from ecclesial, 104–5
  unfolding before our eyes, 106
pneumatic guarantee, xii, 105, 112
pneumatic movement, Christic center
    of, 112
pneumatic partial, suggesting a whole,
    108
pneumatic unity, 105–8, 113
pneumatological discernment, by the
    Jerusalem Council, 21
pneumatological ecclesiology, 50, 129
pneumatology
  articulating sensitive, 50
  connecting different doctrines, 59
  of Ephesians, 122
  facilitating experiential action, 117
  limitations of, 99
  relationship to ecclesiology, 39

polarisation, between maximalist and
    minimalist views, 123
polity, as a feature of the church, 4
power of the Spirit, 38, 41n49, 42n50,
    91, 117, 120
practical theology, writing as a
    systematician and, 33
prayer
  before or after meals, 97
  foundational to the work of
    mission, 88
  healing after, 95
  as like sinking into God's life, 63
  offering to God as a community, 62
  speaking in tongues as a form of, 98
preacher, administering the Word, 97
preaching, 37, 42n51, 46. *See also*
    sermons
Presbyters, as designated ministers, 37
presence, of the Spirit, 8
present era, representing a time of
    mission, 73
pride, Spirit overcoming, 85
priesthood of Christ, xi, 65, 128
priestly dimension, of the threefold
    office, 95–96
progress, involving a questioning of
    authority, 122
progressiveness, of participation in the
    Spirit, 17
properties, of the church, 116, 130
prophecy, response to failed, 103
prophetic dimension, of Christ's one
    office, 96–98
prophetic role, of Christ, 64
Protestants
  account of matters in Ephesians,
    122
  ecclesiologies by Moltmann,
    Pannenberg and Greggs, 117
  ecclesiology as often an
    afterthought, 118
  little attention to various media, 98
  on the Spirit and the church,
    123–30
public worship, online broadcasting
    of, 45
purgatory, 6, 16

purificans, of *Lumen Gentium* 8–9, 121
purity, seeking, 76
purpose of the Father, the Spirit bringing realization of, 7–8

Radner, Ephraim, xi
real presence, theology of, 48
reality, true understanding of, 60
Reason within the Bounds of Religion (Wolterstorff), 59
reconciliation, as a struggle, 95
recovering, experiences of as rare, 95
redemptive mission, of the Spirit, 85
Reformation
  abandoned "one, holy, catholic and apostolic" as distinguishing marks of the church, 129–30
  affirmation of the unity of the church, 7
  challenged Catholic doctrine, 6
  prophetic office in ministry of the Word, 97
Reformed account, of the communion of the saints, 16
Reformed ecclesiology, on digital ecclesial expressions, viii, 35
Reformed theology, vii, 7, 33
Reformed thinking, 100
Reformed-Anglican Dialogue statement, on Koinonia, 100
relationships
  apostolic continuity found in, 81
  forging new online, 49
relics, veneration of rejected, 6
religious claims, dissonance of experience with, 103
repentance, xi, 87
resurrection, bringing life out of death, 85
return and restoration, of divine commitment to covenant promises, 28
revelation, "internalisation" of, 9
Revelation (Book of), 16–17, 75, 80
Ridderbos, Herman N., 13
Riecken, Henry, 102–3
Robinson, Donald, 1–5, 1–2n2
Robinson-Knox ecclesiology, 1–5, 1n1

Rogers, Eugene, 21, 27
roles, of Christ, x, 54–58, 64, 65, 91
rule of Christ, the Church sharing in, xi

Sabbatai Zevi, 102
sacrament(s)
  administered according to Christ's institution, 36
  as an aid to faith, 37
  the church as, 120
  "due" administration of, 47
  fulfilling their office only by the power of the Spirit, 38
  meaning of, 124
  mediation of digitally as contentious, 47
  as "useful aids" to foster and strengthen faith, 35
sacrifices, daily in the temple, 95
saints
  intercession of rejected, 6
  praying for the Church, 16
salvation, 11, 26
sanctification, of the people of God, 76
Schachter, Stanley, 102–3
Schillebeeckx, Edward, xii, 122–23
Schnackenburg, Rudolf, xii, 121, 122
Scripture
  clarifying and constraining this new time, 26
  coincidence of Holy Spirit and church as not at all clear, 106
  describing communion with the Spirit, 9
  employing ordinary language in extraordinary fashion, 32
  interpreting Scripture, 25
  not describing the gift of the Spirit granted to individuals, 11
  reading of in the early church, 113
  the Spirit guiding our reading of, 31
  testimonies to the divine holiness, 74–75
  Trinitarian grammar of, 77
  work of the Spirit strictly bound to, 97

Scripture and Discernment: Decision Making in the Church (Luke Timothy Johnson), 21
Second Helvetic Confession, 74n2, 77n12, 78
Semmelroth, Otto, 125
senior pastor, stints at being, 72
seraphs, in the heavenly temple, 75
sermons. *See also* preaching
  spiritual impact of, 47
sharing, in what God is doing in his church, x
the sign, linked with the Word, 37
Silence (Endo), 111
simul sanctus et peccator, Church as, x
sin, 77, 109
sinful community of the church, 85
sinners, 28, 121
slavery, modern forms of, 95
Small, Joseph, 78, 81
smart phones, as the norm for most people, 49
society of Christ, church as, 35
software, broadcasting a service, 44
the Son. *See also* Christ; Jesus
  "empersoned" by the Spirit, ix
  incarnation of, 7, 70n42
  returning love to the Father through the Spirit, 61, 70
songs/hymns, 45, 66
speaking, as the personal presence of the Spirit, 10
speaking in tongues, 40, 41, 98
the Spirit
  aligning with, 65
  applying the work of Christ, xiv
  bringing attraction to God, 4n11
  coming to individuals, 11
  as continuity between the Trinity and the church, 61–62
  as the deposit and guarantee of life in glory, 16
  displayed and mediated by Christ and the Church, ix
  dwelling in Christians, 84
  enabling us to see the church as truly God's concern, 72
  forming the church as Christ's body, 58
  granting fellowship with one another, 7–18
  indwelling the people of God, 7
  leading the church to speak public truth, 71
  looking through, 59
  mereological resolution of, 108–12
  movement of, 106
  moving outside of the church against the church, 67n38
  not domesticated by any creaturely word or practice, 85, 86n43
  not identical with the human spirit, 10, 10n35
  placing at the forefront of everything, 53
  as the principal divine power, 41n49
  proceeding from the Father and the Son, 29
  reaching individuals and communities, 121
  roles of, 63
  sent of the Word with the Father, 30–31
  sharing the one divine will, 30
  sustaining and enlivening the church, xiv
  transforming the church when celebrating the Eucharist, 66
  transforming us by love, 10
  unified witness to the Word, 28
  work of, viii, 126
Spirit and Church, conference focusing on, 53
Spirit Christology
  as a complement to *Logos* Christology, 55
  on the Holy Spirit as sole agent in the incarnation, 54n6
  informing to pneumato-ecclesiology, 54–58
  moving from to ecclesiology, ix
  as a vantage point to explore the Trinity, 61
Spirit of adoption, 10
Spirit of God, 117, 126

Spirit of the Word, the Spirit remaining as, 86
Spirit-inspired unity, promise of, 21
Spirit's work, polyphony of, 97
Spiritual church, 53, 69, 71
spiritual dimension, to apostolicity, 79
spiritual fathers and mothers, learning from, 21
spiritual feeding, on the ascended Christ, 48
spiritual rebellion, the church engaging her own, 109
spiritual unity, of the church, 113
subjective misperception thesis, on disunity, 100
sung worship, ix, 45, 46
superstition, Reformation critique of, 6
survival, 110, 111, 112
Swiss reformation, 97
"synecdoche" literary term, where the part stands for the whole, 108
systematic theology, 32
Systematic Theology (Pannenberg), xiii, 125–26
systematics, 33

Tamerlane, vicious annihilation of whole peoples, 111
Tanner, Kathryn, 61
temple, metaphor, 91
temple of the Triune God, Spirit forming, 7
temple service, 95, 96
testimony, of divine grace toward us, 37
thankfulness, sacrifice of, 95
theologians, of opposing parties, 123
theological assumptions, history challenging, 102
Third Article Ecclesiology, 54, 54n4, 60
Third Article Theology
    applying, 58–60, 58n16
    broad methodology known as, 53
    compared to pneumatology, 59n16
    looking through rather than at the Spirit, 54n4
time, understanding the nature of, 63–64
tongues of fire, appeared on individuals, 40

Torrance, T. F., 57, 64, 65
tradition and the status quo, "inertia" of, 22
transcending, of physicality, 48
transforming institution, the church as, 71
treasure, found in earthen jars, 83
trinitarian aspect, of divine holiness, 75
trinitarian disunity, Johnson's approach bespeaking, 23
Trinitarian God, unity guaranteed by, 105
trinitarian life, church participating in, 58
trinitarian pattern, God's gift of his presence following, 8
trinitarian question, of how Spirit relates to Word, 29
trinitarian understanding, of the saving work of God, 28
Trinity
    Church in the light of, ix
    different understandings of, 61
    New Testament witness to, 8
    Spirit's role in, 53
    as a vantage point to explore the church, 60–63
Triune God. *See also* God
    disposition toward purity and against sin, x
    external works of as undivided, 30
    holiness of, 75
    working in perfect unity, viii
triune Godhead, 29
Triune life of God, ix
true church, distinguishing from a false church, 36
Turretin, Francis, 7n27, 77

Ukraine, "trust in the Church," 106
unholiness
    of the church, xi, 77, 85
    force of, 74
unholy church, apostolicity of, 73–88
union, with the Holy Spirit, 9n31
unity
    as an aspect of salvation, 12
    Christ creating, 11

of the church, xi–xii, 7, 15, 100–101, 105, 113
of church members, 43
of the Godhead, 30
as one of the greatest foci of felt dissonance, 104
praising God in, 40
of the Spirit, 19, 21, 106
of the Trinity, 8, 105
universal visible church, conceptualizing the fellowship of, 15
Ursinus, Zacharius, 84

Valley of Dry Bones, vision of in Ezekiel, 85
Vatican II, xii, 16, 118
verbal participation, in the Spirit, 9
virtual church, 44
visible church
 communion with the saints focused on, vii, 6, 18
 existing only when it is meeting, 3
 falling into deadly error, 77–78
 subsisting in the invisible church, xiii, 128
visible mission, of the Spirit, 30
Volf, Miroslav, 61, 118

Ward, Peter, 116
Webster, John, 76, 79–80, 81, 118, 128
Weinandy, Thomas, 61
Westminster Confession, 6
When Prophecy Fails, on cognitive dissonance, 102–3
witness of Christ, instruments of, 97–98
Wolterstorff, Nicholas, 59, 61
the Word. *See also* Word of God
 being addressed by, 92
 church as daughter of, 125
 must explain the sign, 37
 showing the church to be a sinner, xiii
 spoken by Peter, 41
Word and Spirit, relationship of as triunity, 28–31
Word of God. *See also* the Word
 church asked to listen and to submit to, 88
 emphasizing, 117
 in mission permeating and to transforming cultures, 82
 purely preached and heard, 36
 taking functional priority over the sacraments, 36n18
work
 of Christ, xiv, 7–8, 127
 of God, 28
 of the Son, 14
 of the Spirit, viii, xii, xiii, 14, 39, 47, 83–87, 97, 126
the world, as the *oekumene* of suffering mankind, 123
worship, 16–17, 63

xenolalia (real unlearned human languages), 40, 98

Zahl, Simeon, xii, 117
Zwingli, Huldrych, 86, 86n44

www.ingramcontent.com/pod-product-compliance
Lightning Source LLC
Chambersburg PA
CBHW071501150426
43191CB00009B/1396